Richard Villar is an orthopaedic surgeon of international renown. Specializing in hip and knee surgery, he is recognized as a leading authority in many fields. He lectures across the world and has also appeared on the BBC's *Hospital Watch* programme. When he is not busy in surgery Richard Villar likes to play classical guitar and go cross-country skiing north of the Arctic Circle. Married to a doctor, with three children, he lives in a haunted house in Essex.

RICHARD VILLAR

Knife Edge

Life as a Special Forces Surgeon

Adam

Best wishes,

VINEYARD PRESS

VINEYARD PRESS

Published by Vineyard Press
The Vineyard
Windmill Hill
Saffron Walden
Essex CB10 1RR

First published by Michael Joseph 1997
Published by Penguin Books 1998
This edition published by Vineyard Press 2002

ISBN 0-9542203-0-7

The moral right of the author has been asserted

Set in Monotype Sabon
Printed in England by St Edmundsbury Press Ltd,
Bury St Edmunds, Suffolk

To Louise, Ruairidh, Angus, Felicity

and

To those I could not save

Contents

Author's Note

Work with the Special Forces, and as a surgeon, makes me doubly restricted. Medical confidentiality and State secrecy are both vitally important. Lives do depend on them. Please therefore understand why I have chosen to fictionalize many names, change patterns of disease and injury, and alter place names, operational codenames and the like. How would you like *your* disease to appear in print? I wouldn't, and I imagine you would feel the same. Lean back now, relax, read on and enjoy yourself. There is a whole world of adventure out there.

Acknowledgements

Those who have written a book will understand what an enormous task it involves. Those who have not, may not. It has been a lifelong desire to write this and it would have been impossible without the help of so many individuals, particularly in a book that covers twelve countries, six major conflict zones, and a whole host more besides. Some have assisted without realizing it, perhaps by casual comment, others have given knowingly and willingly of their time. Owing to the book's content, certain more secretive individuals have been delighted to assist, but would prefer not to be overtly associated with the end result. Having been in the same position, I understand their worries. As all of you are equally special to both me and the book, I have decided to acknowledge *no one* by name. Those who have helped, all seventy-three of you, will receive a signed copy on the day. You are each wonderful, brilliant in fact. I am indebted to you.

List of Illustrations

All photographs not credited are the property of the author.

CHAPTER I

A Brilliant Idea

'Doc! Get over here! Someone's been shot!'

I could not believe it – it had to be a joke. My first day as SAS medical officer and there had been a shooting. Was this really a taste of things to come?

The moment I reached the building, medical pack in hand, I realized this was no test, no trial run. The soldier lay there, blood pumping viciously from a massive wound in his buttock. He looked terrified. Still conscious, he glanced up at me imploringly. 'I'll be OK, Doc, won't I? I'll be OK?"

I was on autopilot by then, mentally checking off the vital functions I had to perform to ensure the man's survival. 'Airway, breathing, circulation – airway, breathing, circulation,' I whispered to myself. I muttered reassurance as best I could, unsure whether or not I could stop the bleeding. Uncertain which nerves, if any, the blast had destroyed.

It had been a shotgun, accidentally discharged six inches away. Most of the buttock was missing. What remained looked dirty, contaminated with grit and pieces of clothing. Around me stood several tall SAS operatives, each one totally relaxed. They had seen it before. A real-life situation it may be, but I was still on test. They inspected my every move. 'How will he do under stress?' I could hear them thinking.

I tried hard to stop my hands shaking as I ripped open the shell dressing, stuffing it firmly in the wound. 'Lean on it!' I instructed the medic who had joined me in my dash to the building. With enough pressure applied, I knew that any bleeding could be stopped. It was important not to lift up the shell dressing to see how things were doing. Keep on stuffing them in, one on top of the other, as hard as you can go, until the bleeding stops, I thought. I had seen many gunshot wounds before. My record had been fourteen dressings to stem the tide. This one needed three.

The soldier survived, thanks to both prompt treatment and his own strength. With a major artery ruptured it can take only thirty seconds to die. Life-saving must therefore be reflex. As a doctor you act first, think later and trust to God that your medical training keeps you right.

I delivered the man to hospital one hour later, an intravenous infusion running fast to replace the blood he had lost. Once the surgeons had taken him over I sat, exhausted, on a wooden bench in the hospital grounds. I felt shattered, both physically and emotionally. Join the SAS? It had seemed a good idea at the time.

I had always wanted to be a surgeon, from the moment my mother gave me a plastic stethoscope on my seventh birthday; I played with it until the toy was chipped and cracked beyond recognition. My only sister, six years my junior, would be exposed to all manner of imaginary operations, homemade splints and carefully applied bandages. For hours I would daydream and ponder, glued to any and every television programme or book that covered the subject. Was there really a breed of person who cut people open for a living? How did they do it? What actually happened during an operation? There had never been a surgeon in my family, even if I went back 300 years, so there was no close relative I could ask. The only exception was an uncle, a charming New Zealander living in South Wales, an eminent chest doctor. He had been decorated following his time as a prisoner of war in Greece and had endless stories of life as a doctor that filled me with passionate enthusiasm about the medical profession.

My father was a highly successful naval officer, having been a sailor since the age of thirteen. My mother, a part-time broadcaster and writer, would chase round the globe in his wake, supporting and holding her restless family together. A thousand times I remember being asked the question by any and every visitor to our various naval homes:

'What do you want to be when you're older, Richard?'

'A surgeon,' I would answer, steadfast in my determination.

'A surgeon? My, that's interesting,' would come the reply, followed by a friendly pat on my head. I soon realized that my ambition was a conversation-stopper. No one knew anything about surgery, so discussing it was impossible. I would have to find out for myself.

To be a surgeon, you have to become a doctor first, so throughout my schooling I concentrated on the sciences. Of all such subjects, biology was my favourite, particularly dissection. Dissection involves cutting open some poor animal to gain a better understanding of how the body works. In retrospect it seems cruel, but in those days I knew no better. You would take a small, unsuspecting frog and insert a needle forcibly into it, just below the base of its fragile skull. This would pith it, such that it was technically dead, or so we were told, but its heart would continue working. You could then cut it open to see how the tiny body functioned. There would beat the firm, pea-sized heart, pushing blood round the animal's circulation. The guts would wriggle and writhe, driving the motions onwards. I was riveted by such things, particularly the act of opening the beast up with the tweezer-like surgical forceps and curved, tiny scissors. From a young age I learned that opening and closing bodies, however small, was not a simple act. It took time and effort to practise. If you were not careful, your scissors could slip and damage an artery or nerve. I learned to rest the edge of my hands on the table while dissecting, to eliminate any sign of tremor. I learned, too, that surgical errors can be fatal. It was with this background, and a now fierce determination to become a surgeon, that I entered my London medical school. I was damned sure what I wanted to be.

At medical school I was exposed to every aspect of doctoring imaginable: general practice, cancer therapy, children's medicine, X-rays, the lot. One specialty, above all others, stood out for me – orthopaedics, the art of operating on bones and joints. I remember the day I decided it was for me. I had barely started my training and had been allocated a two-week period attached to an eminent orthopaedic surgeon's practice. I was by myself in a huge, empty room containing little more than a wooden desk, two rickety plastic seats, and an X-ray viewing box screwed to a dirty wall. Décor has never featured highly on the National Health Service's list of priorities. Outside I could hear the hubbub of conversation as dozens of patients waited to be seen, all comparing breaks and sprains, and the inconvenience of months spent in plaster. I sat nervously in my seat, jammed underneath the viewing box, awaiting the arrival of my consultant.

Consultants? These were powerful, terrifying people, particularly when seen from the position of a junior medical student. You called them 'Sir', bowed and scraped copiously, and prayed they asked their questions of others, not of you. I did not have to wait long. Within minutes a tall, tanned figure strode into the undecorated room, confidently taking his place in the wobbly seat behind the chipped mahogany desk. He did not spare me a glance.

I sat silently, praying this God-like creature would not turn and notice me, even though I was only feet away. Please, I thought, please come and join me, someone. Please come and keep me company. There were meant to be at least a dozen students attending this particular clinic, but I had been the only one to appear. If I stay very, very quiet, I thought, perhaps he will leave me alone. It was a foolish idea, as only seconds later the powerful, white-coated frame turned and looked me hard in the eye. For a brief second I lurched backwards, as if braced for some unexpected assault, but only succeeded in wedging myself still further under the viewing box. Its hard, rectangular frame prevented any retreat. He's going to ask me a question, I panicked. A question! I won't know the answer! Please, someone, help! But no question came. Instead, the hard eyes softened, and a smile appeared. 'You're Villar, aren't you?' came the quiet voice. 'First day?'

I nodded frantically, scraping my head against the underside of the unfriendly viewing box, though I could sense my fear subside. There was something in the voice that made me relax.

'I thought so,' the consultant continued, still smiling. 'The Dean told me you would be here. I hope you enjoy your time with me. Remember one thing, Villar.'

'Sir?'

'Orthopaedics is *fun*.' Then he turned and the clinic began, as he smiled and chatted, greeting each patient as a long-lost friend. I was hooked, firmly and securely. Orthopaedics has been fun since that day.

It is a young specialty when compared to medicine overall. It was only in 1894 that it became recognized in its own right. Until then, bones and joints were handled by general surgeons, who would also deal with the abdomen, chest and other body parts. The situation persisted in the United Kingdom well into the 1950s, and still continues in certain parts of the world.

As a student, I began also to realize that not all surgeons work in major teaching hospitals. Many operate from very primitive establishments, often in basic, unhygienic parts of the world. Third World countries are classic examples. Perhaps it was my restless childhood – my father's postings had sent us to North America, Greece and Malta – but I decided within three months of starting my medical studies that teaching hospitals were not for me. They were too laborious, too political, overconstrained affairs. Or so I thought. I laugh about it now, working in one of the most eminent centres in the globe, but in those days I had set my heart on orthopaedics in the Third World.

How to do it – that was the problem. A London teaching hospital prepares you for many things, but Third World orthopaedic surgery is not one of them. A large part of orthopaedics involves the management of broken and shattered bones, injured as a result of accidents. I not only had to train myself to deal with such things, but also to cope with them when facilities were non-existent or sparse. I thought about it for months. How much easier it would be, I reflected, to be less restless and stay in teaching-hospital surgery. I even felt guilty in the presence of my instructors for considering life outside that of a spotless white coat and gleaming hospital corridors. Then, one day, something happened to send me on my way.

As with most medical students, I seemed permanently short of money. Educating and enjoying oneself always appear to cost more than the sums coming in. To supplement an appalling student grant, I decided to join the University of London Officer Training Corps, the ULOTC. A part-time Territorial Army unit, they not only paid me for what I did, but took me away from London at weekends. This prevented me from spending what I had.

I was surprised to find that I enjoyed the ULOTC. Joining them had initially been a purely financial exercise. Yet here I was having fun on ranges, heavy-goods driving courses and cross-country navigation tests. My time with them reinforced my ambition to do something different with my life. What the ULOTC could not do was show me how to realize my ambition – until my Commanding Officer decided I should parachute. I was horrified. Parachuting. What a pastime. To think that some do it for pleasure.

I was sent on the military light-bulb course. The light bulb is a parachutist's badge, not proper wings, issued to soldiers from non-airborne units after seven static-line descents. Thus it was that I found myself hanging on for dear life in the back of a C-130 Hercules, waiting to leap through the door into the thin air beyond. With me, along one side of the aircraft, lurching round the skies over RAF Abingdon, sat a handful of equally terrified men. Jim T, a good friend from Hull, was one of them. A solid, muscular man, he had approached our earlier ground training with real determination. Right now even he looked scared. Opposite us sat four very confident men. Chatting to each other in a relaxed way, they could have been on the London Underground.

They were dressed differently to us, in blue boiler suits, oxygen masks hanging loosely around their necks. Their parachutes were also different: steerable Paracommanders in their thin, compressed packs rather than our bulky, standard-issue affairs. We were the basic static-line course, scheduled to be thrown out over Weston-on-the-Green at any moment. Eight hundred feet was as high as we would go. They were the HALO group – High Altitude Low Opening – scheduled for a 12,000-foot freefall, learning advanced parachuting techniques for infiltration behind enemy lines. I had naturally heard of them, but never seen them. I thought again. Here were SAS men in the flesh. SAS? Of course! What a brilliant idea.

The parachute jump instructor, the PJI, barely gave me time to think further. The moment the red light glowed to one side of the exit, he pulled open the door. When that happens, your insides work overtime. I was terrified. My legs shook as I felt the slow trickle of urine down the inside of my thigh. Jim also looked bad as I saw him struggle to control a vomit. We were both very frightened. We knew also that we could not go back. I looked across at the HALO team. One of them, the taller of the group, sensed my distress. Smiling, he winked and gave me a cheery thumbs up sign. 'Go for it, lad!' I heard him shout over the din of the aircraft's engines. It was his encouragement that got me out the door, of that I am certain.

A static line is a broad webbing strap attaching the parachute apex to a thick wire hawser inside the aircraft. Naturally, but unnecessarily, I checked that my own was still firmly attached. Behind me I noticed Jim still looking pale, concentration etched on his petrified face. Then the light changed from red to green. 'Go!' shouted the PJI at the top of his lungs, as he thumped me on the shoulder. That was not the time to turn, as I have seen done, and ask 'Do you mean me?' I jumped firmly through the door, feet first, arms folded on top of my reserve. The brave-hearted look back up as they depart, to be sure the main parachute opens properly. I did not. My eyes remained firmly closed throughout. Before I had time to think, I had plunged through the buffeting slipstream into the quieter air beyond. Slowly, hesitantly, I opened my eyes and looked upwards. Thank God! There above me was the perfect hemisphere of my open parachute. The relief was overwhelming. Unfortunately, full parachute deployment does not always happen. A number of things can go wrong.

The commonest problem is the 'twists'. This is what happened to Jim. As he exited the aircraft, the slipstream spun him like a top, rotating him rapidly as his parachute opened. This narrowed the canopy's dimensions, making him fall faster and the parachute impossible to steer. He hurtled past me, thrashing his legs wildly in an attempt to untwist himself. Ground training had taught us to do this, emphasizing how important it was not to panic. Jim seemed to be doing well. As I drifted downwards, I felt how unfair it was that his first aircraft jump should face him with an air emergency. With less than eight hundred feet to go he had to untwist himself fast.

Fortunately, Jim was successful. Though he had left the Hercules after me, he had landed well before me. After my own, very inept, parachute roll, I found him lying on the grass looking up at the sky. His parachute was collapsed, though still attached to him. 'Thank ****, thank ****, thank ****,' was all he could say.

As well as the twists, parachuting problems are numerous. They can include failure to open at all, in which case you are dead; rigging lines caught over the top of your canopy; or someone going below you and stealing your air. That, too, can kill you. In fact your worst enemies in a military static-line jump are your colleagues. It is fortunate the average military canopy is only steerable to a limited extent. A Hercules disgorges more than sixty parachutists in under a minute. Some will have their eyes open, some will have their eyes shut, whatever they are told in training. The thought of sixty soldiers careering round the sky under their parachutes, each with independent steering, is terrifying. It is best to allow the wind, and Mother Nature, to let each one down in a safe, orderly fashion. Full control is reserved for freefallers. There are fewer of them, jumping from a greater height, allowing more room for error.

The final danger is landing. A significant percentage of any parachuting course is spent on how to hit the ground and roll. It is roughly equivalent to jumping off a wall, twelve feet high. Grandly called 'ground training', the various parachute centres are wealthily endowed with devices to simulate heavy landings. Once a freefaller, life is different. It is possible to turn into wind just before ground contact. The lift this provides should give a soft landing. Static liners take what comes. Knees together, feet together, elbows in, chin tucked down and roll. Most of the time they get away with it. Unfortunately casualties do occur, particularly broken ankles, broken heel bones, broken shin bones and the occasional broken back. Alastair, a very good friend and an excellent doctor, managed to break the lot in one go. Parachutists can also develop awful spines by the time they reach middle age as a result of repeated injuries and arthritis. For certain active-service scenarios, to ensure soldiers are not exposed for too long to enemy fire, jump height can be as low as 350 feet. This gives no room for error. Casualty rates of over 10 per cent have been associated with this.

In later years, once I qualified as a doctor and had joined the SAS, my parachuting skills made me fair game for dropping-zone, or DZ, medical cover. I would be thrown out first, wherever we might happen to be, medical kit in hand. Not in hand really. Equipment was attached to two large hooks in front of me, just beneath my reserve. Once clear of the aircraft I would open the two hooks, the equipment falling away, though remaining attached to my harness by twelve feet of sturdy rope. This was useful, particularly when jumping at night. I could hear the equipment strike the ground first, giving time to brace before Mother Earth leapt up and grabbed me for her own. The problem is who provides DZ medical cover for the medics? No one, I am afraid. The first out is on his own.

The purpose of jumping at night is to lessen the chance of detection by the enemy. Even if a parachutist breaks a leg as he lands, he is unlikely to scream about it in the middle of a war zone. He will lie there and suffer, or should do, until help arrives. As a doctor, I became accustomed to listening for the sound of breaking limbs. It is unmistakable once you have heard it. You can see nothing, it is all done on sound. As a parachutist lands there should be two thumps. The first is his equipment, the second is himself. A third sound, usually a high-pitched 'click', following close behind the second, is the fracture. The moment I heard that tell-tale sound, I would prepare my splints, ready to immobilize what I was sure would be a broken bone.

That first day, as Jim and I staggered from the DZ, I began to relax. The intense emotions I had gone through, the total fear, were subsiding. I started to think once more, my head bowed to the ground, as I carried the heavy weight of the parachute in its large green bag on my shoulders. Jim disturbed my thoughts.

'Penny for them.'

'They're not worth it.'

'Go on. Try me,' came the challenging reply.

'The SAS. What do you know about them?'

'Bugger all. Bunch of lunatics I reckon. Why?'

'I'd like to join them. What do you think?'

'You must be ****ing mad, Richard. They're all brawn, no brain and you'll get yourself killed. Anyway, you've got your medical career to think of.'

'It was my medical career I was thinking of. It could be ideal. Why not do both? I mean, why can't you be a doctor *and* join the SAS? Someone must look after them if they get hurt. Just think of all the experience you would get.'

I heard Jim grunt with disbelief beside me. At that point I doubted there was anything he could have said to change my mind. The moment I had seen the small group of HALO parachutists in the Hercules, I resolved that, one day, I would join them and become their doctor. Rumour had it the SAS spent much of their time on active service and real-life exercises. If so, they were bound to have broken bones, twisted knees, dislocated shoulders and all manner of orthopaedic conditions. A major part of orthopaedics was in the management of injuries and major trauma. What better training than with the SAS? Rumour also said they worked extensively overseas. Any doctor with them would be as far away from a teaching hospital as it is possible to go. I would learn how to deal with injuries, from the moment a patient was wounded, until he was evacuated to hospital and taken to the operating theatre. For a young, ambitious orthopaedic surgeon, with his eye on the Third World, I could do no better. For sure, the SAS it would be.

The moment I returned to London, I sought advice about leaving mainstream medicine from a few, highly selected advisers, all of whom were sworn to secrecy. They, and my parents, sided with Jim. They thought the idea mad. I was, after all, already established on the first rung of a major teaching-hospital career. Was it really worth giving up all that for such a whim? I still knew very little about the SAS, but anything I heard convinced me that nowhere else in the world would I obtain such excellent training. I was also young enough to take a risk, barely twenty-one, and had time on my side.

Jim and I parachuted together on several occasions after our basic Abingdon course, though he never fully recovered from the twisting episode at his first jump. His tale of the event, told with a charming accent in various pubs, became more unbelievable at each telling. Whenever we met he would take me to one side and ask, 'Have you thought more about the SAS?'

'Continually,' I would reply. I barely thought of anything else and had read every book available on the subject. There were not many. I daydreamed on ward rounds, endured endless sleepless nights and talked to myself incessantly. To most who knew me, I must have gone mad. It took several months to build up courage and take the plunge. 'I'm going to join soon,' I told Jim on one occasion. 'Now I'm a third-year student, I have a few skills I can offer if they want.'

I remember Jim's look of astonished disbelief. 'So you're doing it after all? I thought you were joking. But no, I can see you're serious. You are mad, Richard. Completely scarpers.'

It was too late by then. I was hooked.

My trouble was that I had no idea how to go about joining. Quite rightly the SAS does not advertise, or didn't in those days. You had to seek them rather than the other way round. There will never be a shortage of people wishing to join the Regiment. That hidden something gripping me, grips thousands of others as well. If you were to believe everyone who says they have been, or are, in the SAS you would have enough manpower for a thousand Regiments. In reality, there are only three Regiments, two Territorial and one Regular. The Territorials are part-timers who combine a civilian job with military service. The Regulars are fully committed, day in and day out, to the SAS. To some extent that still applies now, though a high-readiness Territorial reserve has been created to assist the Regulars on occasion. Selection weeds out the unworthy from both, with more than 80 per cent falling by the wayside. The odds are worse for officers.

There is one major difference between Territorial and Regular SAS. The Territorial SAS soldier will have come in off the street, often without any prior military service. The Regular SAS operative must have come from some form of previous Services background. Those joining the Regulars are thus up to scratch with basic soldiering skills from the start. The Territorial soldier often is not. This difference was initially reflected in the roles of the various Regiments. Whereas the Regulars, 22 SAS, had a more aggressive approach to life, the Territorial units – 21 and 23 SAS – were more passive. Their primary role was one of observation. Their secondary role was more SAS-like, involving sabotage, snatches and the like.

Those who fail the SAS Selection course often bring back tales of deeds and happenings that defy imagination, an attempt to justify why they did not succeed. Such tales are unnecessary. There is no dishonour in failing Selection; you are in good company if you do. The SAS is looking for individuals of a certain type and *you*, however strong God made you, may simply be the wrong person. One thing is certain, the day you first decide to try for the SAS is immensely awe-inspiring.

I decided to join in secret. Apart from Jim, I did not want any colleagues knowing, in case I failed. To my earlier advisers, I had let the matter drop, though my parents knew I was up to something odd. One Thursday afternoon I found the remotest, tiniest, loneliest Army Careers Information Office I could, somewhere in south London, and strode resolutely inside. It was empty, save for one very properly dressed Warrant Officer, sitting ramrod straight behind an immaculately tidy desk. Everything was laid out in perfect order before him. Telephone, blotter, paper clips, files. Each item appeared to be parallel to the one beside it, like soldiers on parade. He looked directly at me as I approached the desk. 'Yes, sir?' he said as I drew near, a tight knot gnawing at the pit of my stomach.

'I want to join the SAS,' I said self-consciously, mumbling terribly – a family failing.

'Sorry, sir?' The man had obviously not heard me. I would have to try again.

'The SAS,' I said, still in hushed tones. 'I want to join it.' I could see the Warrant Officer was struggling hard to hear. His forehead wrinkled deeply as he leaned over his desk, head turned slightly to one side. With his hand he formed a cup behind his right ear.

'Say again, sir. I can't quite hear you.'

My heart sank. We had just spent two weeks learning ear, nose and throat surgery at my hospital, so I knew all about high-tone deafness. Particularly in soldiers exposed, unprotected, to rifle and artillery fire for many years. Surely not? My self-consciousness had by now disappeared. Checking around me to be sure I was still alone, I put one hand firmly either side of the Warrant Officer's inkblotter, and shouted.

'The SAS. You know, the Special Air Service. How does one join it? I want to join.' I was leaning so far forward, my face was only inches from his own.

I was almost hoarse, but could see comprehension begin to dawn on the soldier's face. He removed the cupped hand from behind his ear, raising his eyebrows and opening his mouth in realization. I had broken through at last. From the corner of my eye, on the pavement outside the office, I saw two passers-by stop in their tracks and look in the window. My heart sank still further. For sure, the whole of south London must have heard my request. I prayed the floor would open and swallow me up, but it did not. Instead, the Warrant Officer reclined back to his vertical sitting position, and reached for the pitch-black telephone to his left. 'The SAS, sir? Of course, sir. I'm sure we can help.'

So it was, twenty-four hours later, I appeared at the end of a long line of hopefuls at a barracks in central London. I had decided A Squadron 21 SAS, a Territorial unit, would be the correct first step. It would allow me a better understanding of SAS life without compromising my medical training. After full qualification as a doctor, only three years away, joining the Regular 22 SAS might be a possibility. 'You can take medicine anywhere,' my aunt had once said. After qualification, anything was possible.

My companions in line came from all walks of life. You will never see such a cross-section of society as can be found at the start of SAS Selection. Black and white, straight or gay, rich or poor. Everyone is there from the streetwise mugger to the affluent professional. The one question you never ask is why someone wishes to join. For some it may be an escape, for others it might be a planned career move. You never know for sure. As far as the Regiment is concerned, you pass Selection first and they will ask questions afterwards, though there is obviously a degree of basic security clearance at the start. However, you are not exposed to the more covert, specialist SAS techniques until after Selection is complete. This can be immensely disappointing for some. Several years after I joined, a good friend tried the same. Having passed Selection with flying colours, and all the labour that entails, he was refused entry on security grounds. Whether or not it was due to his wife originating from the then Eastern bloc was never explained.

Standing in line that evening I was, as seems frequently my lot, at its very end. I learned that I had already missed the first two of five Selection weekends, leading to a fortnight away in Wales at a final Selection camp. At that time, the Territorial Selection was similar in design to the Regular, though slightly downgraded. For a civilian it was just as demanding. Nothing less than utter dedication would see you through. In recent years the situation has changed, both Territorials and Regulars taking the same course. The two are separated by speed. Regulars should average four kilometres per hour across country, Territorials three kilometres per hour. A Territorial who can keep pace with the Regulars becomes eligible for a high-readiness Reserve.

I noticed a total lack of conversation in the queue. At the far end, through an open hatch, a cheery quartermaster, the QM, was handing out equipment. His was the only voice to be heard. Everyone was taking this event very seriously. Twenty minutes later my turn came. I could see a vast expanse of empty shelves over the QM's shoulder. He saw my gaze and spoke sympathetically. Sympathetically, that is, for an SAS QM. 'Sorry, son. You're new aren't you? Afraid all the best stuff has gone. Here's a Bergen rucksack and poncho anyway. You'll find rations over there.' He pointed to a pile of overladen, clear, plastic bags, being quietly decimated by the others. 'I'd grab a few quick before they all disappear,' he added. As I turned, the hatch was closed, eliminating any prospect of further conversation. I darted across to the pile of bags, grabbing the final two.

The other applicants, let me call them trainees, had spread themselves and their equipment along the length of one wall. Ponchos were being folded, rations unpacked and repacked, maps covered in plastic. The atmosphere was one of frightening, albeit silent, efficiency. I had no idea what to do. Finding myself a small space in a distant corner I, too, started to reorganize my kit. This was difficult, as no one had told me what to expect. All I knew was that I was to be physically tested, somewhere in South Wales.

The ration packs seemed a reasonable starting point. There were only three choices of SAS ration. Beef, mutton or curry. I subsequently learned that each tasted the same, even to the gastronome. I am sure they were identical. I suspect all the army ever did was to change the label on the pack, in the hope this would persuade the consumer the taste was different. They did not fool me. As I began to separate out my rations, mutton and curry had been my choices, a small orange pill fell to the floor in a tiny plastic bag. I picked it up and studied it, feeling it through the clear plastic, looking for some indication of identity. There was none. It was smooth on both sides, no grooves, no letters, nothing. What on earth was it?

Beside me was another trainee, arranging his kit with alarming speed. A thin, wiry individual dressed in a cream shirt with sleeves rolled up, he looked very much the man who had seen it all before. He sensed my quandary and glanced towards me.

'Suicide pill,' he said, his voice deadly serious.

I could not believe what I was hearing. I must have looked

doubtful, as he started to nod his head sagely and spoke again. 'Sure. It's a suicide pill. All over in less than ten seconds. In case you get caught. You'll probably not need it, but you never know.' Then he turned back to his pile of very orderly equipment, rapidly packed everything away in his Bergen rucksack, and strode purposefully through a door at the far end of the room to join an increasing throng of trainees.

I stood there, mouth open, watching the rear view of the trainee disappear into the room beyond. The trouble with the SAS is that you can believe anything of it. Anything at all. It did not surprise me to find a suicide pill in a ration pack. I was only a volunteer, not a full-timer. What about my medical studies? I may believe in my country, but not enough to kill myself. I had seen various films and read assorted books about the Special Operations Executive in the last war. The use of their lethal pill, buried deep inside a molar tooth, was well known to me. Naturally it made sense that the SAS should have the same. After all, what chance of survival would you have if captured behind enemy lines? It seemed odd to be issued with a suicide pill on Selection. Was this a way out for failures perhaps? Or even a test? Did I honestly have to take the thing when caught? How many had died on Selection as a result? Questions rattled through my mind. What were they going to do to me in South Wales? Would I ever get back at all? I can laugh about it now as I subsequently learned it was a vitamin pill. My competitive self was also secretly delighted that the man who teased me failed Selection.

To the regular hillwalker, South Wales is a paradise. To the SAS trainee it is hell on earth. If you survive Selection, you know almost everything about the Brecon Beacons and Black Mountains by the end. That first weekend, having travelled by tube to Paddington, train to Newport, and four-ton lorry to the Brecon Beacons, it was 2 a.m. on the Saturday morning that we arrived. Unceremoniously dumped by some woods next to an old pub, the Storey Arms, we were told to be prepared for duty by 6 a.m. We should be packed and ready to move by then. That was it. No frills, no help, no light, no hot tea ready to welcome us. Nothing at all. It was pitch dark and pouring with rain. I was soaked to the skin within seconds of leaving the friendly shelter of the four-tonner. What on earth was I meant to do? Even the military parachuting course seemed a welcome relaxation compared to this. Already I was looking forward to Monday morning's hospital ward round that, by tradition, filled most medical students with terror. In hushed tones I promised my Maker all manner of noble deeds if he returned me to London in one piece.

Looking around me I saw the other trainees disappear into the woods, in different directions. 'No lights, you lot,' was bellowed from the back of the departing four-tonner. 'Any lights and you're out,' was added. Bastard, I thought. You come and find somewhere to sleep in this lot. I now realize, of course, that the man who shouted had himself survived Selection. He is also, now, a very good friend. I hated him then.

By the time I had finished fuming at the stupidity of it all, I was alone. Alone, lonely, tired and very wet. Deep within the woods I could hear the cracking of branches and twigs as the other trainees prepared their own sleeping arrangements. I could see nothing. The blackness of a forest at night is complete. I was to learn that again, several years later, with 22 SAS in the Far East. Fed up, with both life and the army, I produced my poncho from a sodden Bergen, wrapped myself in it, lay on the ground, and tried to sleep. I think I cried too.

It was a worse than awful night. The poncho made a half-hearted attempt to keep the worst off me, but by 5 a.m. I was as cold and as soaked as one gets. Every item of equipment I possessed, be it inside or outside my Bergen, was drenched. I had to eat. I knew that was essential. The sky had that dull, depressing lightness about it, when you wonder if dawn is ever truly going to break. Gathering my few things together, I stumbled from the wood to the roadside. What I saw staggered me. The place was a hive of frantic activity. Along a fence beside the road was a line of little green homemade tents. Each was made from an individually erected army poncho. Beneath every one was a soldier, looking as warm as toast, perfectly dry, earnestly cooking his breakfast on a solid-fuel stove. It was my first introduction to the SAS *basha*, a word of Malayan origin. Keeping dry was unquestionably an artform that I had not yet mastered. These men, the training-wing instructors, were obviously professionals at the game.

I can now make *bashas* of any shape or size and erect them anywhere in the world, day or night. In those days I had never seen one. The key is preparation. First, all holes in the poncho must be hermetically sealed. The head hole, for example, can leak like a sieve unless tied off. To small eyelets in each corner are tied lengths of military twine, the so-called 'paracord', looped at the outer end. Two elastic, roofrack bunjees and a few plastic tent pegs are the only extras. The whole affair fits neatly into a Bergen pocket, and probably weighs less than a kilogram. With the wise use of available vertical supports – fences, gates, trees – a *basha* can be erected in no time. It can be of any design, but should be angled into the wind and staked down so that rainwater runs off rather than on to you. For most of the world, a *basha* is all you require to survive. The only exception is certain jungle rainfalls. These can be so powerful they can soak through the poncho material. There is not much you can do about that, except choose a different material.

The delicious smell of cooking filled the air that morning. From one *basha* I could hear the sizzling of meat being fried. How did these guys do it? On a military ration? I obviously had to try for myself. With damp, wrinkled, trembling hands I ripped open one of the ration bags and read the instructions on the packet: 'Reconstitute with water.' There was certainly no shortage of that in Wales, I thought. Though the night's downpour had now turned to fine drizzle, I could have squeezed out my clothes into a cooking-pot if it came to it. Of course, like a rookie, I had forgotten the basic task of filling my waterbottle before leaving London. I had been certain, in the warmth and security of our capital city, that water would be everywhere. In reality, the nearest river was fifteen frozen minutes' walk away. By the time I had reached it, and returned, it was 5.45 a.m. Only fifteen minutes before I had to be ready to move. Around me were instructors and trainees looking highly organized. *Bashas* were being dismantled and packed away, maps studied, bootlaces tightened. I, meanwhile, was feeling much the worse for wear. My kit was by now strewn along the roadside and attempts to ignite a solid-fuel hexamine block with a soggy match fruitless. Time was against me. Already I was beginning to receive irritated looks from the instructors and smug ones from other trainees. I was not a happy man.

I realized then it is self-organization that counts in the SAS. If you are not totally organized, any physical tests you are given appear harder, if not impossible. A simple ten-kilometre stroll can become a marathon if you are wet and hungry, or have lost your compass in the bottom of your rucksack. All the instructors wanted to establish was if I could withstand the physical tests in store for me that day. How I went about it was my affair. The fact I was soaked and starving was irrelevant to them. From their perfectly correct viewpoint my discomfiture was self-inflicted. If I had thought through the problem beforehand I, too, would have been like them. Warm as toast, sizzling sausages in my *basha*. I had only myself to blame for any troubles.

How I got through that first weekend I shall never know. The SAS spat me out once more, exhausted and humbled, late on the Sunday evening at its London barracks. I had learned a lot in a short time and had also seen others fall by the wayside. Of the forty trainees setting off up Pen-y-Fan mountain that Saturday morning, only twenty-eight finished the walk in the time allowed. None of those who failed was actively thrown out by the SAS. Each gave up of his own volition. Whoever you are, the idea of giving up goes through your mind permanently. The whole course is a matter of ignoring the very sensible desire to withdraw. You need to develop a strong streak of bloody-mindedness to succeed.

Selection weekends took place at fortnightly intervals over a three-month period, leading to the two-week camp by the end. Each weekend became increasingly difficult. Distances longer, loads heavier, loneliness greater. The intervening fortnight was a valuable time. Once I realized that military-issue equipment, designed for the standard British soldier, was not up to the rigours of SAS Selection, I went down to the local climbing shop. I bought the place out. Sleeping mats, tiny gas cookers, survival bags, map cases. You name it and I obtained it. I learned to report for duty early so as to be at the front of the queue, not the end. I learned that everything should be covered in plastic to keep dry. In short, I became highly self-organized. I was damned if the buggers were going to beat me.

Exposure or *hypothermia*, a slow decrease in body temperature, often over several hours, eventually causes the heart to stop beating. Exposure is similar to becoming drunk. In the early stages it can be quite pleasant. The sufferer is frequently unaware of the problem. I have retrieved three dead bodies from the Welsh mountains. All of them had been intelligent men in life – all of them had also been very strong. For whatever reason, they had decided to push themselves beyond their limit of endurance. The message is clear. No one is immune to exposure. Keeping dry, and away from the wind, is vital to survival. Exposure can kill. If in doubt, there is no harm in finding shelter and brewing some tea. You are no use dead to the SAS.

SAS Selection is a time of deep and intense friendships. People you would never normally meet suddenly become bosom pals. Mutual suffering throws you together, creating a bond that is essentially indestructible. I would do anything for my SAS friends now. Selection also encourages a healthy spirit of competition. Peter B was my target. A physical education instructor by trade, he was the quiet, silent, independent type. He could keep going for ever, appearing to be incapable of feeling pain. I know now that he was just very self-controlled. Predictably, he passed his course with flying colours. On each walk I tried desperately to beat him. Most of the time I failed, but on occasion I triumphed. He was older and more experienced than I, tolerating my competitive ways with great patience.

Keeping, or getting, fit was another challenge. To cope with Selection you must be able to climb hills steadily, without stopping. To stop walking, for whatever reason, is to invite failure. Captain

T, hero of the Falklands, said to me years later when we took Regular SAS Selection together, 'Balance, rhythm and stride, Doc. Balance, rhythm and stride.' He was right. You need a well-balanced, steady, even pace and any of the walks becomes possible. I was fortunate to work in a large London teaching hospital with a huge tower block as part of it. Training for me involved filling a rucksack with bricks and running up and down the building's many steps as often as I could. Patients and colleagues alike thought I was mad. I am reminded of it to this day, but it did the trick. That, and my regular sport of karate, prepared me for the Selection camp at Sennybridge.

The two-week Sennybridge Camp was split in half. The first week was a sequence of walks, culminating in the infamous endurance march, 'Long Drag'. The second was what the SAS called Continuation training, where those who survive Long Drag are introduced to the basics of SAS soldiering. By the end of the Continuation week you become 'badged'. You are eligible to wear the winged dagger on a beige SAS beret. To be precise, it is not a winged dagger at all, but a winged sword. Nevertheless, the term 'dagger' has become so commonplace when talking of the SAS that I will continue with it. If you walk round the average SAS establishment you will find the minority of soldiers wearing the winged dagger. Most are attached personnel – signallers, cooks, medics, mechanics. They, too, will wear the beige beret, but their own cap badge is attached. It is the badge, not the beret, that separates them from the real thing. To be badged, whether Territorial or Regular, is the ultimate in military achievement. By the time you reach Sennybridge therefore, you can almost smell the badge. It has already become an obsession.

Predictably, the walks become increasingly arduous as the first week progresses. Total organization is the only way to succeed. I strapped my feet, back and shoulders with adhesive moleskin dressing before the week began. A Bergen rucksack is just as capable of creating blisters as an ill-fitting pair of boots. I was early for everything, ate like a horse, did not drink and slept whenever I could. Sex was non-existent. Finally, I did not stop walking for any reason. But the temptation to give in was sometimes enormous.

Halfway through the week we were tasked to make a twenty-kilometre night march. This took place across open country, the use of tracks not being permitted (on live operations tracks are easily ambushed). A typical march involves a series of checkpoints (or 'R Vs' – rendezvous) at approximately five-kilometre intervals. We were sent off individually, every three minutes. It was eleven at night, pitch black and pouring with rain. The usual insistence that no lights should be seen, and no tracks used, was given. That did not mean I was going to avoid using a torch; I had to be sure I was not seen doing so. Who dares wins is the SAS motto after all. A red or green filter over the lens preserves night vision admirably and cannot be seen more than a few feet away.

For the first three hours I had no trouble. I was soaked, but happy to be so and confident I knew my location at all times to within fifty metres. I was headed towards the penultimate R V and lying either first or second in a field of several dozen trainees. This was good, I thought. At such a rate I would be on the first transport back to Sennybridge Camp and in bed before the stragglers had finished. That meant more sleep and a better chance of doing well the next day.

As I walked confidently up the side of yet another windswept mountain, my mind was on other things. I cannot explain why. It never pays to be overconfident. Suddenly I began to fall. I could not see where, or into what. Then an ice-cold hand clamped around my chest as I realized I had fallen from a rocky outcrop into a peat bog below. Peat bogs are dangerous enough by day. At night I knew they could be fatal. I was slowly sinking, the weight of a forty-pound Bergen dragging me down. Each time I struggled I sank further, the slimy pressure of the ice-cold hand becoming ever greater. I screamed and shouted for help, but it was windy. I had no idea where the nearest person was. He could have been five feet away, or five kilometres. I hadn't a clue.

There were two choices. I could either give in and die, in this case a realistic option, or I could fight. I fought, slowly dragging myself hand over hand to the surface until I lay there spreadeagled, sodden and very lonely. Then, suddenly, I felt completely overcome. An overpowering desire to get off the mountain at all costs swept over me. Selection didn't matter, being badged didn't matter, even the penultimate R V didn't matter. I had to get off. Staggering, running, lurching, I dashed from the mountainside as fast as I could go. I recall looking back frequently over my shoulder, as if some evil spirit was pushing me away.

When I got to the bottom I was breathless, but more relaxed. I stood on the forbidden track that led to the final RV, whose lights were twinkling only 200 metres away. Instructors were allowed to use lights. It was trainees who were not. Here, at the foot of the mountain and protected by trees, it was warm and windless. Welcoming. Relaxing. Tempting. This was it, I thought. The SAS was not for me. What a stupid idea. It was time to give up. I would be thrown off for missing the penultimate RV anyway. Purposefully I walked along the track towards the four-tonner at the final RV. There was a definite spring to my stride, now that I had made the decision to withdraw. I was looking forward to seeing my warm London flat again.

It was as I emerged from the wooded track into the clearing of the final RV, that the little voice started speaking. Almost inaudible at first, it became louder, and louder, and louder. For Christ's sake, it said, do you *mean* this? All this effort just to give up now? I tried to ignore it, but it would not go away. For a moment I hesitated at the edge of the clearing, perhaps twenty-five metres from the instructor manning the final RV. He was in the light of his gas lamp, blinded by it. I was in the shadows. I saw him look up and stare in my direction. He put up his hand against the light to get a better view. Squinting, he challenged loudly, 'Who the hell's that? Whoever you are, you're on a track. You've failed. Come here.' Then my little voice took over, a wave of determination rising up within me. Quickly, before the instructor could get to his feet and grab me, I bolted back from where I came. No way, dear SAS. You're not going to get me yet.

I made it in the end, though I had to climb that evil mountain again to do so. I was so late, the penultimate RV had almost closed. Instead of being first back to Sennybridge, I was last. Instead of being relaxed and ready for the next day's walk, I was exhausted and ill-prepared. I had come within a hair's breadth of failing, but was determined the same would never happen again. That little voice has spoken on many occasions since.

Long Drag, the final endurance march, is exactly what it says – tedious. It goes on for ever, or seems to, being at the end of a week that has already exhausted the hardiest trainee. I started it with blisters and when I finished they were worse. The principle is to drag yourself, rifle and forty-five-pound rucksack over a set fifty-kilometre course. For the Regular SAS, endurance came at the end of a two-week walking period and included a rifle and fifty-five-pound rucksack over a fifty-five-kilometre course. I have done both and can promise they were equally miserable. RVs are scattered along the route at regular intervals, the whole event having to be completed within twenty-four hours. It's mad.

Mad or not, if I was to be badged I had to do it. It helps if you find someone else with whom to walk. Peter B was a possibility, but he seemed happier to walk by himself and I did not wish to interfere with this. In the end I, too, walked alone. The advantage of the earlier walks is to allow trainees, if they wish, to separate into various groups. Fast with fast, slow with slow. Only the fast ones are likely to make it to the start of Long Drag in any event. The term 'walk' is actually wrong. If you genuinely walk the various routes, failure is likely. I walked uphill, but jogged along the flat and downhill. I did not stop for any reason whatsoever and that included eating. The Bergen stayed on my back throughout. Any food required was stuffed into available tunic pockets or instantly accessible webbing pouches. My water bottle was only filled to add weight to my equipment, for I drank as I moved from puddles and streams, using my cupped hands, or hat, as a suitable container. Nothing must stop that forward movement.

Psychologically, I had also to be prepared. Fifty kilometres is an enormous distance. It was easier to divide the walk into small psychological packets, congratulating myself after each packet had been completed. Doing it this way, the final R V suddenly appeared and I felt as if I could have kept on going for ever. I managed Territorial endurance in 10 hours 56 minutes – an exhausting experience.

At the end of Long Drag I felt I had conquered the world. The SAS allowed me the perception for about a day. Thereafter I was firmly reminded it was merely Selection I had passed. Continuation was still to come. Even with Continuation complete, I would still be a beginner. Staying humble was a good idea.

The Sennybridge Continuation week introduced me to the basic principles of SAS soldiering, in particular the function of an OP, the observation post. Accurate intelligence is vital to the running of any war. Even with satellites now ten-a-penny, cloud cover can mean the only decent information is from manpower on the ground. The basic principle is to get yourself as near the enemy as possible. Moving very slowly, if at all, a careful record is made of everything that passes by. From time to time findings are signalled to HQ, transmissions being kept as short as possible to avoid hostile direction-finding apparatus, known as being 'DF'd'. Some OPs can be within feet of the enemy. Under such circumstances it is essential to remain stationary for hours on end and to ensure proper camouflage. This includes smell. The world is full of vicious creatures called dogs. They can be killed, but it is best to leave them alone and not let them hear you, see you, or smell you. Washing and shaving are therefore out and food best eaten cold.

The function of the Territorial SAS in the late 1970s was to set up hidden observation posts. Four of us would sneak in after dark to some prearranged location on the front line. We would then work like mad. The aim was to create a fully equipped observation post by dawn. This required a spot for the signaller, a sleeping area, a loo and some form of viewing device aimed at the target. With so much equipment, and four large males, squeezed into a tiny area and expertly camouflaged, living conditions in a hide were friendly to say the least. Fortunately, few of us had to live for long in one. Four days was my maximum. It was terrible, particularly the loo. You get to know each other very well at such times.

By the end of my second week in Sennybridge I was a reformed person. I had learned more than I had thought possible. It was not something I could brag about, as personal security was always a problem. As far as my medical colleagues were concerned I simply belonged to the Territorial Army. Mention 'SAS' and people would either raise their eyebrows in disbelief or ask inappropriate questions. It was best to avoid the subject. The IRA didn't help, as mainland attacks were fast becoming a regular feature of the mid to late 1970s. Territorial SAS soldiers are very exposed in this respect. They do not have a barbed-wire encampment behind which they can hide. Nor do they go overseas for weeks on end, making themselves impossible to detect.

Returning from one weekend away, early in my SAS career, I was tired and I was dirty. Exhausted, I dumped my Bergen in the locker room, picked up my holdall and started to walk towards the nearest Underground station. It was still light, there was little traffic for London, so I wandered at a casual pace, mind on other things. As I walked, I saw a line of five people standing at a bus stop. Two were in a tight clinch. To all intents and purposes they were already in bed. I glanced and smiled at the remaining three individuals who were trying to ignore it all. As I did so I felt a low, but very distinct, rumbling coming from my holdall. By then, with SAS training well under way, I was braced for the possibility of a terrorist attack. My father was also in Intelligence at the time. I had every reason to be a target.

It had to be a bomb. Like a fool I had left the holdall unattended all weekend and the bastards had got me. I had to get rid of the holdall fast. It could blow at any time. I knew my only hope, indeed the only hope for the civilians around me, was to throw the thing away, as far as possible. The bag was heavy, so like an Olympic hammer thrower I turned a rapid full circle, the bag in my outstretched arms, released it and shouted, 'Get down! Bomb! Get down!' As I dived for the security of the gutter, I glanced up at the flying holdall. Thank God, I thought. It had been a good throw. Provided the explosive was not too powerful, the small wall for which I had aimed should protect us all. No one else moved, though the elderly woman at the end of the queue did look somewhat astonished. Then, as the holdall tumbled through the air, straps and handles flapping loose, the awful realization hit me. It was a sick feeling at first, that rapidly turned into uncontrollable mirth. I lay in the gutter laughing. It wasn't a bomb at all but my electric razor. For some reason it had chosen that moment to discharge itself. 'Just testing,' I said to the bus queue as I sheepishly picked up the bag, 'Just testing,' and went on my way. SAS service does wonders for your reflexes.

CHAPTER 2

Surgeon or Soldier?

'If you cut that artery, Villar, I will personally crucify you.'

'This one, sir?' I pointed towards a pulsating tube with the trembling ends of my long, curved, surgical scissors.

'No, you daft idiot. That one. Look. Here. I'll show you.' My tall, intolerant instructor deftly pulled the patient's stomach to one side to reveal the engorged blood vessel behind it. With a perfectly steady hand he took his surgical forceps and rested their blunt tips on it. 'This one. Can't you see? This is the one I want you to avoid. Your scissors have lurched near to it several times. If you damage it by mistake we're all in trouble.'

'Oh! I see. Thank you, sir. Y-Yes, sir. Of course, sir,' I replied uncertainly as I struggled through the operation. I think the instructor felt he was being kind when he let me act as first surgeon. Coming near to full qualification, I would normally have been the assistant, standing where he was now, but for some reason we had today swopped around. It is astonishing how easy an operation can seem when you are assisting, but how difficult it can be when you are at the sharp end, the first surgeon. It was the first occasion I had been allowed to operate on a living patient. Until then I had been confined to laboratory-frog dissections, dead human-body dissections and copious assisting at the real thing. Nothing can ever prepare you for that first day. It often comes when you least expect it. Suddenly, to have prime responsibility for the life of a patient makes the task appear harder. My hands were all over the place. I could barely control them. A tiny tremor of your finger is magnified a hundred times if you are holding long scissors or forceps, six inches from end to end.

It was meant to be a simple task. Find a small nerve, called the vagus nerve, lying near the stomach and cut it. Called vagotomy, it was a treatment for stomach ulcers. We would scarcely do it now, as tablets do the same job admirably, but there was a time when vagotomies were performed by the dozen, every day, in operating theatres throughout the world. This was one of them.

It was an early Tuesday morning and my brain was still fogged from an arduous weekend away with 21 SAS. I had not slept from Friday to Monday and was only just beginning to recover. Certain that all I would have to do was assist, pulling gently on a surgical retractor or swabbing the occasional blood vessel, I had looked forward to a relaxing morning while the first surgeon took the strain. It was as I walked through the doors of the theatre coffee room that I realized this particular Tuesday was going to be different.

'Ah, Villar,' the outspoken instructor had exclaimed, as he lounged in his armchair, booted legs crossed and outstretched. 'You want to be a surgeon, don't you?'

'Well . . . yes . . . but . . .'

'Then *you* can do it. Why not? Excellent idea!'

'Do what, sir?' I asked, still suffering from extreme sleep deprivation, eyes half closed.

'The operation, of course! You can do it. I'll show you. Come on then!' The instructor leapt to his feet, towering over me.

'But . . .'

'Come on, man! Do you want to be a surgeon or don't you?'

'Yes . . . but . . .'

'Look. It's a vagotomy. Even a blind man could do that. Follow me. The anaesthetist has already put the patient on the operating table so we've got to scrub up. Let's go.'

I followed him along the corridor to the operating theatre. That sick feeling, again, ate away at my stomach. A vagotomy? I hadn't a clue. I had no idea what to do. Where was the bloody vagus nerve anyway?

Even scrubbing up, the thorough washing process that all perform immediately before operating, was an ordeal. You may think it is a simple matter of washing your hands – it is not. Scrubbing up is a ceremony. The object is to wash from fingertips to elbows with disinfectant soap, but without touching anything other than running water and soap solution. Afterwards, try donning a pair of rubber gloves without touching their outer surfaces, for example. I can do it now, instinctively, but that morning I was all fingers and thumbs. I dropped gowns, contaminated gloves and knocked over a complete trolley of instruments before taking my position on the first surgeon's side of the operating table. I knew it was not going to be a good day.

Anaesthetists have a habit of making junior surgeons feel unwanted. The vagotomy was no exception. With my instructor bellowing orders from in front, the elderly, eminent anaesthetist did the same from behind. Glasses perched on the end of his nose, he leant over my shoulder, muttering comments like 'Come on, Villar, we haven't got all day. There's a whole operating list to finish by lunchtime.'

Two hours into this normally sixty-minute operation, I was exasperated. My initial fear was becoming anger. With the two of them shouting at me, one in front and one behind, I could have thumped either. I was unable to do so, of course, as that would have contaminated my sterile hands on their unsterile jaw bones. I was not impressed. If this was the type of training you had, it was no surprise it took most doctors a decade or more to become surgical consultants.

My mind was also on other things at times. Now I was badged, and held the Regiment's lowliest rank of Trooper, it was proving difficult to juggle my medical studies with SAS commitments. I would frequently find myself drawing outlines of Soviet tanks on the back of a patient's notes, or calculating ways of penetrating high-security establishments instead of concentrating on ward rounds. Those early SAS days were immensely demanding, mixing my two chosen careers, and yet highly enjoyable.

I knew I was out of my depth. In retrospect it was the instructor's fault, letting someone so junior perform an operation so ill-prepared. Surgical training then frequently meant leaping in at the deep end without detailed experience beforehand. We would shudder at the prospect now, as I barely let juniors do anything unfamiliar without my gloved hands clamped firmly around their wrists. As I struggled with the vagotomy, I realized I had met my match, even if I had passed SAS Selection. I felt a surge of anger overtake me as I turned towards my two superiors, instructor opposite and anaesthetist beside. I tried to look each hard in the eyes simultaneously, though masks prevented me from seeing their full faces. 'Sod you both,' I said, spitting out the words. 'Do the bloody thing yourselves.' With a metallic clatter, I banged my forceps on to the instrument trolley to my left and in a few, short strides moved to the opposite side of the table. My two critics remained silent and motionless, dumbfounded by my behaviour. Medical students were the lowest form of human life in teaching hospitals, and I was no exception. But my blood was up. 'Come on!' I shouted, 'If it's so simple, show me. How the hell else do you expect me to learn?' My instructor took the hint, quietly moving to the first surgeon's position, completing the task with consummate, annoying ease. Needless to say, he never spoke to me again.

Once badged, life opens up for the SAS soldier, be he Territorial or Regular. Enormous opportunities exist, plus a level of comradeship and support unrivalled elsewhere. Training continues throughout a man's career, liberally interspersed with operations and lifelike exercises. You cannot get more convincing than SAS training.

Interrogation is a typical example. I have now been interrogated several times. It gets no easier. The first occasion was late one Friday night. It had been a heavy week in the hospital, allowing little time to concentrate on anything other than medicine. Twenty of us were thrown from the back of a four-ton lorry outside a small village near Hereford. We had each been given specific instructions not to use tracks but to make our way to an RV the far side of some woods. Further orders would be issued when we got there. There were two routes to the RV. One, a safe, tactical journey around the outside of the woods used the available cover of hedgerows, farm buildings and tumbledown walls. The other was a broad, well-trodden bridlepath through the woods themselves. This latter choice led directly to the RV and was very quick.

Despite specific instructions to the contrary, another operative and I chose the track. We calculated it would be possible to dash through the woods to the RV before the enemy had got into position. It was the very start of the exercise and we both knew how long such things took to get under way. Unfortunately we guessed wrong. It was the last time I ever used a track for any form of SAS service.

Leaping from the back of the lorry as soon as it stopped, the two of us ran as fast as we could towards the start of the track. I remember how inviting it looked. Quiet, seemingly undisturbed, a haven of peace and tranquillity. It was as straight as a Roman road, allowing us to see moonlight at its far end, no more than 300 metres away. The remaining trainees chose to skirt the wood.

I remember the exhilarating feeling of knowing we would be first to the RV and thereby ahead of the entire field. The gamble was not worth taking. Within fifty metres of entering the wood, from the blackness to our right came the unmistakable command 'Halt!' My immediate reaction was to turn and run. As I did so, three large figures emerged from the undergrowth. One took my neck, the other my waist, another my legs. There was no arguing, their combined weights being more than 600 pounds. I was thrown sharply to the ground, face down and by then severely winded. 'Keep still you bastard, and don't speak,' one said. A large boot pressed down on the back of my neck, a rifle barrel stuck under my left ear, while my hands were handcuffed behind my back. I can still feel them as I write this. Handcuffs are painful things. My colleague, an accountant at the time, was being manhandled in the same way. I never asked him what he felt, even when we eventually returned to London, but I imagine he rated himself as foolish as I. We had been out of the lorry for barely thirty seconds before being caught. Not what is expected of a trained SAS operative.

We were dragged, blindfolded, along the track to a waiting vehicle. Once a prisoner is captured the aim is to totally disorientate him in time and space. Hooding, or blindfolding, is one such way. I was terrified. My mouth was dry, my heart racing. It was not a pleasant experience. I could sense our captors were experts, but I had no idea what was in store for me. All I knew was that I could only give my name, rank, number and date of birth. I shall call them the 'vital four'.

The UK now has a number of locations specifically designed for interrogation. I was to see them develop in later years. On this occasion, however, such facilities did not exist. It was dark and I was blindfolded. Much of what I describe is thus based on subsequent experience, when I was on the issuing rather than receiving end. I am afraid even doctors who have taken the Hippocratic oath do have a part to play in suspect interrogation.

By now I had lost contact with my colleague. For all I knew he could have been right beside me, but neither of us was going to speak to find out. Once caught, I knew I should say nothing to anyone, except the vital four when faced with my interrogator. I was taken first to the prisoner holding area, a dilapidated barn fifty metres from an equally dilapidated country road. An indelible marker pen was used to write my prisoner number on my forehead, my handcuffs were removed and I was placed in the stress position.

The stress position is the official term for wallstanding. Still blindfolded, your hands are placed at head height, palms forward, a shoulder width apart on the wall before you. Feet are positioned a metre from the wall and a metre apart. There you stand, seemingly for ever. When you first adopt the stress position you wonder what all the fuss is about. After twenty minutes you begin to understand. Your hands go numb, your thigh muscles shake and your shoulders feel as if lead weights are attached to them. Slowly, quietly, in the hope that no one will notice, you let your elbows bend and hands slide downwards to a more comfortable position. What you do not know is that you are in the permanent company of at least one guard. He, or she for all I know, stays silent. No one hits you, no one threatens to kill or drown you, they simply put you back in the stress position whenever you lapse. They do not speak at all.

The stress position is not without medical hazard. Inside the human body, immediately behind the collar bones, lie the major nerves to the arms and hands. When you stretch out your arms, these nerves also stretch. They do not like being pulled and are very sensitive to such things. Normally the human body would not stand for hours on end, arms outstretched against a wall. Should it do so, the prolonged pull on the nerves can damage them, albeit to a minor degree. On a number of occasions, after interrogation, I had tingling in my fingers and hands for several days before the nerves recovered. A worrying time for a future surgeon who relies on his hands to make a living.

Fortunately, not all your time is spent in the stress position. Occasionally, your guards will sit or kneel you on the floor, hands clasped behind your head, elbows and shoulders braced firmly backwards. The floor is normally concrete or gravel and extremely uncomfortable. Thus it continues for at least twenty-four hours, limited bread and water the only food provided. During this period you can expect to be interrogated five or six times.

Interrogation is carried out by the JSIW – Joint Services Interrogation Wing. These people come in all shapes, sizes and sexes and are not the most loved individuals from an SAS viewpoint. They can be aggressive, they can be peaceful. They can be nasty, they can be nice. You never know what they are going to be like until you are left alone with them. Sometimes you are blindfolded, at others you are allowed to see the questioner. It is easier, from a soldier's viewpoint, if you remain blindfolded. That way you can remain in your own little world and allow no one to drag you from it. As with all SAS techniques, the secret is concentration, persistence and bloody-mindedness. Your captors, by fair means or foul, will attempt to drag from you details beyond the vital four. You, as their prisoner, must thwart such attempts.

'What is your name?'

'Villar, sir.'

'What is your number?'

'2419843, sir.'

'What is your rank?'

'Trooper, sir.'

'What is your unit?'

'I cannot answer that question, sir.'

'What is your date of birth?'

'28 April 1958, sir.'

'What is your unit?'

'I cannot answer that question, sir.'

'Come on man. What is your goddam unit?'

'I cannot answer that question, sir.'

So it goes on. To any question concerning anything other than the vital four, the reply is 'I cannot answer that question, sir.' It is important not to be drawn into long discussions with the interrogator. These people are highly trained for the job and can tie you in knots given half a chance. They are looking for that tiny chink in your armour to work on, so as to open it up into a huge chasm.

That first weekend I nearly gave the interrogators their chance. It was entirely my fault. The interrogator had been going at me with rapid-fire questions for ten continuous minutes. All he asked was the vital four, nothing else. It felt as if I was entering the spirit of competition, trying to answer his questions as fast as he put them to me. I was verbally stumbling to keep up. Then, unexpectedly, he asked 'What is your unit?', just as if it was one of the vital four. Immediately, I replied 'Twenty . . .' and then stopped instantly. I had been a fraction away from saying 21 SAS. My military career would have been over if I had.

Overconfidence is your worst enemy. Years later it got me again, in yet another remote farm building, though this time in northern Scotland. Like a fool, I had allowed a guard dog to catch me trying to break into an ammunition storage depot. I should have killed it, but could not separate it from its handler. I thought I knew it all at that stage. I had already been through interrogation several times and felt I had seen anything JSIW could throw at me. I was wrong.

It was a routine interrogation. The questioner was being moderately unfriendly, thumping the side of what I thought was a riding boot with his swagger stick. I could only judge by sound as I was wallstanding and blindfolded. I was sure we were alone. Just the two of us. You put up a wall around you during interrogation – an invisible skin that you make as impermeable as possible. Gradually, the interrogator's thumping lessened and his voice quietened. He began to sound almost reasonable, his questions again on the vital four. He even started to joke.

'You're a hitman for the Brownies, Villar, aren't you?' he asked, whispering into my right ear.

I laughed openly, hesitating before giving the standard, obstructive reply. I was totally relaxed, particularly as I was sure we were both alone. Then, suddenly, a loud voice shouted into my left ear 'Answer!' I jumped. It was an enormous shock. We had not been alone at all. Someone had broken my impermeable skin. I shut up immediately at that stage and put up the barriers. I had learned, however tempting it might appear, never to lower them again.

Interrogation appears a one-sided affair. All advantage seems to be with the questioner. Your only consolation is knowing it has to end some time. It is not pleasant and there is no point in pretending that it is. You can make life difficult for your interrogator, however. Beyond firmly, but politely, refusing to answer anything other than the vital four, you can make yourself a very unpleasant specimen with which to deal. Peeing in your pants, and all down your trousers, is a good way. It makes you stink and puts the interrogator's mind on other things. An alternative is to stay silent. Answer nothing at all, not even the vital four. Pretending to be ill, or inducing yourself to vomit, is another way. Again, it makes you smell and you are entitled to see a doctor at any time. This can offer a brief reprieve. However, the JSIW interrogators may not be SAS-trained, but are very shrewd. They have seen most of it before, but are also human and can have their own weaknesses exploited. Unfortunately, it is particularly uncomfortable standing for hours in the stress position with urine-soaked trousers. I have tried it. If you get it wrong and attempt to upset an interrogator who may be devoid of emotion, then you stand there feeling very silly indeed. Be careful when peeing in your pants. It does not always work.

Despite the enormous mental strain to which a soldier is subjected during interrogation, injuries are fortunately few. Apart from nerve damage, the main worry is psychological. For the SAS trainee or operative there is much at stake if he talks under pressure. It is the end of a Special Forces career.

Nothing emphasizes the loneliness of SAS service more than survival training. This is the art of staying alive, for indefinite periods, away from the normal lines of resupply. In the normal, 'big' army you will, or should, receive a regular supply of food and essentials. For an SAS operative, inside enemy territory, the situation is different. Resupply may not be physically possible. Even if it is, the act of resupplying may highlight the presence of an SAS patrol. The same applies should an operative escape after capture, with little more than the clothes in which he stands. Knowing how to live off the land that surrounds him is vital. This is the skill known as 'combat survival'. Courses are run in various locations throughout the world. To be totally realistic, survival training should take place under hostile conditions. Not only should you survive, but you must not be caught doing so.

I learned my survival on a tiny Scottish island, when working alongside the Special Boat Squadron, or SBS. I cannot remember the exact mechanics, but one September the SBS engineered that four of us should be captured. We were unceremoniously tied and locked into a gents' lavatory somewhere on the mainland coast and held prisoner for several hours. Then, at dead of night, we were manhandled on to a motorized fishing vessel, an MFV, and taken out to sea. It was very dark. We were made to strip, all clothes being taken from us, including underwear. This was a tragedy. The well-prepared SAS operative should have items of survival equipment littered over him. If surprised when behind enemy lines, the first thing to be ejected is the heavy Bergen rucksack. With it go the normal comforts of SAS covert life. To compensate for its loss, the operative should at all times wear his belt escape kit, with his slingless rifle never more than one arm's length away. Within the escape kit should be sufficient equipment to survive for as long as required without resupply. Lightweight ponchos, minicompasses, flints, razor blades, fishing-hooks and line. The list is long. You can spend months tinkering with your escape kit, trying to squeeze as much as possible into the tiny spaces a military webbing belt will allow. Sometimes you would talk for hours with SAS colleagues on the best type of fish-hook or gill net, or the ideal form of windproof match. Escape kits are very personal things. Everyone has his own idea on the perfect design. Finally, in the unlikely event an operative should ever be separated from his escape kit, various items should be sewn into his clothes, boots and pockets.

Anything is fair game as far as survival is concerned. Even when fully stripped, it is your task to smuggle through as much as you can. You still have the inner folds of your cheeks, your anus, and your vagina should you be female, left to play with. The less squeamish spare not even a second thought when inserting a cigar tube laden with survival equipment up their tail end. It is probably my medical training, but I have always balked at the idea. Public-school education perhaps. You must be careful when placing items up your anus. Having once spent six months of my civilian life working for a tail-end surgeon, I have seen all manner of things put in that never make it out again. Not without help from a doctor that is. Screwdrivers, spoons, whole vibrators, broom handles. Diversity in human taste never ceases to amaze me. The female vagina is effectively a blind-ended tube. Most items that go in will come out again easily enough. The anus is different. It is the bottom of a very long, open tube, starting with the mouth at the top. Should you pop something up it, it can keep going upwards rather than stay where it is. Lost for ever, until a surgeon opens your belly to retrieve it. You have been warned.

That night we were cast ashore on an unidentifiable Scottish island. There was me, a policeman, a doctor and one other. In exchange for our nakedness, we were each given a pair of laceless, ill-fitting army boots, some coarse army trousers and a buttonless shirt. That was it, though we were also told not to swim to the neighbouring island. Gruinard Island, the SBS advised, had been used for anthrax experiments in the last war. It was still uninhabitable. The anthrax bacillus can survive for decades in soil. It is a particularly nasty way to die, causing large pustules and damage to your skin and other vital systems. There has never been anything fair about germ warfare.

Your first reaction, when cast ashore in the middle of nowhere, is to become obsessed by hunting for food. It is the wrong approach. Your priority, particularly in Scotland, must be shelter. You can easily survive for a couple of days on water alone. Exposure can kill you.

Near our landing we found a tiny cave, well sheltered from the wind in its small cove. My mistake was to build a fire at the back of the cave, rather than its entrance. Within seconds I had smoked the place out. The four of us coughed and choked for hours. I had managed to smuggle a small book of matches past our earlier search. The match supply was not limitless, so once lit, a fire had to be kept burning. The survival books are full of many different ways to light fires in the wild. Flints and tinder, bowstring and stick, and many more. In practice, anything other than a match is a challenge.

By the afternoon of our first day, the cave was well organized. We had arranged a somewhat flexible rota for keeping the fire ablaze and could then start looking for food. My first thought was to kill one of the few wild sheep I could see wandering the hills. I had no weapon, but if I could get close enough I did not think it would take much to break its neck. Two of us set about trying to catch the animal. Fortunately, no one else was there to see us.

I had always thought sheep were dumb, daft creatures whose sole contribution to life was to leave slimy droppings over Nature's mountainsides and to give good company to mint sauce. Scottish specimens are different – and extremely tough. We had decided the best approach would be to corner it at one end of a small peninsula and drive it over the edge to its death on the rocks below. We forced it to the peninsula easily enough, but no sooner did it reach the edge, it turned. It had small horns and very dark eyes. It looked first at me, then at my companion, then back to me. I was obviously the chosen one. With a loud 'Baaa!' it charged, going full tilt. I could not stop it and was knocked flat, winded for the umpteenth time that year. My companion could not restrain himself and rolled around in uncontrollable mirth for ages. We decided at that stage a diet of seagulls' eggs, limpets and dead cormorants was a safer, wiser choice.

The doctor was a problem. A charming man, he was qualified, unlike me at that point, and tried to apply logic and common sense to the situation. Sometimes it does not pay to think too much about the merits and disadvantages of SAS service. Sitting in the cave, tending the fire, he claimed searching for food used up more calories than were actually found. There was therefore no point, he argued, in looking for food at all. You would die quicker if you looked for it than if you sat and did nothing all day. He had a point, though none of us wanted to admit it. Sit he did, helping himself to the food the rest of us brought in. If you had spent eight hours bringing in a dozen limpets, two dandelion leaves and a cormorant's egg, only to have them eaten by someone else, I assure you it would drive you over the edge. I nearly cracked. Likewise the policeman. To this day I do not know if the doctor was right in his analysis.

In this vegetarian era, shops are full of books on what can be eaten from the land. Buried at the bottom of my Bergen was a copy of Richard Mabey's *Food For Free*, but the rucksack had long ago been confiscated. When that happens you have to experiment. As I found to my cost, overconfidence does not pay. When faced with an unfamiliar food, you should first place it in the space between your lower lip and teeth. Keep it there for at least a minute. If it tastes reasonable then swallow a very small amount. Wait and see what happens. If you are still alive five minutes later, then swallow the lot.

Bored with our now established diet, I felt it was time for a change so went searching beside the small freshwater lake our island haven supplied. To one end of the water were some light green, rushlike plants. I have no idea what they were. By then I had already found several dozen new ideas to take back to my companions. None of my earlier finds had been any trouble, so I took a large handful of light green plant and ate everything. I would have done credit to a cow. For a brief moment all was fine, but then the agony hit me. A furious, sharp, searing pain shot down my gullet. I could hardly breathe. I broke into a ferocious sweat and then the most intense stomach cramps overwhelmed me. I retched and vomited everywhere. Nature has a strange way of protecting us and vomiting is an excellent method of eliminating poison. I had broken the rules and had paid for it. I do not know what it was I ate. However, if you are tempted to live off the land, do avoid those tall, thin, rush-like things at the end of a freshwater lake. They will make you sick.

It is all very well finding food, but your catch has to be cooked. The books say you should find a metal container washed up on the beach and use that. Something akin to an old oil drum would do, once suitably cleaned. Real life is not so helpful. Have you ever tried to find a *metal* container on a beach these days? Everything is plastic and plastic melts when you heat it. We were saved by the policeman. Somehow he had managed to smuggle past our captors a complete messtin and a packet of rice. I have no idea how he did it and he was not letting on. For sure these are not items that would fit easily into a cigar tube.

We made it in the end, a week later, somewhat lighter and significantly unkempt. The SBS did send out helicopters to look for us while we tried to survive. They are another factor you can do without. The secret is not to look up when one flies over you. They make a loud noise and should give you reasonable warning to lie face down, camouflaged against Mother Earth. Its pilot, navigator or loadmaster will nevertheless be looking for you. Not only do they look forwards and sideways, they also look backwards. Consequently, if you look upwards once it has flown over, your white face will be perfectly contrasted against the green vegetation. You will be seen. It is essential to keep your head down until they have flown well past.

You are not allowed to rest on your laurels in the SAS. A special skill, preferably more than one, is mandatory. The typical, traditional, SAS patrol comprises four men: demolitions, signals, language and medical. The medical man is usually called the patrol or SAS medic. In practice, each operative needs a grasp of every skill, but you need one who is in overall charge of each specialty. My first shot, being a medical student, was to become a patrol medic. I thought it would be easy. After all, I was dealing with medical problems every day in my civilian life. I was wrong. I had not realized the level of sophistication of SAS medical training delivered by its various medical courses. Needless to say, the teaching given by the UK's medical schools to their students is no use whatsoever to the SAS medic operating behind enemy lines. The medical student learns to deal with patients on a hospital ward. The SAS operative may be working under a hedge somewhere, without the trappings of modern medical care. I failed my SAS medical course, I am ashamed to say. It was a failing I was happy not to advertise at the time. It was due to no other reason than my cockiness. I felt certain a medical student was bound to know all the answers. In the event, I failed as I did not know the dosage of certain commonly used medicines. Aspirin was one of them. I felt suitably chastened and did not attempt the course again.

For the first time I began to have doubts as to whether my ambitions were viable. The vagotomy operation had highlighted how difficult it was to develop the skills a surgeon requires. If I were a patient, I would go for a manually adept surgeon for my operation, not necessarily a clever, hamfisted one. Intellect and manual ability do not always go together. It was difficult enough to become a surgeon, without the added complication of developing SAS skills as well. A small voice, Satanic this time spoke in my ear. I worried if I would ever make it. At times I even wondered whether I should forsake surgery altogether and take up soldiering full time. The SAS was certainly demonstrating there was an excellent, challenging life outside medicine. I would feel this way most often when I returned from SAS activities around the land. The moment I re-entered my hospital, however, I knew I could not turn my back on medicine. The Third World still beckoned and also orthopaedic surgery. I would simply have to find a way of doing them all.

Having failed the SAS medical course, I decided instead to become a signaller. It was a skill I thoroughly enjoyed. An SAS patrol is no use to anyone if it cannot report its findings to headquarters. I learned everything I could and was soon fortunate to win the Regimental signals prize. Morse code was vital. It is impossible. Dah, dah, dah, dit, dit, dit. The various combinations of dahs and dits are enormous. Eventually, I learned it from the back of my motorbike. To and from work every morning I would transpose the number plate of the car in front into Morse. Dit-dah, dah-dit-dit-dit, dah-dit-dah-dit, it might go. There I would be, ditting and dahing furiously at traffic-light stops all over London. Whatever my fellow commuters felt, it was an excellent way of learning the code.

The aim of the signaller is to send his message in the shortest possible time. Out there are people who want to know what you are up to. Spending too long on the air allows them to work out both your location and who you are. The way a signaller handles his Morse key is as unique as a fingerprint. Everyone uses the same dits and dahs, but the way they can be sent over the air is variable. A trained operator, working for the other side, will pick this up and specifically identify location, signaller and unit from the nature of the dits and dahs. This is direction finding, or 'DFing' for short. Being DF'd is not a good idea. It is difficult to imagine, when you are in the back of beyond, that anyone can be listening at all, but they are. On one occasion I was asked to test a new military radio. It was big and bulky, but had all manner of knobs and buttons that allowed you to change frequencies as often as you liked. The earlier SAS radio, the PRC-316, had only a limited frequency choice. As a result it was easier to DF, despite being a lovely machine to use. The new design was meant to avoid such troubles.

I took it to some woods near London and started sending fully encoded messages to our radio base. I do mean fully encoded. Fast, efficient message keying in numerical format, using destructible one-time pads, held by me and the radio base only. Security was as foolproof as it gets. And yet it wasn't. Within five minutes of keying my first message, an unidentifiable but strong Morse message came over my set. Dit-dit-dit, dit-dah, dit-dit-dit. Dit-dit-dit, dit-dah, dit-dit-dit. Those are the Morse symbols of the letters 'S.A.S.' Someone, somewhere, had identified me on this new, marvellous, supposedly undetectable radio. Not only had they isolated my frequency, but they had established my unit, something a trained signaller would never transmit uncoded. I had been DF'd well and true. A very spooky feeling when stuck in gloomy woods near south London. Furthermore, it was impossible to say who had DF'd me. Russians, Americans, Chinese? I had no idea.

As a trained signaller, many doors are open to you. It is not a skill that everyone takes to. However, security tests were my interest. Some were easy, some not so easy, but I soon became master at breaking into all manner of civilian or military establishments. I remember one very well. Our patrol had been tasked to penetrate a storage depot in western Scotland, in order to lay dummy charges against some missile warheads. The depot was miles from anywhere, frequently patrolled by Ministry of Defence personnel, the MOD police, with doghandlers and some military support. They were all told we might attempt an attack. Other SAS patrols meanwhile were ordered to infiltrate alternative establishments around Scotland, including the sabotage of a nuclear submarine. The submarine group was completely successful.

We decided to infiltrate by night, reconnoitre ('recce') the place, and return twenty-four hours later for the definitive attack. Aerial photographs had been given to us, the primary target of the warhead store being barely 100 feet from the MOD police base. We were also given a secondary target, a transformer, in case our efforts on the warhead store failed. As part of our pre-operation planning we had established that the primary target's main door was secured by a huge, bulky padlock. Carrying a thermolance, a device like a welding rod, was impractical, so the technical boys in London made a special tungsten carbide hacksaw blade. We were assured it would cut through anything within ninety seconds. That would be fine, I agreed.

The recce went well. Dropped off some distance away by Land Rover, we approached the depot across country from some ten kilometres. The area was largely uninhabited, which was good to see. Locals can be the enemy on occasions such as this. They notice if even a blade of grass has been moved and are on the telephone immediately to the police. The annual exercises in Scandinavia were classics in this respect. There, the whole civilian population was warned, well before the SAS ever arrived, that UK troops would attempt to sabotage their various key establishments. Advertisements would be pinned up everywhere. The result was the entire civilian and military populations would be mobilized to catch you. Families would go for picnics, dogs would be taken for a walk, in the desperate hope they would stumble over an SAS trooper.

The guard routine at the depot was predictable. Every fifteen minutes someone would visually check the door, though would not necessarily go right up to it and inspect it. An occasional patrol van, complete with searchlight, would drive round the large remaining expanse of depot to ensure security of the smaller, outlying buildings. Armed with such information, I signalled London that all was in order, while the patrol laid up for the day. For a signaller there is no such thing as 'lying up'. This is when other patrol members, during daylight hours, sleep or cook. In this lying-up position, or LUP, totally camouflaged, the signaller is still hard at work. As a radio operator, sleep is an impossible luxury. Being exhausted becomes a way of life.

We had positioned the LUP one kilometre from the target, to avoid unexpected perimeter patrols. The day passed uneventfully and by dark we were again ready to move. The approach to the depot went easily, save for one thing. Bullocks. During the day a local farmer had unexpectedly placed twenty of them in the field immediately adjacent to the depot. That night they were extremely frisky. On the one hand we were four heavily armed and camouflaged SAS soldiers crawling towards a highly secret government establishment. On the other, were twenty boisterous animals refusing to ignore us. They cramped and crowded us, butted us and pawed the ground incessantly. By the time we reached the fifteen-foot security fence we had gathered a crowd of not-so-admiring onlookers. If there is anything good to say about them, they were at least silent.

The security fence was a latticed affair, with three strands of barbed wire leaning backwards at the top. You can either go under or over such fences. By under I mean tunnelling through the ground underneath the latticed portion. However, on this occasion the fence was well bedded into the earth, so tunnelling was impractical. Cutting a hole through the wire would have been an idea, but our aim was to get in and out without detection. Leaving a gaping cavity in the security fence would have been an advertisement for all to see. So over we went. At least, over three of us went. Number 4 could not make it, however hard he tried. He was not strong enough. Fifteen feet was too far. Poor man. Here was the supposed super-human SAS, surrounded by bullocks, struggling to get past only the first hurdle the MOD had thrown at us. Fortunately it was dark and no one else could see. Number 4 eventually gave up and waited for us at our emergency RV. There was an obvious limit as to how long we could remain at the fence waiting for him to cross.

When designing the depot, the MOD had, perhaps, the welfare of the saboteur in mind. There was the occasional hedge, and frequent earth mound, to hide behind. It did not take long to find a position immediately outside the MOD police base, directly opposite the target store. Beside the door was a metal dustbin, the entire area being bathed by orange spotlight. The angle of light, however, meant that part of the door was in shadow. At last it appeared things were getting better.

We waited for the next MOD patrol to pass. To say 'pass' is optimistic. It was a windy night, not conducive to staying outdoors, unless really necessary. The MOD patrol thus consisted of a policeman putting his head outside the base's door for several seconds, checking all was in order and disappearing inside again. You rely on human failings on such occasions.

As soon as the policeman's head had disappeared inside the warmth and security of his base, we set to work. Two of us stayed in the shadows opposite the target, to act as early warning of patrols for the third, whose task was to cut the lock. Ninety seconds was all it would take, the technical boys had advised. The lock was taped rapidly to a small, hand-sized piece of chipboard to allow it to be held securely. Number 3 set about cutting the hasp with the new, magic saw. Ninety seconds later he had barely made any impression. He dashed over to join us in the shadows.

'Jesus! The bloody thing's useless!' he said. 'What the **** are we going to do?'

We knew we had several minutes to play with, so decided to keep going, certainly until the next patrol was due. Number 3 returned to his task. The remaining two of us could always over-power anyone who became too inquisitive, though our element of surprise would then certainly be lost.

By the time we had warned number 3 of an impending patrol, judged by the shifting noises emanating from the police base, it had become apparent our task was going to take a long time. The lock was now bound to a block of wood, and partially cut. All it would take was a close, visual inspection and our efforts would have been wasted. MOD's technical guys were not popular with us that night.

Yet somehow, for reasons I still do not understand, no close inspection was made. I can only suppose it was the weather that kept the guards inside. We took it in turns in the end, in twelve-minute shifts, waiting for the next head to appear before resuming our task. On one occasion a policeman did come very near to the target door, when number 2 was sawing the lock. The patrol, if that is what I can call it, was unexpected. Number 2 got the fright of his life. We had decided, if caught, to abandon everything and run. The SAS operative thought he had been rumbled, throwing the hacksaw firmly into the dustbin beside the door. As he did so, the dustbin lid slid off, landing with an enormous crash on the ground. The noise went on for ever. Number 2, meanwhile, was stood in the doorway, bathed in orange light, as clear as day. I can see the policeman now, looking disinterestedly our way. He missed number 2 altogether, ignored the clattering dustbin lid and returned to his warm base. Perhaps he felt the wind had been responsible for the noise. After all, no self-respecting SAS patrol would make such a din, would they?

After ninety minutes, not ninety seconds, we were successful. The lock had been cut, dummy charges laid and we were away, heading towards the secondary target. Perhaps we were being overambitious, but by now our blood was up. It was as we approached the transformer that the police discovered evidence of our successful primary attack. All hell broke loose. Sirens, lights, cars, dogs. You name it and they had it. The number of times a searchlight passed directly over me that night was horrifying. On each occasion I froze and on each occasion it passed me by. We had now been rumbled, though not captured. It was time to beat a hasty retreat if we could, though via the transformer, our secondary target. I almost made it there, but had to go to earth ten metres away when a dog patrol arrived to inspect it. Now, at last, the police were taking their job seriously.

The dog went crazy, jumping, leaping, growling and barking. I could hear it straining at the leash, pulling hard on the handler's shoulder. I lay there, inches away, completely motionless. On one occasion the animal came so close its saliva hit my neck, but it was dark and the transformer had no floodlights to illuminate it. Several times the handler shone his torch at me, and over me. Each time he failed to see me. I knew I was there, the dog knew I was there, but the handler did not. A guard dog is only as good as the person controlling it.

Target attacks like this are the staple diet of any SAS soldier. They can be immensely challenging and at times dangerous. No holds are barred on either side. I remember well a night attack on a dockyard, near Southampton. We were successful, in that charges were laid on several naval vessels. The security forces, however, were certain two of us had taken shelter under their main quayside, having approached it from the sea. They were right, though could not prove it. It was high tide, but there was a tiny pocket of air between the water's surface and the underside of the quay. It was a perfect place to hide, allowing easy access to the boats moored each side. The security people were not to be deterred and ran their patrol vessels up and down the water either side of the quay at top speed. If we were there, I am sure they felt, their wash would drive us out. Their ploy nearly worked. The two of us hung on for dear life, being thrown forcibly and repeatedly against the barnacled underside of the quay. Like a fool, I had not worn gloves and so had to grip the razor sharp barnacles with my bare hands for protection. In my frantic efforts to prevent my head from being smashed to pulp on the quay's underside, the skin from two fingertips was ripped completely away. They have since recovered, but made surgery impossible for several weeks thereafter. I still cannot feel properly as a result.

Throughout these events, I was part civilian, part soldier. The transition from one to the other was frequently difficult. As a medical student, neither bosses nor colleagues had any idea of what I was up to. It was best kept that way. Jim T, my parachuting friend, had long since returned to Hull after his confirmation of my insanity for joining the SAS at all. I noticed my loyalties slowly changing. Civilian friendships began to fade, while military ones developed. Relationships with girlfriends struggled to survive. I was either working all hours God gave in hospital or miles away from London on SAS training. I was engaged to be married, but my wife on this occasion was the SAS. I imagine those girls who knew me must have thought I was gay. The reality was simpler. I was more interested in medicine and the SAS than lifelong liaisons or carnal satisfaction on a Saturday night.

For my last six months at medical school I packed away my camouflage uniform and studied hard. The final medical examination is no laughing matter and needs endless hours of book work and research. Twelve hours of reading a day would not be an exaggeration. Having failed my SAS medical course I was determined not to do the same with its civilian equivalent. I found the only way truly to concentrate, apart from the vivid terror of forthcoming examinations focusing my mind, was to remove all distractions from around me. Non-medical books, guitars, pictures on the walls. All had to go, otherwise I would find an excuse to tinker with them rather than deal with the prime object of qualifying as a doctor. A medical colleague taught me a particularly good way of staying awake during the endless book work. He, too, would remove all extraneous distractions from around him. For maximum concentration he had to sit facing a blank wall, the one relevant textbook open on the desk before him. He would place a scalpel vertically, blade upwards, beside the textbook and rest the palm of his hand gently on the tip of its cutting edge. Each time his concentration lagged, or should he fall asleep, his hand would sag and the blade would jab him awake. It was an excellent method of cramming in the book work over the shortest possible time. Painful, occasionally bloody, but a brilliant idea. I take no responsibility should you try it.

I was fortunate to qualify at the first attempt. Now, grandly, I could be called *Doctor* Villar, Bachelor of Medicine and Bachelor of Surgery. It sounded tremendous. My chest was puffed with pride. As with SAS Selection, however, such feelings last for barely a day. Suddenly you realize that these grandiose qualifications represent only the beginning of medical life. You have not yet treated any patients at all. So far it has been theory, plus closely supervised instruction. The real thing, making life and death decisions, is far more terrifying. Becoming a surgeon, particularly an orthopaedic one, was still a long way away.

It was a difficult time for the UK's National Health Service. Healthcare is a political football, from whichever country you originate. You must become accustomed to rules and regulations changing almost every year, often for no apparent reason. Despite my deeply held ambitions to become a full-time SAS doctor, it was still hard to take the final plunge. Until now I had always the option to switch between SAS or civilian medicine at will. To leave the warm, parental feel of my teaching hospital worried me, even if I also felt the place was too constrained and political. Six months away from SAS activities while I qualified had put tiny, infinitesimal doubts in my mind. They did not last long.

I had the good fortune to have the British monarch's surgeon as my first boss. He, and his colleague, were charming and professional, but their job immensely demanding. A 120-hour week was routine. That would not be accepted now, but in 1978 was regarded as normal. The moment I realized the intensity and impracticality of such a rota, I welcomed an alternative. Within six weeks I had volunteered for Regular Army service. The NHS, well used to its junior doctors showing signs of strain, did not bat an eye.

I was not allowed to join as a soldier, irrespective of what military skills I possessed. My recent medical qualification prohibited it. I did not wish to anyway. It was SAS medicine that interested me now. I had long ago decided that 22 SAS Regimental Medical Officer it would be. 22 SAS only had one doctor. At that time the route in was through the Royal Army Medical Corps, the RAMC. As before, the civilian world thought me mad, advising against stepping outside the bottomless rut of NHS hospital practice. By then it was too late. I had already applied to join. Determined, and with a chest full of anticipation and ambition, I arranged to meet 22 SAS's commanding officer, Colonel M.

Despite extensive experience with the Territorial 21 SAS and all manner of Special Forces activities over several years, I had only ever passed through Hereford's Regular 22 SAS camp for very brief periods, usually in transit elsewhere. I was invited to join Colonel M in the Officers' Mess bar. He was a huge man, positively charming. He explained that the SAS doctor's post used to be the most unpopular in the British Army. Now, for some reason, he said, 'Everyone wants to join.' He was right. There was a list of applicants as long as my arm, including one who had left 22 SAS several years earlier, specifically to train as a doctor. My heart sank. He was bound to get the job, I thought. In the event, it was I who was successful. I do not know why. Whatever the reasons, I was shortly to embark on the most astonishing journey of my life.

CHAPTER 3

Press the Bleeding Button

Entering the main gate of 22 SAS's Hereford Camp, an immense wave of awe overtakes you. Instantly, you become aware that the place is special. Few ever have the chance to enter. Those who do guard this privilege jealously.

Unsignposted, and surrounded by a housing estate in Hereford's suburbs, the then Bradbury Lines was a forbidding sight: a central encampment, consisting largely of slatted wooden huts, surrounded by twelve-foot high unfriendly fencing. The Officers' Mess, my home when I started as Medical Officer, stood apart from the rest. Again wooden, again fenced, it struck a lonely figure immediately beside the main camp. It was drizzling, cold and misty. It is always drizzling, cold and misty in Hereford. I remember one year when the sun did not appear until May. Despite being a fully badged member of 21 SAS I knew this occasion was different. No longer did I have the security of civilian medicine. I was now committed to full-time service with the most feared and professional military unit in the world.

With a trembling hand I approached the reinforced gate, aware I did not have the magnetic card which would allow me to enter. I pressed the button to one side. 'Yes?' came the instant, crackly, male reply from its adjacent loudspeaker. I withdrew my hand immediately, as if I had received an electric shock. I could see no one. No cars. No lights. No pedestrians. No guards. No dogs. Just me, and a gate in a fence, standing twenty yards from a lonely wooden building. Taking a deep breath, I bent towards the loud-speaker and whispered, glancing either side of me as I spoke. I was imagining all manner of things in my insecurity, including hidden

IRA men lurking in nearby hedging, telescopic sights aimed to kill.

'Villar, Dr Villar,' I said, voice as low as I dared, praying someone would come and help. It was reminiscent of my day in the south London Careers Information Office, though this time there was no deaf Warrant Officer. Just me, the loudspeaker and the gate.

There was no answer. I stood transfixed, staring at the loudspeaker, but it remained silent. Worried, forehead wrinkled, I looked through the wire gate to the building beyond. When I had paid my earlier visit to Colonel M, I had not noticed these security arrangements. Nothing moved in the Officers' Mess. Its unlit, darkened windows gave no clue as to what, or who, lay beyond. Silence persisted. Then, suddenly, the loudspeaker broke into life once more. 'Yes? Who is it? Come on, speak up! I haven't got all day!' it crackled.

Again I leaned forward, whispering 'Villar. Dr Villar. I-I'm your new doctor.'

'Oh for Christ's sake,' replied the loudspeaker. I could hear voices talking in the background, despite the electronic fuzz. At least there are two of them in there I thought. The loudspeaker continued. 'I don't know who you are, but for God's sake press the bleeding button! We can't hear until you do.'

My heart sank. It was so obvious. I looked again at the loudspeaker, now seeing the small, aluminium button to one side. I pressed it and tried again, feeling suitably humbled in my attempt to give a good impression on first arrival. 'Dr Villar,' I said. 'You're expecting me?' Perhaps it was a mistake, I began to think. Perhaps a joke. The Army never intended to post me to 22 SAS at all. Perhaps there had been significance in the posting major's wicked smile when my Regimental attachment had been announced at London's First Avenue House, dominating one side of a dreary High Holborn.

'Doc Villar?' came the reply. 'We're expecting no Doc Villar. Who are you anyway?'

My heart sank still further. For years I had trained for it and it had come to this. 22 SAS were not expecting me. I had been set up after all. It was as I turned to leave that the loudspeaker crackled noisily once more. 'Wait one!' it shouted. 'Doc Villar? Yes. Here we are. We got the notification today. I'll send someone out to let you in.'

An overwhelming sense of relief overtook me. I turned to face the gate once more, looking through it at the main entrance door beyond. I broadened my shoulders, stood as upright as I could and wiped my sweating palms surreptitiously on my trousers. I wanted to be sure I could respond in kind to the firm, muscular handshake I was sure to receive from whichever SAS operative allowed me in. David Stirling himself, perhaps, the founder of the SAS? I stood even more upright, now preparing what steely-eyed gaze I could muster. The drizzly weather no longer made any impact.

With a thump the Mess front door swung open. I waited for the tall, confident figure who would greet me. I had, after all, forsaken an entire civilian medical career to come here. I was sure the SAS would roll out the red carpet as welcome once they knew I had arrived. It was as the figure appeared I began again to have doubts. No uniform. No weapon. No steely-eyed stare. 'Doc Villar?' it said as its small frame waddled towards the gate. 'I'm Anna, one of the cleaners. Wait just a moment and I'll let you in.'

Despite my initial experience, I learned to love the Mess in no time. Home from home, it was lovingly tended by two permanent staff members. The officers would come and go on their various attachments, but the permanent staff were its continuity. With SAS officers in short supply and overseas for much of their time, the place was often like a morgue. Its walls were littered with trophies of various Regimental actions around the globe. Kalashnikovs, killing knives, flags, and pictures of assorted buildings and embassies in disrepair. The prize trophy, certainly from my viewpoint, hung from the barbed wire over the entrance gate. A small, decaying strand of worsted wool. 'What's that?' I once asked an SAS colleague as we walked from the Mess to the main camp opposite.

He smiled. 'It is the only medical trophy we allow to be displayed, Doc,' he replied.

'I don't understand.'

'Doc B's trousers,' he continued. 'One of your predecessors. He snagged them trying to climb into the Mess one night. I think it was his attempt to escape a lady friend led to that.' He pointed upwards to the limp woollen strand, blowing jerkily in the wind. I realized then it was not only your medicine the SAS assessed, it was your whole personality. Doc B was possibly the most respected SAS Medical Officer in the Regiment's modern life. For a long time my own efforts were judged by standards he had set years earlier.

The epicentre of any Officers' Mess life is the bar, no matter how warlike the regiment concerned. In Hereford, this was a simple wooden arrangement. VIPs and politicians from every party could be found there on occasion. Some of the most successful SAS actions of recent times started off life as ideas over a pint in that room. Civilian clothes were frequently worn, so it was impossible to know who was who most of the time. Often, officers would seek my medical advice at the bar, rather than coming to my official clinic, where they would be in full public view. As a doctor, you were also regarded as the resident scientist, frequently being asked advice on matters that only rarely formed part of earlier medical training. I was naturally keen to make a good impression.

At the end of my first week, and still terribly earnest, I remember discussing heatedly over a drink with a troop commander how to administer local anaesthetic when stitching up an open wound. If truth be known, I knew very little about it. The officer started firing intelligent, searching questions I found hard to answer. I had not at that stage learned that 22 SAS makes short shrift of bluff. It will see through you instantly, to your great discredit. I started to hum and ha, hypothesizing furiously in my attempt to appear all-knowledgeable. It was a mistake. So heated and blustered was I becoming that I failed to notice someone entering the bar area behind me. I had thought the troop commander and I were alone.

'That's bullshit, Richard,' came a voice I was sure sounded familiar. 'Absolute cock in fact. Lignocaine doesn't work like that at all you know.'

I turned to meet the challenge, somewhat ashamed I had been caught out. There before me, smiling broadly, was the dynamic and powerful James R. We had been at school together, though had lost touch once we had left. The decade or more we had been leading our separate lives melted in an instant. We shook hands briefly and then, suitably humbled, I listened to James the non-medic, lecture me, the doctor, on the exact mechanics of lignocaine's actions. I never bluffed again.

Over the years I saw many outsiders trapped in the same way. An SAS operative, whatever rank he holds, assumes a responsibility far greater than the equivalent rank outside the Regiment. It would be completely normal for a young SAS Captain to negotiate directly with a senior politician, for example. Such a situation would be unheard of outside the SAS. This responsibility makes an operative question everything. Nothing is assumed and nothing is taken at face value. It is one of the major attributes of SAS success.

The SAS, particularly its officers, forms a tightknit community. Everyone is bonded like Superglue by mutual discomfort, danger and extreme responsibility. During my first days in Hereford I was astonished how many old friends I met. Friends I had no idea were involved with the Regiment. Not only was there James R, but another close school friend and two operatives who had been my playmates as a child. It was like some grand family or school reunion, bumping into one familiar face after another. SAS friendships are particularly intense. There are Regimental friends I have now for whom I have the deepest affection, even though we left active service long ago. It is a bond I cannot logically explain, but James R certainly formed part of it. This is a problem for a doctor. His friends are patients and his patients are friends. It is not possible to hide behind the impassive wall of the civilian practitioner. As an SAS doctor you are involved, to the hilt, emotionally and professionally, in everything that happens to your patients. It is an enormous obligation, the greatest I have assumed in my life.

Security was vital. Not so much personal security, which by now was intuitive, but the ability to keep what you were told to yourself. Times have changed since then, as one so-called secret revelation follows another. But whatever is written, whatever is said, I cannot imagine any SAS operative knowingly putting his colleagues in danger by speaking out of turn. The Army takes it particularly seriously and puts all such operatives, and their doctors, through a process known as vetting. Vetting can be normal, the so-called 'NV', or positive, the so-called 'PV'. I imagine the Army is unaware that the initials 'PV' stand for vaginal examination in medical jargon. My own PV came a few days after I first arrived in Hereford.

I do not know from where the security system obtains its vetters. However, to a man they are very easy to talk to. They have a way of making you pour out your innermost thoughts and secrets without hesitation. My vetter looked like a retired policeman. Mid fifties, ordinarily dressed and well-spoken. It did not matter what I said, studiously he would record my details without raising even the tiniest eyebrow.

'Ever had VD?'

'Of course not.'

'Slept with anyone's wife?'

'Of course not.'

'Drugs?'

'I give them, not take them.'

The object was to go back in time at least five years, justifying every action and deed for each day of that period. Referees had to be given for anything I reported, so I dragged up old schoolmasters, holiday tour operators, even the occasional casual acquaintance. I heard later that many had been approached and asked to verify my stories. Heaven only knows what they thought I was up to.

The beneficial spin-off from vetting is the immense feeling of inner cleanliness with which it leaves you. All of us, however eminent or otherwise, have a few dark secrets we will take with us to the grave. They may be simple, such as forgetting to brush your teeth on your eighteenth birthday, or more sinister, such as an approach for information by an overseas power. Whatever the secret, the vetter has to know it. Consequently, by the time a vetting session has finished, you feel completely expunged, purged of all guilt and conscience. It is a marvellous feeling. I strutted around for months afterwards, a bounce to my step, as if I could do no wrong. I felt the system had given me its blessing to accumulate another pile of sin before the next vetting session.

If you hear nothing from the vetter once he has left you, then all is fine. Every so often he will return to update his records, though I would often wonder who vetted him. He will also return if, for any reason, you choose to let the side down. I did once and will for ever feel guilty as a result. It was years later, away from Hereford, when I was sitting in a surgeons' coffee room in southern England. A senior colleague walked in, handing me a letter his son had received that day. It invited the young man, barely twenty years of age, to form part of a statistical survey in central London.

'What do you think of this, Richard?' my colleague inquired. 'Does it mean anything to you?'

I knew at once. I only had to look at the letterhead to see the address of Century House. Often called Gloom Hall, and now no longer functional, it was then a major headquarters for our spies. The letter was obviously an initial recruiting approach. I told my colleague so. He went away satisfied, never mentioning the matter again. However, within forty-eight hours, I had received a telephone call from my vetter, asking for updated information. He never once mentioned the letter, but the point was made. It was a warning shot across my bows to shut up and keep silent, of that I was sure. SAS service taught me very rapidly that nothing is ever what it seems. The most unlikely people can do the most unlikely things for the Government.

It did not take me long in Hereford to establish how different my practice was from others around the world. The responsibility was immense. There was me, fresh from basic medical studies, assisted by some of the most capable RAMC medical assistants in the land. These were different to the badged SAS medic. There was intense competition to provide medical support to the SAS. The job attracted all sorts, united by a deep commitment to see things through to the bitter end. We had our stresses, we had our strains, but got to know each other well. Officially I was their leader. In practice, my Medical Centre, often called the MI Room, was run by its sergeant. If you did not take his advice you were mad.

With SAS squadrons scattered throughout the globe, one doctor cannot be everywhere. Hence the need for specialist medical training. The skills of a fully trained SAS medic are remarkable. By the time he has completed his medical course he should be able to do everything expected of a civilian paramedic, and more. Drips, chest drains, setting of fractures, all become routine. Such skills are combined with a detailed theoretical knowledge that can put even a junior doctor to shame. Hence my lecture on the effects of lignocaine by James R. Occasionally enthusiasm can go too far, once the SAS operative has been blooded. For some, to qualify as an SAS medic was licence for anything. Once, when I was running a hearts and minds operation in the Middle East, a small glass pot arrived from an outlying SAS patrol. Inside, floating in liquid formalin, was a yellow, spherical lump. Two stitches had been expertly tied at its north and south poles, securing what must have been the blood vessels feeding it before excision. To the black top of the bottle was fixed a small label that read:

'Doc – found this inside an Arab's forearm. Grateful if you could tell me what it is. Thanks. Signed B.'

Out there, somewhere in the vast empty quarter of the desert, an SAS medic was in full throttle, operating on anything he could find. Trooper B was a first-class soldier, well able to cope with the demands of independent, minor surgery. He highlighted the very high levels of ability developed by SAS operatives once their medical training was complete.

You could be certain the SAS would face you with the exotic. My first day in post, not only did I have to deal with a close-range shotgun injury, but diseases such as leishmaniasis, giardiasis and march haematuria came through my door. Few who read this book will have heard of them. They are incredibly rare in UK civilian practice. I certainly had not come across them in those days.

As a doctor caring for such widely travelled individuals, I had always to remember that not every patient in my clinic would have an English disease. Much of what I saw was acquired outside the United Kingdom. Tim M demonstrated this admirably. He came to my clinic one morning looking very concerned.

'Doc. I've got this ulcer on my cheek. I can't get rid of it,' he said, his Geordie voice trembling. However tough one is physically, a realization of mortality can be frightening for the hardiest of people. As he spoke he removed the crisp, white bandage from his face. I had seen him around camp for the past few weeks sporting the dressing and had assumed one of the MI Room medics had been responsible for it. As I looked closer, I realized it was not one of our own and had probably been bought from one of the pharmacies in town.

With the dressing removed I could see the huge ulcer on Tim's cheek, in glorious Technicolor. About two inches in diameter, it was pinkish-violet with rounded edges. Its centre was filled with bloody slough and dead skin pieces. It looked revolting and was obviously getting bigger, not smaller. It also smelt.

'Does it hurt?' I asked.

'No, Doc. Just keeps on growing. If it carries on like this it'll have eaten half my face away within a few months.'

I nodded. Tim was actually right, though I doubt he realized it. I had seen this before: leishmaniasis, so favoured of Central America. It was a small parasite, injected into the skin by the sandfly. Gradually and insidiously it eats away at its chosen area. Healing is slow or non-existent and eventual scarring severe. Even though Tim had not taken his SAS medical course, he knew something was wrong. He was understandably petrified. At least I could reassure him, I thought, even though treatment would be lengthy and painful. We may not be able to undo the damage it had already made, but we could at least stop it getting worse. Traditional, everyday medicines would not touch it. Leishmaniasis demanded big guns if it was to be cured. Antimony, a poisonous metal, was given. It made hair fall out and did all manner of terrible things to the liver, but slowly the ulcer would fade. It could sometimes take six months or more to disappear.

It took the Army a while to acknowledge the threat of leishmaniasis. When you wake up one tropical morning covered in itchy bumps, there is no way of telling which particular insect has caused which particular bump. The majority of bumps will be completely innocent, minor, inconsequential mosquito bites. Some might herald the onset of strange diseases like dengue fever, Chagas's disease or filariasis – all equally unpleasant. It was only when we realized each man had acquired his ulcer on return from the same operational area that the diagnosis became clear. Mosquito nets are hopeless as the sandfly is small enough to fly through the holes. That is why nets are now impregnated with insecticide. The net stops the mosquitoes, while insecticide vapour kills the sandfly. Much of the original research on these insecticides was performed on SAS jungle troops. They only had to look at the ulcerated skin of their colleagues to know that cooperation was in their best interests. Prevention was better than cure. For the men who acquired leishmaniasis treatment was possible, but not easy. Tim would settle in the end, I was sure of that. Ahead of him was a long, painful road.

Selection courses were medical mayhem. It was a busy time. As well as the course, I was running clinics, negotiating promotions for my staff and trying to set up antiterrorist medical support. There were not enough hours in the day to do everything. Once, early one morning and in my usual rush, I was summoned to a soldier's room. One of the most promising Selection candidates was unwell. I had got to know him briefly and liked him. I was sure he would pass and eventually become the type of man who would do the Regiment proud.

Though it was 7 a.m. I was already late for my first appointment and knew I had little time to spare the poor man. As a doctor you learn rapidly how to maintain a calm exterior for your patients, even though inside you are worried sick. That was me. I looked at him briefly. He was pale, vomiting, with a gradually distending stomach. My initial diagnosis was one of mild gastroenteritis, gut rot, that would get better soon. All it would need was a day away from the rigours of Selection and he would be fine. I issued some tablets, smiled confidently and briefly, and turned to go. However, there was something nagging at the back of my mind. I could not explain what. Something did not feel right. Though most diseases in medicine have classic textbook signs and symptoms that we are all trained to detect, occasionally you must base your actions on instinct. Rather like a dog's nose. If it is cold and wet, the animal must be well. As I turned to leave, I hesitated and then glanced back. 'Look,' I said, 'this may be over the top but I'm going to send you into hospital. It'll do no harm.' The poor man was looking so ill he did not have the strength to object, even though the mention of a hospital admission was normally sufficient to send the sturdiest soldier running. He nodded his consent, so I rapidly wrote out the worst, most unprofessional, referral letter of my medical life:

Dear Doctor,
This man has been vomiting for 24 hours. I do not know why.
Please see and advise.

(Signed) R. Villar

When you refer a patient as a doctor, you like to give the impression of comprehensive care. Single-line referral notes, such as I had written, are frowned upon. I had not suggested a diagnosis, nor had I described what there was to find on examination. To any receiving hospital doctor, it looked as though I had not bothered to give the problem more than a second's thought. The truth was that I had no time to perform a full examination, and had no clue what was wrong.

Leaving the note with him, I made a brief telephone call to my RAMC medics to arrange his transport to hospital and went on my way. It was a frenetic day as I was out on the hills with Selection, dealing with the many injuries that such a course can create. It was when I returned in the evening that I received the message to ring the hospital. I recognized the extension number immediately as that of Intensive Care. Intensive Care? Who did I have on Intensive Care? Surely not? But yes. The man had just made it in time. Life-threateningly ill, his vomiting had been a sign of kidney failure. Urgent dialysis, blood cleaning, had been required to save him. He was the first-ever case of kidney failure caused by over-exercise reported in the world. His condition was subsequently widely reported in the international medical journals. Toxic chemicals, released by over-exerted muscles, had coursed through the bloodstream and clogged up his kidneys. He had been lucky to survive. Had I ignored my sixth sense he would surely have died. Dead and no one would have known why.

Diseases did not always affect one patient at a time. My record was forty-seven. Again it was a Selection course. Soldiers from throughout the world had come to pit their might against the mountains of South Wales. For me, the day started routinely with my normal clinic, or sick parade. Lumps and bumps, piles, varicose veins or the odd runny nose – nothing particularly challenging. At least my London training had prepared me for these.

In designing Bradbury Lines, the architect had obviously not had the welfare of the doctor in mind. The M I Room was positioned immediately beside the helicopter landing pad. This made it impossible to hear anything a patient was saying and totally impractical to use a stethoscope. It was as well that heart and lung conditions were rare in the S A S. I could not have diagnosed them had they appeared. Whenever a helicopter was landing or taking off, you either had to abandon the clinic altogether or shout instructions to your patient at the top of your voice. On this occasion, fortunately, the helicopter had decided not to fly.

An hour into the clinic, quite unexpectedly, I heard the sound of vomiting outside my window. It was a painful, forced, almost projectile affair. I looked out to see the large figure of a Parachute Regiment soldier clutching his belly, writhing on the tarmac in agony. He was in obvious, extreme pain. By the time I had dashed outside to help him, a four-ton military lorry pulled up. In the back lay a dozen further bodies, groaning loudly in their misery. Vomit was everywhere. The floor of the lorry was awash with the stuff. The stench made even my cast-iron stomach heave. Nappy changing and vomit are two things I find very hard to tolerate as a doctor. Within seconds another lorry appeared. Then another and another. Each contained the same sorry story. Large, highly-trained soldiers, clutching their bellies in pain.

This was gastroenteritis in full flood. The men had barely made it to the Brecon Beacons before the first casualty occurred. Only a handful escaped the agony. Forty-seven were returned to Bradbury Lines. My quiet, routine day had suddenly turned to chaos. MI Room staff had to work fast. Drips, stool specimens, blood tests and the opening up of extra latrines. I soon realized that the ones to escape had been those who had missed breakfast. Few bugs attack the gut so viciously and suddenly as this. One that does is called 'staphylococcus', named thus because it looks like a bunch of grapes under a microscope (Greek *staphule* = grape). Each victim recovered rapidly, though not without significant misery and discomfort. It was then that the witchhunt began. In the Army, and that includes the SAS, there is no such thing as bad luck. Everything must have a reason. It seemed likely the bug had come from contaminated milk. My casual suggestion to MI Room staff was instantly passed up the line. Before I knew it my idea had become fact and the cook was being disciplined in the Kremlin, Regimental Headquarters. The poor man. We never did prove he had infected the milk. For that matter we never proved the milk was the true source at all. Despite this, judgement was instant. The cook was out and negotiation impossible.

I could always guarantee Selection would keep me busy. Not only did I have to provide medical support on the hills of South Wales, but my clinics would be full of ailing candidates at the end of every day. Many were seeking an excuse to fail. A few had serious injuries they could not ignore. The determined candidate would not go near a doctor for the duration of Selection, whatever his state of disrepair. Pain was inevitable and injury likely. To pass SAS Selection without one, other or both was impossible.

One evening, after a lengthy clinic was nearing its end, I looked out of the MI Room window. There was no sign of life, save for one lonely, uniformed figure walking slowly towards the Selection billets. I could see the man was in pain. Dragging his feet, barely able to lift them more than a millimetre from the ground, his rounded shoulders slouched terribly and his head hung low. He looked awful.

'What's wrong with that guy?' I asked the MI Room Sergeant. 'He doesn't look too well.'

'He's not, boss,' came Sergeant R's clear reply. 'We can't get him to see you. God knows we've tried.'

'What's the problem?'

'Blisters, boss. Terrible ones. The silly bugger wrapped all of his body, and his feet, with sticky tape at the start of Selection two weeks ago. He hasn't taken the stuff off since.'

'So?'

'It hasn't worked. He's developed blisters *under* the sticky tape. We can't take it off without removing most of his skin.'

'Ask him to come and see me,' I encouraged. 'I'll think what I can do to help. Maybe we can soak the tape off.'

'We've suggested that, boss. He won't have it. Says he'll put up with it until Selection is over.'

I rolled my eyes Heavenwards. There was no point in arguing or forcing the man to see me. For better or for worse, the candidate had set his own course of action for attempting Selection. He would have erected his invisible shield, determined to pass, irrespective of the consequences. The fact his overladen Bergen rucksack had worn the skin of his back away to underlying flesh, the fact the blisters on his feet now exposed tendons and bone, was irrelevant. If he needed plastic surgery to heal the damage once Selection was over, so be it. That was the price of ambition.

I can understand such determination. It was no surprise to learn the man passed with flying colours. It took us three days to remove the sticky tape once Selection was over. Under it lay massive, infected, oozy sores that took several weeks to heal. Such tenacity shows why some die in their efforts to become badged operatives.

It was not a requirement that the Regimental Medical Officer took 22 SAS Selection. Nevertheless, I volunteered to do it. It made good sense. For credibility's sake it seemed right. You are open to criticism when you make a decision like that. Some saw it as my attempt to be a soldier rather than doctor. My MI Room staff, none of whom had taken Selection, thought it an excellent idea and I believe were proud once I passed it. Having earned my Regular badge, however, I decided never to wear full SAS uniform when in camp. My self-appointed style was a badged SAS beret and RAMC belt. It meant a lot to me. In particular, it allowed me to address the hordes of candidates eager to take Selection and speak with the voice of both experience and authority.

I, too, developed blisters. My rucksack's lumbar strap would dig away at the low spine until the skin eventually gave in. Once the skin was broken you could not afford infection to enter. With so much mud, filth and mire, this was not an easy task. My solution, at the end of a long day's Selection walk, was to go to my MI Room staff, expose my bare raw back and ask them to pinion me face down on the examination couch. They would then pour neat iodine on to the Bergen sores while I screamed, and screamed, and screamed. I never did ask if they enjoyed mugging their boss. I imagine their answer would have been 'Yes.'

The rucksack had a lot to answer for. The shoulder straps in particular would pull forcibly downwards on each collar bone. If the straps were not continually shifted in position by the soldier as he walked, the intense pressure would paralyse the nerves to the shoulder blades. Called 'winging', whenever you tried to push an object away from you, your shoulder blade would lift off the back of your chest like a bird's wing. It usually improved, but only after months of rest and strict avoidance of heavy load carrying. If you wish to stay healthy, do not take SAS Selection.

Not everything an SAS doctor does is medical. There are certain things that would make the General Medical Council squirm. None more so than providing medical assistance to the combat survival courses. Someone has to be sure that no soldier has hidden anything up his tail end. I was always the favoured choice. Doctors were supposed to enjoy such things. In my civilian days I had only to perform half a dozen rectal examinations in a day. Even then, I had found such things hard. Particularly so, as the Rectal Clinic I attended always took place on a Thursday morning, immediately after I had eaten a full fried English breakfast. On combat survival, however, with upwards of a hundred runners from assorted countries, everyone had to be examined. No one was exempt. Worse, they all had to be seen within thirty minutes. I hated it. The only way of dealing with the large number of soldiers was to take everyone's trousers off, bend them across a table and get on with it. Down the line I would go, one backside after the other. Glove on, finger up, feel and pull. Glove on, finger up, feel and pull. It was terrible, both for me and the troops. Particularly the Italians. As a nation they did not seem to welcome rectal examinations on exercise.

A most enjoyable part of the job was assisting with officer Selection. In the SAS, officers are called 'Ruperts', and are a very closely analysed and inspected breed. Ruperts were given an extra week of misery, over and above the normal Selection walks. During this so-called 'Officers' Week' they were sleep-deprived, physically stressed and forced to perform in public. For example, an officer might have been kept up all night on a cross-country march before returning to barracks. Lulled into the impression he could then go to bed, he would suddenly, and unexpectedly, be ordered to attend the lecture theatre within thirty minutes, in full Regimental uniform and spotless boots. He would be tasked to give a ten-minute résumé of his life story. The entire Regiment was at liberty to attend and frequently did so. They could interrupt, harass, insult and say what they wished.

I felt sorry for the poor men, but despite this it was an important time. I was able to see things from a non-military point of view. Occasional weaknesses would appear in an otherwise unyielding exterior. I recall one officer who was performing excellently. He spoke clearly and succinctly, seemingly impervious to sleep deprivation. I could tell his SAS audience was hooked by the widespread silence. Something in his voice demanded attention. On this occasion it was my sixth sense that again spoke, as more than half of the life story he gave was describing his wife and family. For a potential SAS officer it sounded strange. It was more usual for an applicant to concentrate entirely on himself – some would regard this as selfish. I remember one very flamboyant individual telling the assembled throng how wonderful he was. How he could free-fall parachute, deep-sea dive, speak eight languages and defend himself against a second Dan black belt in karate. He was floored by a very senior member of the Regiment who stood up from the audience in the middle of the officer's presentation. 'Excuse me, sir,' the operative shouted, 'have you ever thought of becoming a spaceman?' The poor fellow failed.

Feeling uneasy, I whispered my misgivings to the selection team, but was overruled. The officer was through. I was not surprised, some time later, to find he had left the Regiment, apparently unable to cope with the rigours of operational life.

Medical tuition of SAS operatives was my overall responsibility, though in practice it was capably run by two Royal Army Medical Corps non-commissioned officers. Both were brilliant and much admired by the Regiment and me. I would often turn to them for medical advice, once I realized my civilian medical training was inappropriate for this new, strange life of mine.

A major part of the medical course was an attachment to a civilian hospital. Before an operative could be fully qualified as a medic he had to complete one month working in a casualty department. We naturally did not advertise the fact the men were from the SAS. Arrangements were generally made directly, and informally, with the various casualty consultants involved. Some were openly hostile to the idea of SAS operatives working in their departments, but many were welcoming. For the most part, the intelligent SAS operative was an asset to a casualty unit, well able to give as much training to the civilians as they could give him. Sometimes their presence was life-saving, such as the letter of commendation I received from a hospital in the west of the country. It ran something like this:

> We wish to acknowledge our grateful thanks to Mr W for his prompt action in saving the life of one of our nurses recently. A patient ran amok in the department, eventually taking the nurse hostage and holding her forcibly against a

cubicle wall, a scalpel to her throat. Mr W capably and reliably disarmed the assailant, who is now in police custody.

I later discovered their letter was a gross understatement. Mr W was, in reality, *Sergeant W*, and an expert at unarmed combat. The poor hostage-taker would not have stood a chance. He could have been armed with a Samurai sword for all Sergeant W could have cared. Predictably, the Regiment's response to this event was one of disapproval. Sergeant W should not have attracted attention in the way he did. My own approach, one I made known to those in power, was supportive. Sergeant W had done us proud and the hospital was delighted.

It was important to make those civilian consultants who helped us feel involved, reinforcing the special position they held in our eyes. By offering their services they exposed both themselves and their departments to some risk. You can never truly tell what a terrorist will do next. In those days the media was not over-invasive. Now, the incident with Sergeant W would probably be headlined 'SAS THUG ATTACKS DEFENCELESS HOSPITAL PATIENT' or some such line. I therefore spent many hours visiting the various hospitals, updating their consultants on what we needed, and why. We also held meetings for them in Bradbury Lines, demonstrating our military skills for their interest and enjoyment. It was wonderful to see casualty consultants, and a handful of nurses, blasting away with Browning automatic pistols at terrorist targets in the killing house, our indoor range. They loved it. Perhaps there is a streak of aggression in everyone, however caring they may outwardly appear.

As well as training others, I had my own career to consider. I knew that one day, however much I enjoyed it, my time with the SAS would end. Though I had done much practical surgery, I needed the qualification to go with it. The qualification is called Fellowship of the Royal College of Surgeons. Now a three-part examination, it was then a two-parter, involving book work night and day for months. An isolated SAS job is not the best training environment for such a qualification, so I would travel weekly to

Birmingham to study alongside civilians there. My Birmingham colleagues had no idea what I did, but it was good to see there was life outside the military.

Examination day eventually arrived. At the time I was very hyped up. We had just completed the successful Iranian Embassy assault and I had been required to go overseas for a short tour. Consequently, I was fit, very alert and looking unbearably healthy. The moment I walked into the examination room, giving the examiner a confident smile combined with a bone-crushing hand-shake, I knew I had failed. Around me were dozens of young civilian surgeons, each looking like death. For months they had been burning the midnight oil and were now bulging with knowledge. I could not compete. The examiners failed me with dignity, but fail I did. Cheeky and impatient to the last, I asked our Adjutant to send a letter, on fully badged Regimental paper, requesting that I be considered a special case and allowed to pass. At the very least, I said, my examination fee should be refunded. The College of Surgeons, of course, had seen it all before. Unimpressed by such a request from the hard-nosed SAS, my failure was reaffirmed. For the resits six months later I made certain I looked the part. I read and revised endlessly, staying indoors for a complete fortnight. I drank endless whisky, smoked myself halfway to an early grave and attended the examination looking terrible. I passed with flying colours.

One major advantage of its Hereford location is the physical separation from the rest of the Army given to the SAS. Medically, this was vital. The Army is rigid in the way it classifies diseases and injuries. Large books exist that contain the name of every disease imaginable and what it means to the service potential of a soldier. A knee-ligament injury, for example, means you are no use to them. Loss of an eye, or an amputated arm, makes you highly suspect, and so on. Physical grades, P grades, are given to every soldier, with P1 being superfit and P8 being disastrous. At P8 your next step could be the grave. For some reason no one can ever be P1, the best you can reach is P2.

If a man is injured, his P grading is adjusted upwards, depending on his degree of incapacity. He will go back to P2 once fully recovered. If your P grading goes *up* the Army calls this a *down*grading. Only those with a P2 grade can officially take part in high-level, physical, military activities. Grades P3 and above mean a man is not permitted to do much physical activity and his chances of promotion may be severely curtailed. The Army insists that each soldier should be categorized into an appropriate grade. Consequently, as a military doctor, if you refer a soldier to a military hospital, he may return from his appointment having been medically downgraded. To an SAS operative this was an unacceptable fate. As a result, I only rarely referred patients to military specialists and hospitals. The nearest was more than a 100 kilometres away. Moreover, the local civilians were brilliant and were well capable of handling anything. It meant I could receive an instant opinion, from a leading expert, whenever I needed one. More importantly, the operative's medical grade remained untouched. Likewise his salary and promotion prospects.

I hated the medical grading system, as did my patients. Partly this was because I could barely understand it. I had no time to wade through the pile of reading material needed to categorize an injury accurately. More importantly, the system never took motivation into account. Nowhere in the world will you find people more inspired than in the SAS. Superficially, to examine many senior Regimental operatives is like reading a walking pathology textbook. Over many years they have acquired all manner of different diseases, injuries and strange conditions. Pieces of limb have flown off here and there, joints are wobbly and worn, but mind and will-power are as strong as ever. It is these that carry them through, which is why Everest can be climbed without toes and Military Medals won without fingers. An astonishing crowd.

Women were a problem in the SAS – the lack of them in particular. I had not realized it until one morning more than a year into the job, when a gentle knock on the consulting-room door disturbed me from some paperwork. Slowly I heard the door open, my eyes still firmly on the paperwork before me. Whoever it was walked quietly to the patient's chair at one side of my desk and sat down. After a moment's further hesitation I looked up. I was dumbfounded.

'B-but you're . . . you know. W-well, you're a *woman*,' I said, completely lost for words. I can remember that astonished feeling even now.

'That's right, doctor. Well done. I'm a woman. Is there anything wrong?' She was gorgeous. Small, very petite and clad in tight jeans and baggy sweater. I recognized her as one of the operatives from 14 Intelligence Company, the covert Northern Ireland people. The sweater most likely covered her holstered pistol.

'No,' I replied, trying hard to regain composure. 'It's just that . . . well, it's just that I don't know much about women, you see.'

'What on earth do you mean? You're a doctor, aren't you?'

'Yes, that's true. But I've sort of specialized. In *men* you see.' I indicated a crowd of male SAS operatives outside my window, waiting for a helicopter to take them elsewhere. I prayed the floor would open widely and swallow me up. The trouble was that she was right. It had not crossed my mind before, but since becoming 22 SAS's doctor I had never treated a woman.

Her request was for a supply of the contraceptive pill. That, too, confused me. I had no idea of names, dosages or side-effects. In the end I confessed ignorance and asked the local general practice to help. Had she arrived with a gunshot wound or worms, malaria or any other tropical disease, I would have managed admirably. The Pill for a woman? Not a hope.

In a male-orientated environment such as the SAS, maintaining any form of adult relationship with the opposite sex is as difficult as Selection. Away for months at a time, in largely male company, I was as hopeless at talking to women as one gets. Civilian girl-friends had not been able to cope with their changed partner and went their own way within weeks of my arrival in Hereford. A few would telephone in an attempt to keep things going. That was disastrous, as quiet conversations would frequently turn into noisy arguments when I was unable to tell them what I was doing. I was also fairly sure that telephone calls into, and out of, the camp were monitored. The last thing I wanted was Her Majesty's Government knowing what little remained of my love life.

On one occasion, and in the wake of the Iranian Embassy assault, I was elected Regimental stag. I do not know why. A young woman wrote, asking if she could meet an SAS man in the flesh. I was duly chosen. In retrospect it was a dangerous move and could easily have been a setup. However, I requested that Special Branch did a search of their records to ensure she was genuine. This proved to be so. Several weeks later I arranged to meet her, somewhere near London's British Museum. I asked that covert surveillance also be given, in case of trouble. I never saw the followers so must assume they were either very good, or did not appear at all. The girl was, in the event, good fun and genuinely interested in what I did. We saw each other on several occasions thereafter. However, like any relationship I had while in Hereford, my attitude and absences made it die before it ever began.

There was one woman who did attract me. Of course, I had never met her. It was her reputation that did the trick. Apparently, somewhere in Northern Ireland, the RAMC had a medical officer working for a cavalry regiment. She was infamous for her large, out of control English sheepdog, curvaceous figure, encyclopaedic knowledge and total fearlessness when under threat. Why, I thought, do I never meet a woman like that?

Special Forces units around the world are two-a-penny. The SAS, however, sets itself apart from the rest. As a result Hereford is frequently visited by outsiders. Selection is regarded as a model on which many others base their own – the United States for one. Their Special Forces are different to ours. Larger, noisier, less covert. Their SAS lookalike is the Delta Force, beginning to form during my Hereford days. Whereas the US Special Forces would arrive thoroughly crewcutted and barely able to remain upright due to the number of medals they wore, Delta was different. The Delta operatives I met were pleasant, hard-working people. Their boss, Colonel F, was a muscular, confident, powerful man. His second-in-command, Major N, was somewhat younger and romped around our Selection course as if it was a mild inconvenience. His only faults, some would say attractions, were a deep Southern accent that was impossible to understand and the disconcerting habit of chewing and spitting tobacco when talking to those in authority. We followed the development of Delta with interest, in particular their attempt to rescue the Teheran hostages some time later. Putting names, friendships and personalities to some of the bigger military operations of this century does make you see them in a different perspective.

Maintaining one's own personal security was a continuing process. It was plain fact that many terrorist groups around the world would have given anything to take a shot at an SAS man. For the IRA in particular this was a great challenge, but from their viewpoint would have been a difficult task. Not only had the Regiment let it be known that any such attempt would lead to instant reprisal, but the entire Hereford population acted as a giant security cordon. Walk into any shop, pub or garage in the Hereford area looking or sounding remotely odd, and the Regiment will hear of it before you arrive within a mile of their camp. The local people are fiercely proud of the SAS and are immensely supportive. We were frequently stood ready, and then stood down, because an Irish couple on holiday might have stopped to fill their petrol tank fifteen kilometres from town. The last thing Hereford wanted was a bomb in its midst, so it went to great lengths to avoid it.

Eventually, you become accustomed to living under constant threat. Rank and regiment disappear from letterheads and envelopes, uniforms were forbidden outside camp, and long hair with stubble actively encouraged. The best approach was to follow simple instinct. If it felt wrong it was likely to be so and was therefore best avoided. You develop a sixth sense for these things. No more so than my mother who one day received a long, thin, unidentified package from the Republic of Ireland. Her first and natural reaction was to telephone the police. At the time, letter bombs were being regularly received by various public figures in the land.

'A parcel's arrived,' said Mum. 'I don't like the look of it.'

'Oh, I'm sure it won't be a problem, madam,' replied a sleepy police sergeant. He had already received four such calls that day, from over-anxious folk seeing a terrorist in every corner. None had the least reason to be targeted. Here was another, I could imagine him thinking. 'I would just open it very carefully,' he advised.

'But what if it's a bomb?'

'It won't be a bomb, madam.'

'But supposing it is?'

'It won't be. I can assure you of that. Anyway, why should anyone want to blow *you* up? What have you done to deserve it?'

'Well, I have a son in the SAS, you see. Oh yes, and my husband is in Intelligence. Does that make a difference?'

The telephone went silent and within minutes Bomb Disposal was on its way, alerted by an embarrassed police sergeant. The parcel? I am afraid it is true: a controlled explosion of a box of smoked salmon. We never did learn who sent it.

To keep the local people on one's side, it was important to be as helpful and cooperative to the public as possible. Boat Troop would thus turn out to rescue flood victims, while the mountaineers would help with Brecon Beacons' rescues. Meanwhile I would do my best to advise several overseas expeditions what to expect when in far-flung lands. I was right most of the time though still feel guilty about my bad advice to a team aiming to canoe through North Africa. I gave them a list of diseases, medicines and vaccinations as long as my arm, but forgot the fearful schistosoma. Schistosoma, sometimes called *bilharzia*, is extremely common in certain parts of Africa. Found in water, the tiny parasite penetrates human skin and makes its way to the blood vessels of the gut and bowels. There it stays, clogging the vessels and destroying intestines and liver. It can slowly kill. Treatment, with potentially toxic medicines, is both dangerous and unpleasant. I understand one canoeist developed the condition, but was fortunately cured before its effects became too severe.

I also did not endear myself to my next-door neighbours. I tried hard, but lost much ground when trying to take an aerial photograph of my house. Living on a housing estate twenty kilometres west of Hereford, I persuaded Jim F, our brilliant helicopter pilot, to hover immediately over my house for several minutes so that I could take a photograph. He did the job beautifully, but neither of us noticed the estate's entire complement of washing, hung out to dry, flying everywhere. Sheets, socks, knickers, took to the air and I do not believe were ever recovered. My local credibility plummeted, I thought as far as it could go. Unfortunately I was wrong. A few days later, I misbehaved again.

It was outwardly a straightforward day. I was late for work and was driving my small, metallic gold Renault 5 faster than normal. Exiting the housing estate, I turned right down a narrow country lane, high green hedges on either side. Suddenly, completely unexpectedly, a tabby cat shot out from beneath the hedge going from left to right. I could not avoid it and felt two gentle thumps as my wheels ran it over. I was horrified, looking in my rearview mirror at what I had done. There lay the poor creature, thrashing its last on the roadway, in obvious mortal agony. I knew I had to put it out of its misery, so stopped the car and got out. The road was quiet, the air was still. It was just me and this poor, wretched creature. Certain I was alone, I picked up the dying animal, two hands around its neck. Its body hung limply downwards, twitching only gently at that stage. Rapidly I squeezed its neck and within seconds it was out of agony. Upset, though pleased I had been able to dispatch it so quickly, I stood for a moment thinking what I should do with the body. My two hands were still around its neck, my arms extended forwards, with the lifeless form hanging vertically. As I stood there I realized I was not alone. Someone was behind me. I turned to greet whoever it was, my arms still extended, the corpse dangling. There before me stood a woman, middle-aged and very distressed. I knew I had to act first.

'Do you know who owns this cat?' I asked, inclining my head towards the limp creature still within my grasp.

'Oh God!' she cried. 'She's mine! You've killed her! You ****! How could you?'

'B-b-but . . .' I tried to explain. It was no use. Standing in her garden beyond the high hedge she had not witnessed me run over the animal at all. She had only seen me stop the car, stride towards her pet, pick it up and strangle it. 'SAS murderer,' she hissed as I went humbly on my way. From that day on 'Killer Villar' was my local name.

A single-handed doctor cannot be everywhere at once. The SAS highlights this admirably. With four squadrons, each with different functions and each split into smaller groupings throughout the world, it is impossible to keep track of everyone. I thought I had been busy with a 120-hour working week in my London teaching hospital. That was nothing when compared to the SAS. I even developed chest pain on one occasion, standing outside the CO's office and was quite convinced I was about to have a heart attack at the tender age of twenty-seven. It was unquestionably a false alarm, but it did highlight the stresses of the job. Everyone wanted you with them. Whether they were in Germany or Greece, Australia or Austria, Canada or China. When they could physically see you they thought you were marvellous. When you were somewhere else you were shirking your job.

In the pre-terrorism days it was easier. The Regiment had one major conflict zone with which to deal, say the Middle East, and all efforts could be directed towards that. By the mid-1970s, and to a greater extent now, the Regiment could have operatives in a dozen countries at any one time. The doctor had responsibility for them all. In the morning I could be arranging medical training for an operative in central Scotland. At lunchtime I might be discussing hostage extraction from Concorde with a major airline. By teatime I might be counselling a distressed couple with an ailing marriage and by nightfall be in an airplane to the Far East. Such a day did actually occur. Jobs do not come any busier. No wonder the Regiment has increased its complement of medical staff in recent years. It frequently crossed my mind, albeit briefly, to return to the civilian National Health Service for a rest.

Wherever an operative is located, it is important that a secure medical home base is available to him. He must know this, and trust it, wherever he is. Should he be injured or diseased, he must have faith in the individual handling his care, even if he is 12,000 kilometres away. A significant part of SAS activity takes place many miles from the UK. Whatever we might otherwise think, few countries in which an SAS operative is likely to work have a medical system as good as the British NHS. Much of my time was thus spent overseas, being certain the Regiment had access to the best care I could find. If nothing was available locally, I had to provide it myself. Being single-handed, the moment I left Hereford to visit far-flung lands, the home-based operatives lost their doctor. Consequently, doctors from a local civilian practice would stand in for me when I was gone. They were excellent. Unvetted, they did not talk out of turn and could be relied upon to maintain the medical grade of a sick operative. Without them my job would have been impossible.

The nature of SAS work lends itself to disease. Covert operatives, working in a civilized environment, may be an exception. However, the majority of SAS personnel undertake more traditional, soldier-like activities in strange parts of the globe. In many such countries, severe, debilitating diseases are rife. No more so, perhaps, than the jungle. If I had known how awful it was, I doubt I would ever have gone there.

CHAPTER 4

The Bastard Jungle

'He's going to die, Doc, isn't he?' said Tony's distraught wife as she squeezed his limp hand tightly in her own. 'God, what am I going to do?'

I had been up all night with the patient. Tony was a senior SAS staff sergeant. The sort of guy legends are made of, who had been in every major SAS action of the past ten years. He was ill, desperately so, and I had no idea why.

'Where's he been, Jill?' I asked, trying to sound as calm as possible. I had already sought the advice of the best physician the country could offer. Even he had drawn a blank. Jill rolled her eyes upwards, shrugging her shoulders, as if to say 'How do I know?'

Tony would not say. He had returned only five days earlier from a highly classified military operation. Despite being his doctor and badged myself, he would tell me nothing. Seconded to a specialist defence agency, his work was of a nature that could bring down Governments if made known. I was frantic with worry. His temperature was sky high, well over 40 degrees, as he sweated and shuddered his life away. His neck was as stiff as steel. Already I had tried antibiotics on the assumption he had developed meningitis, but they had not touched it. This powerful man was deteriorating rapidly before me.

Then, for a second, Tony stopped his shuddering. His breathing, once irregular, quietened. 'Venezuela, Doc,' he whispered. 'The bastard jungle. Can you hear?'

It had been enough. As soon as he had spoken I knew. Cerebral malaria. A killer if you cannot treat it fast. 'I've got it, Jill!' I exclaimed. 'Chloroquine! We've got to use chloroquine! I'll be back!'

Tony and Jill lived almost next door to me, twenty kilometres west of Hereford. The drive that night, to and from Bradbury Lines to obtain the intravenous chloroquine, was the most frightening of my life. Rain obscured my windscreen, wipers struggling uselessly against it, as I slithered along the country roads trying to prevent the ampoules from breaking in my pocket. By the time I reached the house once more Tony was worse. His breathing had now become shallow, his lips blue, his pulse barely palpable. I did not bother to measure his blood pressure as I knew it would be unrecordably low.

It is difficult to keep a steady hand at times like that, but somehow I managed to insert the intravenous drip first time. Tony was a muscular man when healthy and had a large vein along one side of his forearm. The needle and plastic cannula slipped into it with ease.

As the first batch of chloroquine went in I knew I had the diagnosis correct. It had been Tony's only chance and without it he would certainly have died. Slowly I could see the colour return to his lips and fingernails, his breathing deepen. Ten minutes later his eyes opened and he managed his first effort at a smile. The relief I felt was overwhelming. Tony had probably been within minutes of dying. Once I knew control had been established, I ordered an ambulance to take him to the hospital as full recovery would naturally take several days. For months afterwards Tony would keep asking why the first thing he remembered was seeing his wife and me by his side, Jill with tears streaming down her cheeks. Relief is a powerful emotion.

Next to SAS Selection, the jungle is the end of the earth. Unfortunately, in the Regiment, you cannot escape it. My turn came unexpectedly, two days after Tony's crisis, one foggy Hereford morning. As I staggered sleepily towards the Kremlin for my weekly operations update, I was waylaid by Major P. 'Doc, Doc!' he said urgently. 'I thought I'd catch you here. We need you in Delight.'

'Delight?' I asked.

'Yes, Operation Delight. You know, Central America. They've got problems down south and need you to set up hearts and minds on the border. When can you go?'

'Tomorrow, I suppose,' I replied doubtfully, praying the local practice could stand in for me at such short notice. I had all manner of things organized for the coming weeks in Hereford, including careful follow-up of Tony's illness. Despite this, the nature of SAS service was that you had to move quickly should the need arise.

'Good,' Major P replied. 'I'll get it organized.'

So it was that I found myself seated on an RAF VC10, facing backwards as was traditional, heading across the Atlantic to Central America. It is the nature of operational codenames that they should bear no connection to the operation itself – Cloud, Prince, Bee, Rodent, Gravel. Who dreams these things up I shall never know. Putting SAS operations in Central America under the codename of Delight was typical. At that time it was a very pestilent place. If a disease featured in a medical textbook, it could be found in those fungating jungles. When you earn your living from human misery, as I do, it could be fascinating. Delighted? I think not.

The SAS has a long history of jungle warfare. Borneo and Malaya were major testing grounds for the Regiment – long periods of isolation for small SAS patrols, deep within enemy territory. This was the era of the SAS jungle specialist – the 'jungle bunny'. The jungle brings out the best, and worst, in people. If you are claustrophobic, thrive on company or are in the least bit disorganized, it will defeat you. That is why the Regiment insist jungle training should form part of a trainee's Continuation assessment, before he joins his Squadron. However powerfully he may walk across the Brecon Beacons, however well he resists interrogation, the jungle represents the ultimate test. Every year, a handful of individuals, and even the occasional trained SAS operative, are returned to their parent units for failing to withstand the rigours of jungle life.

Hereford Hospital loved the jungle trips. They were a mine of pathology once the operatives returned from overseas. The laboratory staff would run competitions, trying to guess which country in the world was involved, by identifying the large number of infecting organisms the men brought home. You can get a good idea where someone has been by looking at his stools, or his watery eyes, even his nasal discharge.

Gut rot, or gastroenteritis, was the commonest illness. This is a waterborne disease. A jungle animal, or more likely a local native without an understanding of hygiene, defecates into or near a jungle waterway. The excreta may be teeming with bacteria. Salmonella is particularly common. The SAS operative, in all innocence, creeps to the water's edge to fill his waterbottle, praying that he will not be seen. High humidity has dissolved and destroyed his sterilization tablets and he cannot boil the water for fear of being detected by the enemy. He must drink it as it comes, salmonella going straight from tail end of native to stomach of operative. Florid gastroenteritis is the result. I learned to recognize salmonella by the smell. It has the most pungent, foul, penetrating odour imaginable. Routinely I would walk round the Squadron latrines once jungle trips returned home. I needed no laboratory support to diagnose the disease. The sound and smell of fifteen backsides excreting the stuff was enough. It was disgusting, though largely curable.

Some operatives appeared to have greater resistance to jungle pestilence than others. The experienced jungle bunnies, those who had served many times in the tropics before, were best. I became so worried at the disease rate of returning jungle troops at one stage, I insisted each man underwent a full medical examination on his return home. I remember one Squadron medical session, fifty-five men in all, each staggering dishevelled and unkempt into my Spartan office. Fifty-three were covered from head to toe by insect bites and skin rashes. Two were entirely blemish-free. Both had served in every jungle campaign worldwide for twenty years and were as at home in the rainforests as on the main streets of Hereford. I am not surprised that one of them later produced a best-selling survival book. He cannot only write about it, he can do it too. For three months he had been isolated in the globe's thickest jungle and yet I could not see a bite nor a bump on him. Remarkable.

The Regiment maintained a regular presence in Central America, in case of insurgence by the other side. There had been some noisy sabre rattling in the mid-1970s when the United Kingdom felt sure the opposition was about to cross the border. Immediately, the SAS was mobilized, experienced jungle troops being sent on their way to set up cross-border ambushes and observation posts. Not knowing what to expect, the operatives prepared themselves for action from the moment their Hercules landed. Fully tooled up, M16s on automatic, grenades hanging from their webbing, camouflage cream applied, they hurtled from the aircraft tailgate ready to take on all-comers. They were greeted by a sleepy, relaxed, RAF groundcrew. 'Haven't you heard?' a flight lieutenant asked.

'Heard what?' queried the gruff SAS troop sergeant.

'The war's off. Cancelled. Finished. Didn't they tell you?'

It was a classic example of one hand not knowing what the other was up to. During the long flight to Central America the politicians had negotiated a settlement, though no one had thought to tell the SAS. The operatives, every muscle tensed for the action they were sure they would find, could barely believe what they had been told. In the Army one becomes accustomed to occasional inefficiencies, even in the SAS. It is to their credit that the operatives rapidly disarmed themselves and enjoyed life in the sun before returning home. Operation Delight had been born.

As my VC10 thumped to earth south of San Carlos, it was as if the same, sleepy, RAF groundcrew were still there. Someone held up a large white board, the black number '7' displayed for all to see from the windows as we slowed towards the end of the runway – marks out of 10 for the quality of the pilot's landing. How bored they must be, I thought.

The main military base was at Tayola Camp, a short drive from the runway. If the airfield was sleepy, the camp was unconscious. Here the limited SAS presence mixed with the regular Army, though tried to keep separate for the sake of sanity. The place was full of soldiers bored to tears. The troops barely ventured from the camp into the jungle around it. If they did so, it was for no more than a few hours at a time. Whitewashing of the camp's kerbstones was a regular punishment – this was the Army I wished desperately to avoid.

Despite its sleepiness and pestilence, Central America was still a region that had taken its Regimental toll. None more so than Paul J. You could not find a nicer man. Aged barely twenty-five, he was an outstanding soldier. His fiancée was a sweetheart. Following a particularly sensitive border operation, his patrol was celebrating before returning to the UK. On his final night in the country Paul J walked back from the party, held near to Tayola Camp. I never did learn the full story. He was found, lying face down, by the side of a nearby track. He was alive, barely so, but could not move. Paralysed from the waist downwards by a forceful blow from behind, his spine had totally dislocated. The bones had flown so far apart that his spinal cord had ruptured, a situation from which recovery was impossible. Everything below the point of dislocation was paralysed – feet, knees, hips, bladder, rectum, the lot. Within seconds this capable, ambitious man had become useless to the Army.

As the doctor you have to pick up the pieces. I tried hard to do so, showing him friendship and support. I helped with compensation claims, rehabilitation and appliances to make him walk again. Paul J joined an ever-increasing list of Regimental paraplegics. I admired him tremendously, feeling almost guilty at my own health. I see him now, struggling into my medical centre, on his two crutches, a huge brace around his waist and legs to hold him vertical. Every ambition he ever held had to be abandoned. It says much for his resilience and single-mindedness that he painfully dragged himself back to an independent life. When it goes well, SAS service is a great adventure. When it goes wrong, it certainly hurts.

We had received information of illegal border crossings in the south of the land. Apparently some immigrant loggers were not all they purported to be. Whether it was drugs, or an attempt slowly to establish a military presence, was not known. Whatever the reasons, it was felt a hearts and minds presence on the border would help. I would establish myself in a central location while the operatives attempted to find out what they could. The small jungle village of Joaquín was chosen as our base. Thirteen kilometres from the border, it was close enough, but not so near that an international incident would be created if an SAS presence was discovered.

Four of us went in. Tom, Roger, Jim and me. In keeping with a long SAS tradition, though I was the only officer, I was not in charge. Tom was my boss. Though only a sergeant, he had seen it all. As far as I was concerned, whatever Tom wanted was fine by me. We took with us a local twelve-year-old boy, well used to the tracks and waterways of the southern areas. He was our guide. With him came the FINCO.

The FINCO is the Field Intelligence Non-Commissioned Officer. Central America was full of them. Their task was to blend with the surroundings and pump the locals for whatever intelligence they could obtain. Information would be passed back to Headquarters at Tayola Camp and from there, if necessary, to the UK. FINCOs came in all shapes and sizes, but would often grow their hair long, wear civilian clothes and carry hidden weapons. They were largely confined to the main towns – Celoni, San Carlos, Ricos and others. Only rarely did they venture into the jungle itself. Few were jungle-trained in depth and able to withstand the days and weeks of isolation that jungle living required. It was in the deep, inner jungle the real intelligence was to be found. The result was that up to the minute information could only infrequently be obtained from FINCOs.

Our FINCO was no exception. He was a charming individual, but apparently overwhelmed by his involvement with a fully trained SAS jungle patrol. His 9mm pistol was of no use in such an environment and he remained permanently terrified of attack by wild animals or snakes. The twelve-year-old boy, meanwhile, was an invaluable asset. Not only did he speak all local dialects, but was a crack shot with a catapult. Snakes, birds, even frogs and toads, fell to his accurate shot as he guided us confidently along the unmarked tracks. We had been landed by Puma helicopter at Punta Cabello, ten kilometres to the north of Joaquín, and made our way slowly through the rainforest towards our objective.

Central America does have a number of dangerous animals. So-called immigrant loggers are not the only foe. Two, in particular, worried me. The fer-de-lance snake and the black widow spider. The fer-de-lance is a huge beast and totally illogical. Most snakes run away when they hear you coming. The fer-de-lance may not. It can attack anything and anyone on sight, including a passing Land Rover. Forcibly it will inject its venom via two retractable fangs. Death is a guaranteed result, usually from kidney failure and bleeding into the brain.

The black widow, however, is different. She has a tiny body but huge, long legs. Her favourite spot is under the overhang of a toilet seat. Her favourite target is the juicy male scrotum as it hangs downwards, its owner peacefully relaxing at stool. One bite and it is all over. Death, again, is assured. One has to sympathize with the FINCO. I never once saw him open his bowels.

It took us two days to reach Joaquín, a thriving little community on the south bank of the Dabacho River. The place was unique. Throughout the jungle could be found dozens of rundown villages. Dirty reed huts, mud-splattered paths, filthy water supplies and mangy dogs. Joaquín was different. It was immaculately clean. There was also Helen. Helen must be the most God-given creature on earth. A young nun, it was said that at the age of eighteen she had ridden by donkey into the heart of the jungle, stopping when she felt tired. It was Joaquín's good fortune that she chose to stop there. Over the years she had struggled to educate and improve the lot of the locals. Five years later she had succeeded. Always dressed in immaculate white, however filthy the jungle near by, her influence extended throughout the region. However trained and warlike the SAS might be, nothing was possible without Helen on side. As I shook her smooth, perfectly clean hand, I knew I was in the presence of someone very remarkable.

In my travels round the world I have met many missionaries, enough to know the job is not for me. Of them all, Helen competes for top position. She did not force religion at you, but simply concentrated on being friendly, leading by example. Gradually her flock began to follow. Before long the whole area was on her side. I was not allowed to tell her we were from the SAS. In fact she never once inquired who I was, who we were, or why we were there. Unquestioning, she took us at face value, judging us by our attitude and demeanour.

At first sight we looked a frightening lot. Unwashed, unshaven, heavily armed, we formed a tight-knit, withdrawn group. Our twelve-year-old guide, passport to the area, left once we reached Joaquín. Likewise the FINCO. Whereas Tom had led us here, through the thick, slimy jungle, now it was my turn to run the show. A hearts and minds project is a complex affair. The aim is to win over the local population in as short a time as possible, offering them facilities they would not normally have. Medical care is usually top of the list. Once the word gets out, people flock in their hundreds to you, wherever you may be. Clinics can be huge. It is not unknown to see more than 200 patients in a day. So it was with Joaquín. At such times it is all hands on deck and thank God for SAS medical training. Tom, Roger, Jim and I threw ourselves into the clinics with gusto. I knew the others had little knowledge of the sometimes complex tropical diseases that faced them. However, SAS confidence is a wonderful thing. Within minutes they were making all manner of diagnoses, many I imagine invented and had created scores of delighted patients.

Naturally, every patient must leave a hearts and minds' clinic with something in hand. There is a profoundly held belief amongst most of the world's primitive peoples that an illness can only be cured by a tablet or injection. In the developed world we know this to be nonsense. Many are best cured by the medical manoeuvre of 'masterly inactivity', letting Nature take her course. Diarrhoeal conditions often respond quicker to rehydration and cleanliness than to any tablet on the market. In the jungle, many diseases are created by viruses and parasites, not by bacteria. Antibiotics, being ineffective against such beasts, are a waste of time.

In hearts and minds you have to move fast. You have a short

time on site, and in that period you must win the confidence of the locals and do the best you can for their healthcare. As everyone wants a tablet or injection, you take with you a large supply of placebos. Placebos are medications that are safe to give, but without proven therapeutic effect. At least without proven *physical* effect. Their psychological advantage cannot be underestimated. Sugar tablets are best. I have used them for all manner of things, including marital disharmony, male impotence, even the common cold. Should you have to inject a patient, for whatever reason, it is sometimes worthwhile making a ceremony of the occasion, particularly if a village elder is involved. The event gives them an opportunity to demonstrate strength and confidence in front of their people. You can help by freezing the skin before you inject and using a tiny, thin needle. This makes the procedure almost painless and ensures the elder does not flinch. Excellent for his credibility and standing. Excellent, of course, for the gathering of information and intelligence by an SAS hearts and minds patrol.

Roger, in particular, was a real enthusiast. The most unlikely looking medic, he was in his element. At one point I saw a thin, tired old man dragging himself away from Roger's clinic area, supporting himself wearily with a long bamboo walking pole. Around his forehead was swathed a large crêpe bandage. 'What's that for?' I shouted across to Roger. 'Has he cut himself?'

'No, Doc,' came the reply, barely audible over the noise created by the gathered throng. 'It's what you would call bedside manner. He's got a headache, that's all.'

'A headache?'

'Yeah. I've bandaged an aspirin to his forehead and told him to keep it there for a week. He's feeling better already. Look!'

I glanced across again at the elderly man. When I had last looked he had seemed distinctly the worse for wear. No longer. Already I could see life returning to his face, confidence in his stride. The bamboo pole was barely being used. Roger had effected a most thorough cure. It was not for me to interfere.

It is a feature of hearts and minds operations that, whatever it takes, you must do as they do. You must never inflict on local peoples an insistence that the English way is the only one. If they drink from a filthy well, ignore the use of toilet paper and routinely sleep for three hours after lunch, so must you. Never question their behaviour and way of life. It is reasonable to take precautions behind the scenes, but outwardly you should fit completely with their lifestyle and be as humble as you dare. Slowly this will give the opportunity to change the ways they use. In particular it will give them the confidence to speak to you and provide that valuable intelligence you seek.

I had first come across this concept of total involvement in local culture thousands of miles from the jungles of Central America. I was in the North-West Frontier of Pakistan, on its border with Afghanistan. There was political chaos, with the Russians building up to their invasion of the land. Two of us had been asked to prepare a full report of the area's medical facilities, in case of subsequent need. We found a small valley, south-west of Chitral, and arrived to announce our presence to the local Kalash tribespeople. Inexperienced at the art of working with such individuals, my own manner was perhaps too officious and condescending. I did not do well as a result. In the same valley, however, and preparing a thesis on local dialects, was Michael D. Michael and I had been at school together. To meet again in the Rumbur Valley of Pakistan was one of those coincidences that can only happen once in life. In contrast, he had thrust himself into local culture and customs. He spoke their language, ate their food, prayed to their idols, and lived their life to the full. He was an outstanding success and taught me a lot, though I doubt he realized it. His skills I have used worldwide, even to this day.

As part of our attempt to be involved in all of Joaquín's activities, I felt it would be a good idea if we went to church. Already Sister Helen had asked me to talk in the local school, watching bemusedly as I struggled through a lecture on good hygiene to an audience that barely understood English. But church? That was a different matter. Whatever one thinks of the SAS operative, however good or bad he may be, regular churchgoing is not a strong point. My companions looked horror-struck at the prospect but they, too, were as impressed by Sister Helen as I. So to church we went.

On SAS patrol, attending church can raise problems. You are trained never, whatever the reason, to abandon your weapon. Irrespective of circumstance, it should never be more than one arm's length away. Quietly, the four of us filed into the back of the chapel area once the service was under way. Sister Helen smiled, acknowledging our presence, though I could tell from her stern glance that our weaponry was not welcome. Taking the hint immediately, we leaned the M16 rifles against the rear wall and took our seats on the back row of wooden benches laid out for the congregation. At most, there were a dozen people present. The M16s were now at least five arms' distant, but near enough to get at if trouble arose. You could never tell with Central America, particularly in border areas. The immigrant loggers we had been sent to investigate may well have been armed soldiers in disguise. Anything was possible and we were on our own. Jim would send out his twice daily signal to Tayola Camp, the sitrep, but it would have taken a long time to get help to us if we ran into trouble. Hereford had told us that Tony was now recovering well in hospital, so that was at least a relief. Beyond simple messages such as this, communication with our leaders was sparse.

The service progressed as they always do. Mostly my mind was on other things – the clinics, loggers, jungle wildlife. For the religious sloth, church is an excellent time for reflection and thought. Then, suddenly, within my daydreams, I heard the command 'Let us pray.' Reflexly the SAS fell to its knees, facing forwards towards the cross. The remainder of the sparse congregation did the exact opposite, taking to its knees, but facing backwards. I have no idea why. As I looked up towards the cross I found myself staring directly into the eyes of a clean-shaven young missionary to my front. He looked horrified. I knew I was not a pretty sight and to the regular washer must have smelt terrible. I could see his eyes flicker nervously, as I had crept in behind him at the start, without his realizing I was there. He looked first at me, then at the others and then he saw the rifles. You could not miss them. There knelt the congregation, fingers clasped and palms together, praying to our four, tidily arranged M16 carbines. To their credit, no one mentioned it, but I was mortified. It was no surprise that Sister Helen took me aside after the service to say it would be better to hold our clinics outside Joaquín. It was her polite way of saying the SAS had outstayed its welcome.

The following day we made our way to the village of El Morinto, barely a kilometre from the opposition's frontier. Word had now spread that the British soldiers were here and there was free medicine for all. Wherever we went we would be followed by long lines of sickly natives, some genuinely ill, others perfectly fit but wishing to see us nevertheless. Sister Helen, dressed in radiant white as always, came with us, helping Roger and me to run an overcrowded clinic in the village town hall – the *cabildo*. Meanwhile, Tom and Jim disappeared to see what information they could gather on border activity.

The *cabildo* clinic was the worst of my life. I dream of it even now. Sister Helen, Roger and I stood at one end of the primitively constructed reed hut. It was no more than fifty feet long, its open door at the far end. No sooner had we taken up position than the entire population of El Morinto tried to join us, squashing and cramming themselves into the tiny space. Dogs, children, adults, more than 200 in all, crushed themselves in to be with us. Worse still, a gastroenteritis epidemic had struck the village. Everyone, young and old alike, was smitten. We could not cope. No space, insufficient medical supplies and appalling human suffering.

One mother forced herself to the front of a non-existent queue, misery and distress etched on her face. In her arms she held a lovely little girl, no more than eighteen months old. Diarrhoea streamed down the child's thighs and legs, dripping disgustingly on to the earthen floor. The girl's sunken eyes, her wrinkled, desiccated skin meant that death from dehydration was not far away. I knew there was nothing we could do and turned to Sister Helen, if nothing else for moral and spiritual guidance. I could see the agony in her own eyes as she, too, realized the situation was hopeless. Then the most terrible thing happened. As the child died, so a pack of emaciated dogs began to sniff at the limp, frail legs, licking the diarrhoea from her thighs and from the puddle on the earthen floor. It was awful. A great wave of revulsion and nausea welled up inside me. I could sense Roger, to one side, being similarly overcome. Neither of us spoke, but together we forced our way through the crowd into the open air beyond, retching and vomiting on to the ground outside. That child died a horrible death, an end from which we were powerless to save her. The jungle can most certainly be a terrible place.

The little girl's death at the *cabildo* clinic ruined Central America for me. I was glad to leave, and as soon as Tom and Jim returned we exfiltrated to Celoni by boat along the Dabacho River. From there it was to Tayola Camp and, two days later, the UK and Hereford.

True to form, the SAS barely gave me time to unpack. On this occasion it was Major Y who disturbed my peace, putting his smiling face around the door only thirty-six hours later.

'Far East, Doc? What do you reckon? We could do with you out there.'

I rolled my eyes Heavenwards but realized I could not refuse. I knew Major Y's Squadron well. Scheduled to remain in deep jungle for several months, medical cover was a necessity. This time it would not be Central America, but a Far Eastern frontier. As was traditional with the SAS, it was only happy when poised beside a border somewhere. The more political and precarious the position, the more the Regiment appeared to thrive.

We were inserted by Huey helicopter, of Vietnam war fame. Their rotors really do go 'thump, thump, thump', being audible for miles. It is an aviation classic and a joy to travel in. One might imagine that jungle insertion is a simple affair. It is not. The lush green jungle canopy extends for miles. Clearings do not exist and any that are present may easily be compromised by the opposition. The Regiment has dreamt up many ways of infiltrating deep jungle, but abseiling from a helicopter is perhaps the easiest. Clip your figure of eight descender on to the rope and away you and your equipment go. Strangely, the process is fun. I remember feeling upset that, once down, I could not go back up and try again.

At one time the SAS went through a phase of parachute jungle insertion – tree jumping. The principle was simple. You descended by parachute into the trees, crashing through the branches until your canopy snagged and broke the fall. You then either climbed down the tree or released your reserve parachute. The latter's rigging lines made an excellent rope down which you could slide. This was simple in principle, but hazardous in practice. As the parachutist descended rapidly towards the trees, there was a real risk that upward pointing branches would skewer his private parts. Before leaving base a thriving Black Market in telephone directories or extra towels existed. Anything that could be stuffed down a pair of jungle trousers to ensure the SAS's ability to procreate remained intact. Abseiling was safer.

Getting out, or exfiltration, from the jungle was equally troublesome. An overflying helicopter would find it impossible to identify the exact location of troops on the ground. The Search and Rescue Beacon – the SARBE – was one choice but could again be identified by enemy signals personnel. An orange marker balloon, floated up through the jungle canopy was a silent way of identifying ground position. Operatives could then be winched upwards, assuming the winchman could steer the sling through the branches. If tactics allowed, plastic explosive could be used to fell sufficient trees and permit a well-controlled helicopter to land. This was a time-consuming, dangerous and messy business.

Problems with jungle insertion and exfiltration highlight the one major feature of the environment. It is dense. Jungle can be primary or secondary. Primary jungle is as God designed it. Thick, mature trees, close to one another but without much smaller vegetation between them. Secondary jungle is what happens once man starts to remove the primary trees. A morass of thinner, tangled, smaller trees and bushes regrow. Making headway is nigh impossible. Then there is bamboo. If you wish to creep up on someone unheard, bamboo will let you down. It is frighteningly noisy. Step on a piece, or move it to one side, and you will hear a noise like rifle fire. The plant must have been responsible for more deaths in the world's secret wars than any other. Soldiers struggling through bamboo are a giveaway.

The Far Eastern jungle felt a friendlier place than its Central American equivalent. The jungle warrior's bible, *The Jungle Is Neutral* by Spencer Chapman, was written in this part of the world. However welcoming and neutral the rainforest may be, it is still rich in wildlife, not all of which is friendly. I had barely detached myself from my abseiling rope when the first case came to me. It was Jock, a huge, massive Scotsman with hands like spades. He had formed part of the advance party, preparing the abseiling site prior to our arrival. He had killed the beast that had bitten him but was now suffering the effects, the insect's venom already beginning to circulate round his body. It was a large centipede, as long as the palm of my hand. Despite being crushed by Jock's jungle boot, a few of its legs still twitched. Jock was not well. Within thirty seconds of being bitten he had collapsed, his chest wheezing, his forehead sweaty and yet his skin clammy cold. Nowhere had my military medical training told me what to do with centipede bites. From an RAMC viewpoint, if you did not suffer from a standard NATO illness then they could not recommend a cure. Despite this, Jock was obviously in a bad way. Antivenom, if indicated or even available, was nowhere to be found. So steroids it would be. All I had was an injection called dexamethasone, mainly used in civilized societies for the treatment of severe head injuries. Nevertheless it worked wonders for Jock who, within forty-eight hours, was back to his usual massive self.

The one beast dominating the jungle was the leech. Everywhere and anywhere the little horrors could be found. These were not the big, black bull leeches so favoured by Hollywood film producers, but their smaller, browner brethren. Stop for a matter of seconds on patrol in the Far Eastern jungles and the ground will come alive with these wriggly creatures. Purposefully they make their way towards you, determined that you, above all others, will be their meal. They get anywhere, often where you least think of looking. The first you know of them is after they have had their fill. Scratch your backside, or brush your neck, and you will feel the self-satisfied lump of a bloated beast, only too happy to be flicked to the ground and begin digesting your blood cells. They can sometimes be dangerous too.

Mac, a new addition to the Squadron's ranks, found it impossible to urinate one morning. He had never had such troubles before and was beginning to get anxious and distressed as his bladder enlarged. I was preparing to plunge a needle through his abdomen into the bladder to remove the urine when I thought to examine his penis. There, under the foreskin and very self-satisfied indeed, was an inflated leech blocking Mac's urinary passage. Fortunately a small piece of tail still protruded, giving me something to grasp with my surgical forceps. Mac lived to pee another day.

It is a lonely life in the jungle. You are about as stranded as you can get. Movement is slow, communications poor and claustrophobia common. For the married men it was particularly difficult, as any form of contact with home was impossible. You need a very understanding wife in the SAS. For the unmarried ones, like me, jungle trips represented a succession of broken relationships. Whenever I went I could be sure a girlfriend would shelve me. At the start I thought it was just me until I looked around at the gathering of sad faces after the infrequent mail delivery had, literally, been dropped in. Dozens of the single men, and a few of the married ones, had glum faces after reading their letters from home. On this occasion I had already received and read mine. Glancing around me I saw Trooper Mark S looking shocked. I went over to him.

'What's the matter, Mark?' I asked.

'It's Tracy. She's given me the elbow,' he replied, his voice low.

'I'm sorry. What are you going to do?'

'I can't do much from here, Doc,' came the sorrowful reply. 'I'll just have to make a new start when we get back. She says she's got a new bloke. Doesn't ever want to see me again.'

I put my hand on his shoulder, as reassurance. It seemed the right thing to do. This large, powerful operative was completely shattered by what had happened. The frustration of being able to do nothing in response, stranded deep within humid jungle, was naturally immense.

As I stood beside him, uncertain what I should say next, I saw Mark's saddened form slowly begin to change. He was well known to be a very determined soldier. I could almost sense his renewed strength course through my hand. I withdrew my arm as he stood up, his jaw now set. 'Bloody hell, Doc. It's ****ing ridiculous. What the **** can I do about it anyway? Come with me. I've got an idea.'

I followed him through the jungle to a spot fifty metres from our base, in jungle terms a very long way. He stopped by a large, knurled tree stump, perhaps four feet high. It was black, half-rotten and stood beside its decaying trunk, the result of a deadfall months or years earlier. This was the area of our jungle range. I stood behind him, fascinated, silent and completely motionless. I watched Mark slide the long combat knife from its webbing pouch, hold the now sodden letter from Tracy against the stump, and plunge the knife through the paper into the rotten wood behind. Then he took six steps backwards, flicked his M16 safety to automatic and fired. It was frustrated fire, not aggressive. Gunfire in tight jungle surroundings is explosive. I winced with the agony of the noise, thanking Heaven that the nearest non-SAS person was reported as many miles away. I tried to remain impassive as I watched Mark empty several rounds into the letter, softened bark, sharp wood splinters and pieces of paper flying everywhere. Then, as rapidly as the noise had started, it stopped. Total silence once more. The letter hung in tatters from the trunk, though still held secure by the ugly combat knife. Mark turned, his face now smiling, contentment in his eyes as he looked directly at me. 'Doc,' he said, removing a full magazine from his ammunition pouch, 'here are some rounds. Let's have the letter. Now it's your turn.'

I have to admit a sense of warped satisfaction, returning my 'Dear John' letter to its sender full of bullet holes. It was a wonderful therapy. I did it twice, on two successive jungle trips. When upset, the Dear John tree saved the day.

Much of a jungle doctor's work is to do with worms. These tiny creatures, frequently invisible to the human eye, show no mercy. SAS operatives are certainly not exempt. Nor am I, I am ashamed to say. Worms form a very diverse family – tapeworms, hookworms, guinea worms, threadworms. The list is long. You get them either from infested food or by walking through contaminated water. Take Brian, for example. His small stature belied an enormous, hidden strength. On patrol he could keep going for days while others might stop and rest. One morning he came to me. Overnight he had developed several large, red, linear streaks on his legs. I looked at them. Almost like marker pen lines on the skin, I was sure they were getting longer as I watched. They were also very itchy. Great weals and skin flakes littered the area where Brian had scratched furiously in his sleep. I was annoyed with him for that. Break an intact skin surface in the jungle, by whatever means, and you are assured an infection. High humidity and filth are a wonderful breeding ground for bacteria.

'Creeping eruption,' I explained. 'That's what it is.'

'Creeping what?' he asked, somewhat unconvinced.

'Creeping eruption. It's a type of hookworm.' I went on to explain the problem. Certain types of animal hookworm do not have the power or strength to penetrate the human body. A normal human hookworm can get anywhere – lungs, guts, everywhere. Animal hookworm, particularly from cats and dogs, penetrates the skin from infested water and stays just under the surface. It wanders anywhere it wants, leaving long red weals wherever it goes – the creeping eruption. The difficulty is in establishing the direction the worm is headed. At which end of the red line is the beast to be found? The best way, and the one I used for Brian, is to mark each end with a black, indelible pen. Then send the patient away and ask him to return the following day. The direction of travel is then obvious, remembering the red line follows the worm and does not go ahead of it. Brian was easily cured. Once I had found the worms, they were quickly killed when I injected local anaesthetic into the skin around it. The process was painless and over within minutes. I think Brian was somewhat disappointed when I eventually killed his uninvited companions. By the time he had marked the red streaks and followed their movements, he was beginning to become quite fond of the little horrors.

One must be patient to deal with worms, especially the guinea worm infesting our storeman. Like the creeping eruption, this is to be found just beneath the skin. A small lump appears, then a hole, then the worm sticks out its head. Somehow it never appears when you want it. Like a watched pot, you can sit for ever looking at the hole with nothing happening. The beast must be coaxed out. In the storeman's case, I covered the hole with an antibiotic ointment. This distresses the worm sufficiently to force it further out than it would normally wish to go. As soon as a decent length of worm has appeared – they can be several inches long – you stick its head to a piece of sticking plaster. Once firmly stuck, its body is then wrapped around a matchstick, the stick being turned 360 degrees each day. Slowly the entire worm will be pulled free. It is important not to break the beast's body as the piece that stays behind will fester and become infected.

Worms are usually little more than a nuisance, though if you are trying to remain motionless in an ambush position, the last thing you need is a creeping eruption irritating your leg. Occasionally they can be life-threatening. Some migrate to the lungs and stay there. The patient may be unaware of their presence. At worst he might have a mild, dry cough. Give that patient an anaesthetic to treat a major illness or gunshot wound and before you know it the worms break loose and clog the breathing tubes or airways. Obstructing a patient's airway is a killer – I have seen it happen. It was for this reason I insisted jungle troops were dewormed before returning to Hereford, just like household pets. Many different medicines exist to do the job, some good, some not so good. My favourite was Alcopar, little granules delivered in a small sachet. It tasted filthy, but was effective. The only way to ensure my patients took it was to promise a tot of whisky to wash the granules down. They might arrive home drunk, but they were at least parasite-free.

My function in the Far East was to keep the operatives fighting fit. Unfortunately there was one operative who did not do particularly well. I am ashamed to say it was me.

It began as soon as I arrived. Having settled Jock's centipede bite, I spent the remainder of the first day erecting my A-frame. The A-frame is a permanent, home-made jungle shelter. Designed from carefully cut wooden logs, it comprises a hammock, built-in food store and rifle support. Everything is kept off the ground, the whole arrangement being covered by a waterproof poncho. I say waterproof, but the daily jungle rain can penetrate almost anything. Certainly a standard Army poncho leaks like a sieve. The experienced jungle bunnies make their own from impermeable material, the kip sheet, normally used for lining nuclear fall-out shelters. Even the kip sheet can leak jungle rain on occasion.

That first night I slept like a log, waking at dawn to hold my sick parade. There was only one patient – me. Something had decided to make a feast of my right eye, though I had not felt a thing. As a result my eye had puffed up like a football in such a way that I could hardly see. I did my best to put on a brave face. I was not in pain, so coped with sorting out the Squadron's other medical conditions as best I could.

The next day the same thing happened again, though this time affecting my left eye. That, too, swelled up enormously. As the Squadron commander highlighted, I now looked more like a moth than a soldier. Trying not to be downhearted, I volunteered to join a patrol into the surrounding jungle. The object was to identify the various tracks and paths, and to make sure we were alone. It was hot, and very humid, so I patrolled with my sleeves rolled up rather than down. That was a mistake. We had gone barely fifty yards, creeping our way forwards with me in the rear, when I scraped my right arm against a rough, irregular tree trunk. Immediately, almost within seconds, my arm began to swell. Not to be outdone, it appeared, my other arm, and then my cheeks, began to swell in sympathy. In a very short time I was stranded like an inflated whale in the heart of the jungle. Huge, swollen arms, puffy cheeks, bulging eyes. It was impossible for the operatives to take their task seriously as they delivered their doctor back to his A-frame, looking more like a Michelin man than a human being.

I now know that a small jungle fly, with a predilection for

eyeballs, had caused one part of my troubles. My swelling arms had been in response to an allergy against a variety of jungle tree. At the time I was worried, not fully understanding what was happening. As soon as I realized I still felt healthy, despite looking very odd, I relaxed. Slowly my various swellings settled and within four days I had recovered. The Squadron loved it. Each morning they would meet, the so-called Orders or 'O' group, to discuss the activities of the day. Their prime concern, and a source of high amusement, was not patrolling tasks or ammunition supplies, but what illness their doctor had today acquired. I think they were rather disappointed when I returned to peak fitness.

Insects and allergies were not my only enemies. The jungle contains many different four-legged animals, most of which steer clear when they know mankind is around. There are exceptions. Late one night I was woken by the sound of scratching metal, very near to my A-frame. It was probably no more than three feet away. Before going to sleep I had made myself a chocolate drink, consumed it in one gulp and left the metal mug on the jungle floor. That was a mistake. Something fancied the dregs and was using its claws to scrape up the chocolate. I was petrified, but could see nothing. The jungle at night is as black as it gets. There is the occasional fluorescent leaf, but otherwise you are unable to see anything at all. Whatever it was, I realized it had sharp claws and was likely to make a meal from me as soon as it had finished the chocolate.

As quietly as I could, I reached for the M16, perched on two forked sticks beside me. Slowly, I swung it round in the direction of the scratching and flicked off the safety. The clunk of metal echoed through the jungle night as I did so. Immediately the scratching stopped. The animal had heard me, or perhaps sensed me. I imagined it looking around, well able to see in the darkness. I, of course, was completely blind. Then I felt its breath against my cheek. It was a warm, forceful, powerful breath now only inches from my face. I could not shoot. So black was the night that I could easily have shot myself, or a colleague, by mistake. I had no idea in which direction my rifle barrel was pointing. Then the breathing stopped. I sensed that whatever it was had begun to look around him. The next thing I knew, or felt, was a large, reverberating shudder as the beast leapt on to my A-frame. It had obviously spotted my food store and was aiming for that. I had tolerated enough. Against all standard operating procedures, SOPs, I threw my M16 to the ground, grabbed my machete from under my head and flicked on my torch. There it was, the beast in question, rifling through my valuable food supply. A large, very startled, civet cat. As I lunged at it with the machete, nearly amputating my foot as I did so, it snarled and ripped a large hole in my hammock with its claws. Instantly it disappeared into the night, leaving me shaken and blinded by my own torchlight.

Added to my various illnesses, the Doc's adventures with the civet cat went through the Squadron like hot gossip. For those who had doubts about the jungle themselves, my misfortunes provided added strength. I was not the only one to suffer, I was pleased to learn. Perhaps the civet had made the operatives more aware of jungle wildlife, perhaps not, but Jack S had one very worrying night indeed.

Jack was a thin, wiry man, highly expert in CRW, counter-revolutionary warfare. Most of his SAS life had been spent in civilian clothes, trying to blend with the background scenery as best he could. He certainly did not look like the archetypal SAS man. His time in the Far East was to update him in more traditional SAS soldiering techniques. Heavily decorated for his part in a variety of covert wars, nothing could rattle him. Until that night, of course. The night following his return from near the border.

It was 2 a.m., pitch black and totally silent as he lay in his hammock. Around him, well hidden and tactically positioned, were the other three members of his patrol. As he awoke, Jack knew he was not alone. On his chest he felt the smooth, coiled body of a snake. It was stationary, lying motionless as his chest rose and fell with breathing. Jack was horrified. He knew he could not move. If he did so, with the snake only inches from his neck, he was sure to be bitten. He had to summon help.

'Pssst!' he went. 'Pssst! Pssst!' trying desperately to wake his colleagues for help. 'Pssst!' He was sure the snake shifted slightly in position when he made the noise and could feel his heart thumping uncontrollably in his chest. He was surprised how warm the animal's body felt, having never been so close to a snake before. He could feel his hands become wet and clammy, his mouth dry. Worse still, he wanted to pee, though knew it was anxiety that made him feel it. 'Pssst! Pssst! Pssst!' Still no answer.

Jack lay there until dawn, four hours later, frightened rigid. He could barely breathe and could only urinate by wetting himself. All it would take would be one unexpected movement, the snake would startle and that would be it. He would have to wait until his colleagues awoke, or pray the animal moved on. The more he silently begged it to depart, the more it remained committed to stay. As first light began to appear and the tips of the huge trees turned from black to grey, he tried again. 'Pssst! Pssst!' This time he was successful. Lofty, the patrol signaller, sleeping ten metres away to his right, awoke. 'What's the matter?' he inquired, his voice a loud whisper.

'For ****'s sake get this thing off me,' replied Jack, still not daring to move. Lofty peered through the gloom towards his friend, though could not make out the problem. Quietly, he slid from his hammock, knife in hand, to see what he could do. Getting closer he, too, could make out the grey cylindrical shape coiled on Jack's chest.

One could never fault the SAS for indecision, even when faced with problems completely outside their experience. Lofty leapt firmly into action. Grabbing his jungle blanket, he dived across Jack's chest, seeking to smother the animal before it could retaliate. He braced himself for a ferocious fight, aware that some jungle snakes could struggle harder than a man. It was as he landed across his friend, as the entire hammock collapsed to the ground, that he realized what it was. No snake at all, but a camouflage face veil coiled neatly and tidily on Jack S's chest. Somehow it had slipped downwards from Jack's neck as he slept. The jungle can certainly play wonders with the imagination.

Not everyone was as resilient as Jack or Lofty. For some, the psychological strain of jungle service was more than they could take. The Army has long recognized the mental stress created by long periods of isolation in such a cramped, low-light, diseased environment. Psychologists were even attached to the SAS at one point, to analyse the effects of the jungle on the human mind. The SAS survived, the psychologists did not, having to be treated for stress once back in UK.

I had one psychiatric casualty in the Far East. Mick, a most unlikely individual for such problems. I had not realized, but he was obviously a man who kept his feelings bottled in. Not one to join in the general banter of SAS life, the continual teasing and cajoling that goes on between men used to long periods away from society. One of his patrol called me to see him in the early morning, several weeks after the incident with the civet cat. I found him lying, rigidly still, in his A-frame. 'I can't take it, Doc,' Mick whispered. 'I thought I could, but I can't. I'm feeling all shut in. I've got to get out.'

I had never considered claustrophobia, a fear of confined spaces, to be a problem in the jungle, but with Mick it obviously was. We were so deep within the rainforest I could see how it might happen. The nearest clearing was fifteen kilometres away, the trees tightly packed and tracks non-existent. Progress on foot was painfully slow: 100 metres per hour was considered speedy.

In the UK I would have given Mick several days' sick leave and sent him home. Such a course was not open to me now. I tried talking him out of it and for a moment thought I had succeeded. After two hours of quiet counselling he appeared to relax. However, the moment I turned to leave, he grasped my wrist firmly. 'Don't go, Doc,' he pleaded. 'Don't go.' Cruel though it may sound, with an entire Squadron to care for there is a limit as to how long you can spend with one man. I tried counselling again, feeling Mick relax once more. Yet, as soon as I tried to leave, my wrist was clasped tightly. Eventually, the only way of solving the trouble was to sedate him, first by injection and then by tablet. Sedatives are an essential part of any SAS doctor's toolkit. However controlled and well-trained an operative may be, anxiety always lurks around the corner. Particularly so after gunshot wounds, when a sedative can be life-saving. The Army is well aware of the psychiatric effects of remote and active service and takes such things very seriously. Training for its doctors is now quite detailed. I put Mick to sleep for the best part of two days, just as the Americans did for their battle-stress victims in Vietnam. It cured his trouble, but I could not allow him to stay with us once he awoke. Next time he might not have a controlled breakdown, but an uncontrolled one. That could lead to anything. I thus recommended that Mick be evacuated as soon as possible, waving farewell to him as he was winched to safety by a hovering Huey. I never saw him again. By the time we returned to Hereford the Regiment had discharged him, returning him to his unit. There is no space for those who cannot take it in the SAS.

Returning from the Far Eastern jungle, it was traditional to pass through Hong Kong. At that time, Chinese handover was barely considered, the colony concentrating largely on money-making and enjoyment. It was a wonderful place to be. Particularly for SAS operatives who had been stranded in deep jungle for several months. For the single ones amongst us, doctors included I am afraid, thoughts tended to veer towards the opposite sex. I love my male colleagues, but not in any sexual way. Three months, surrounded by damp and trees, in the company of smelly, unshaven masculinity, does little for male hormones. I had heard that Macau was the place to go. Not only could one gamble, but the Portuguese colony was full of massage parlours. Having received my Dear John letter there was little reason to hasten home, so I decided that Macau it would be.

Having clambered from the hydrofoil that plies between Hong Kong and Macau, I immediately started searching for a massage parlour. I did not have to look far. The place was stuffed with them. 'Special Massage', 'Total Massage', 'Heavy Massage', 'Massage With Relief', were signposted everywhere. I did not understand this strange, new massage language. Guide books were understandably unhelpful.

Confused, I eventually narrowed my search to one tiny street and three adjacent buildings in particular. Each was a massage parlour and each looked equally attractive. Or disreputable, if you see things in such a way. The choice was impossible. How does one select these things? Eventually I went for the one with a flashing, neon arrow, pointing obliquely downwards at the parlour's open glass front door. 'Extra Massage' it flashed. 'Extra Massage' sounded ideal – so in I went.

The parlour was everything I expected one to be. Behind the stained Formica reception desk sat a full-breasted creature, gorgeous in every outline, filing her nails. Her long black hair curled gracefully over her shoulders, her smooth, crossed legs exaggerated by the tiny red skirt. I doubt she spoke English, or if she did made no effort to communicate. Chewing visibly and obviously on gum, she indicated briefly a wooden panelled door to one side of her desk. 'Please Enter' was stencilled in several different languages near its top. I nodded my appreciation, now feeling almost sick with anticipation, as I entered this very unfamiliar world.

Closing the door behind me, I could see the narrow corridor leading away to my front. To each side were several curtained cubicles. All were drawn closed, save one at the far end on the right. Its striped orange drape lay wide open, beckoning me to enter. Tentatively I walked the short distance to the vacant cubicle, passing the closed curtains as I went. From behind each I could hear the sound of female giggling, or grunting. The air had that distinct smell of bodily sweat. This, I thought, is definitely it. This is 'Extra Massage'. This is what happens when you receive a Dear John after three months in the jungle. Quickly, and silently, I followed the faded English instructions on the sign above the cubicle's black, vinyl couch. 'Remove your clothes and lie down,' they proclaimed.

'Remove my clothes?' I thought as I stood in my underpants. All of them? Every stitch? I looked around briefly in the hope there might be someone to ask. Though I was surrounded by grunting and giggling, by many obviously satisfied customers, there was no one I might disturb. Anyway, it was obvious, I thought. Stop being so damned timid, Villar. You've travelled thousands of miles for this. So, with one swift move of my hand, I removed my underpants and lay face down on the icy couch.

As I lay prone, head in my arms, listening to those around me, I began to think. This was unquestionably a first experience. Life, after all, was a matter of gaining new experiences, was it not? Even so, I was starting to worry. Maybe this was not such a good idea. No one from the Regiment knew I was there, my girlfriend had shelved me and my parents thought I was still safely ensconced under military control. Anything could happen and no one would know. Mugging, murder, Heaven knows what. Then there was VD. God help me if I caught that. I had treated it dozens of times in my medical life, in all manner of individuals. Syphilis, herpes, molluscum contagiosum, Vietnam Rose – one diagnosis after another flashed past me. I began to feel sick, unfolded my arms and gripped the sides of the slippery couch firmly. I needed strength. Then, as I began to relax once more, a wave of doubt flooded back over me. Like the night I nearly failed 21 SAS Selection, I knew I had to escape. I had to get off that mountain, I had to get off that couch. It was a ridiculous idea anyway. I should know better. What on earth was I doing here? The sound of giggling and grunting disappeared into the background as I now concentrated entirely on my predicament. It was time to leave.

As I lifted myself with sweating, trembling arms, I suddenly felt a large hand push down hard between my shoulders. It was useless to resist. The force was overwhelming. 'No leave, sir. Sorry, sir. Many people, sir. I too busy,' said the deep, male, Oriental voice. 'You want massage, yes?'

Male? A man? A bloke? What was this? Anyway, it was too late. I had decided to go. Determined now, I pushed up once again with my arms. This coincided with a hard thump from the man's knuckles between my shoulder blades. 'No problem, sir. I here now. I massage. You stay still,' he insisted.

'B-But . . .' I turned my head as far as my prone body would allow, to see my assailant. The last thing I had been expecting was a man. From the power of his hands I imagined a huge, muscular frame with bulging forearms, as hard as iron. What I saw astonished me. He was small, with perfectly groomed hair. Smartly dressed in a spotless white coat, gold buttons gleamed at me on its front. He was pummelling hard now, an irresistible force, smiling down, as I attempted to look up. I was being kneaded from head to toe, like mutton being tenderized.

The man smiled, and spoke again. 'You OK, sir? This good, yes? We good massage parlour. Not bad. You understand? I see you worried. No need. This good extra massage. Nothing funny. You fine with me.'

I succumbed at that stage. Small though he was, resisting was useless, his hands and technique totally professional. Nothing strange happened, nothing odd. Just a simple, straightforward massage. Unwittingly, and thankfully, I had chosen the one parlour in the row where peculiarities were not on offer. It was a near miss, not to be repeated. I returned later that day to Hong Kong, feeling refreshed, relaxed and glowing.

My experience in the massage parlour highlighted one thing in my mind. SAS life was lonely. The Regiment looked after you well, but emotional support was something you largely had to find for yourself. Naturally, if there was a crisis – death, divorce, illness – the SAS would pull out all the stops. You still need support at other times, however, a sustained feeling of belonging or being needed by something or someone. With the odd life I led, added to the many visits overseas, I found anything other than casual relationships impossible. You never physically plan to settle down as a man, or I never did, but it does occasionally cross your mind. Particularly after some life-threatening incident when the continuity of Villar genes was imperilled. Procreation is a strange, instinctive thing that I do not pretend to understand.

Each time I met a woman, and there were not many, I would naturally enjoy the moment. I would be less than human if I did not admit to the thought of whether this particular individual was right for life. Usually the conclusion was 'No', probably more my fault than theirs. Of course, those I found most attractive were the ones seemingly unattainable. Like the fearless cavalry doctor in

Northern Ireland I had heard of before, or the paediatrician working in Hong Kong's military hospital. A top-flight professional, my colonial contacts vouched, she was said to have five boyfriends simultaneously, three on the same rugby team. So clever was she that no boyfriend knew the others existed. Now there was a challenge I thought. Did anyone know her name?

CHAPTER 5

Desert Impotence – My Secret Cure

I could not stop the bleeding. The girl had been haemorrhaging for three days. Not fast, just a steady, persistent ooze. The poor thing could only have been sixteen years old, but with vaginal bleeding you cannot get at it. No artery to press on, no spot for a shell dressing to be applied. Without surgery I estimated she would last another twelve hours. I had to get her to hospital – fast.

It was a postpartum haemorrhage, a potentially life-threatening bleed that can occur after childbirth. From between her legs flopped the now gangrenous umbilical cord, the child having long been detached and handed to its grandmother. The lower part of the girl's belly felt hard and distended as the womb clamped down to expel the now useless afterbirth, the placenta. It would not come. The Arab midwife had been pulling steadily on the cord, but the placenta held firm. It was stuck.

This was the village of Haruj, stranded deep in the south of the Bawiti Sands, the Ramlaat Bawiti. Already I had been there for two months. Bedouin Arab families around had heard of the new medical facility we had opened and would come in their droves each day. The young girl had come from Dilma, a tiny village more than 120 kilometres away. Bundled into the back of a Toyota Landcruiser she had been accompanied by more than a dozen screaming, chattering women, none of whom I could under-stand. Though my SAS Arabic course had been helpful, it had not covered the hundreds of different dialects existent in this part of the desert.

At first all I had seen had been the pile of old blankets in the back of the open-top vehicle. A bundle of tatty, brown rags. But when the hysterical women had dismounted I picked up the tiniest flicker of movement from beneath the pile. A foot, I think. Slowly I removed the blankets, gently, one by one. There, exhausted on the grimy metal floor of the Toyota, lay the girl. Her normally pigmented face was deathly white, her breathing shallow. Her eyelids flickered faintly, as she did not have the strength to open them. I felt her now cold, clammy wrist for signs of a pulse. None. Her blood vessels, desperate to stop the bleeding, had constricted down hard. I moved my hand to her neck. There, thank God, was the feeble, thready thump of the carotid artery. Feeble it might have been, but its rate was phenomenal. Her heart was beating furiously, trying hard to push what little blood remained round her rapidly fading body. The girl was in shock, and the nearest operating theatre was across the sea, sixty-five kilometres away on the island of Greboun. What the hell could I do?

'We've got to get her out,' I said, turning towards John, the SAS signaller now beside me. 'Can you call up HQ and get a casevac under way?'

'Sure, Doc,' came the confident reply. 'Get on with what you have to do. I'll see if we can get a Skyvan to take her out. Where to? Greboun?'

'Greboun will do. Or Koussi if that's easier. She needs a surgeon and operating theatre fast. I can't open her up here. The place is too filthy. She'll die under anaesthetic for sure if I do.'

John nodded and walked away through the dirty sand towards the patrol base. A ramshackle building, roofed with corrugated iron, it had been a bad choice. With desert temperatures often over 40 degrees Celsius it was like working in an oven for most of the time. One of the best with a radio, I was sure John would be able to raise Squadron Headquarters in Koussi's Messouda Camp in no time. I turned back to the young girl. I would have to do what I could to save her.

'Ergometrine,' I muttered at the Pakistani dispenser who was also standing beside me. 'Can you draw some up? It might just do the trick. And a drip. Haemaccel fluid, I think. Can you run one through?'

The dispenser nodded his understanding and strode purposefully towards his Portakabin dispensary, only twenty metres away. The girl was too sick to move, so I would have to use the back of the Toyota as my resuscitation room. Within minutes the dispenser had returned, syringe in one hand, drip in the other. It took no more than a minute for me to insert the small butterfly needle into the back of the girl's forearm and start running the lifesaving fluid into her. Human blood would have been best, but I did not have access to any in the middle of the desert. A plasma expander was my only alternative.

With the Haemaccel running I tentatively lifted the coarse, black material of the girl's dress. Not a dress by any Western standards, but a thick cloak-like affair covering her from neck to foot. Her veil had long been cast aside by the futile attempts of others to help her. Bedouin etiquette demanded that I did not expose her. So, with a degree of groping, I felt for the smooth flesh of her outer thigh, disinfecting it with the disposable alcohol swab before plunging in the needle. It was a big needle, long and broad, to ensure accurate placement into the muscles of the thigh. The attached syringe was small, ergometrine injection only being tiny in volume. Even so, it was a powerful drug, well able to force a womb to clamp down hard on the placenta, reducing any blood loss. The clear fluid emptied into the girl's thigh rapidly, though I could see her wince as I pushed the plunger.

Removing the needle and syringe I placed my hand on the girl's stomach, massaging her lower abdomen slowly. Gradually I could feel her womb beneath my hand contract tightly, becoming still harder as each second passed. Good! The ergometrine was doing its job. Then, with my bare hands, I reached up under her dress once more, fumbling now for the blackened umbilical cord. I felt it with the back of my hand, wrapping it around my fingers to get a good grip. Then, still massaging the belly with my other hand, I gently but persistently pulled. Nothing happened at first. Then, slowly, I felt the placenta give way, releasing its tight hold on the inside of the girl's womb. There was a loud gurgle as it was finally expelled. Old, smelly, black, clotted blood followed it.

By now I was covered with blood. My fingers, forearms, even my legs and desert sandals. Blood goes a long way when it decides to spread. The girl was still breathing shallowly, her eyes closed. At least she was alive. I laid the placenta on the floor of the Landcruiser to examine it. Damn! It was not intact. At one corner I could see an irregular rent. That meant a piece was still stuck inside her. There was no way I could get that out without surgery. The girl was in desperate need of medical evacuation. In spite of my efforts she would die for sure if she stayed in Haruj much longer.

Two hours after her arrival we were still no nearer to arranging the evacuation. John had tried one frequency after another, but to no avail. We had been warned that Russian ships off the coast might try and jam our signals. This was obviously happening. John sat there continuously, doggedly hammering away at his Morse key, praying that Koussi would respond. There was no answer.

It took seven hours to get our message through to Squadron HQ. Some bastard off the coast was taking pleasure in imperilling the life of an innocent civilian. I was frantic with worry, likewise the women who had accompanied the girl. The combination of ergometrine, Haemaccel and my extraction had improved her visibly, but she was still not yet out of trouble. Three days is a long time to bleed, however resilient and youthful you may be at the start. She could still so easily die.

Eight hours later, a military helicopter arrived from Greboun, landing with a flurry of sand beside the dispensary. With its arrival, our problems were still not over. The girl's husband, who had arrived late and had not witnessed the drama unfold, refused to allow her evacuation. This was deep, traditional, bedouin country. What the husband decreed was gospel for his spouse, even in matters of life and death. It needed an armed SAS medic to force both patient and husband on to the helicopter at gunpoint. The soldier held an accurate aim at the man's head, fortunately with the support of several bedouin onlookers, until the aircraft left the ground. Bedside manner can take a variety of forms depending, of course, on circumstance. The girl reached hospital within an hour and was on the road to full recovery the following day.

The Squadron's work in the Middle East added to a comprehensive history of SAS desert warfare. The Regiment was created in the deserts of North Africa during the Second World War and since then had spent much of its life in the desert. The Jebel Akhdar, the Musandam Peninsula and Operation Storm in Salalah were all major features of SAS life. This visit, Globe Trotter, was the Regiment's first major trip to the Middle East after helping win the Dhofari war in 1976. Largely a training mission, behind it lurked several clearly defined tasks. Fish smuggling was one. It appeared that fish were being pulled from the Gulf of Greboun and illegally shipped across country to a welcoming neighbour. To help stop this, as well as reinforcing support for the Sultan in the rural areas of the land, local militias had to be strengthened. Basing our activities on a hearts and minds facility, we were to recruit bedouin Arabs to work as a local militia – the *firquat*. Few recruits for the army came from the Ramlaat Bawiti, a trend the military hierarchy was keen to reverse. Border and internal security were, and are, significant issues in the Middle East. At the time of Globe Trotter there was a major border dispute in the north with a neighbouring power, while armoured dhows from an unfriendly Arab cousin were often being chased from oceans near by. No one could accuse the land of being quiet and peaceful, however beautiful it might appear to the untrained eye.

Our task was to set up the hearts and minds facility. Unusually, we had time to prepare. It started, as always, with a casual approach from the Squadron commander, Major A. He was an unassuming man. Highly professional, extraordinarily nice, it took others to tell you of his medals for gallantry or of his command and control of the Iranian Embassy siege. He had no reason to boast and was highly respected as a result. 'I want to do this one properly, Doc,' I recall him saying. 'You'll have time to train the lads. We can really make it work.'

Train I did, both the operatives and me. The Squadron was well-endowed with medics, most of whom needed simple updating.

For myself, it was veterinary training I sought. I felt I knew human beings pretty well, they were my trade, but animals I barely understood. We had only had a dog for eighteen months during my childhood. The dog, a hamster and a few goldfish were all I could muster. Even the goldfish I had managed to kill. I knew how much the bedouin Arab relies on his animals. I was bound to be faced with veterinary problems at some point.

So off to Melton Mowbray I went, the home of the Army's Veterinary Corps. They were very helpful, teaching me how to hold and shear sheep, deliver foals, clip the nails of rabbits and even shoe a horse. Unfortunately, camels and goats were not their forte, so though I left Melton Mowbray much enlightened, their instruction was not a great help for the Middle Eastern wastes. I was to run into trouble later as a result.

Then there was Arabic. French I can handle, even Latin or Greek. Arabic was a different matter. I have never understood how or why people read from right to left rather than left to right, nor use a script that to many is little more than a squiggle. That is, of course, a reflection of my own ignorance. However, if I was to communicate with my patients, Arabic it would have to be. The SAS Arabic course was fascinating, even if many of the phrases it teaches involve moving machine-gun positions, priming grenades and showing local soldiers how to stand to attention. None of these were the least use to a doctor attempting to establish the cause of a bedouin's abdominal pain. Nevertheless I enjoyed myself. What is more, I passed top of the class, an utter rarity for me. I loved the sequence of greetings and lengthy conversations required before business is ever discussed.

As-salaam alaykum (peace be upon you)
Wa alaykum as-salaam (peace be upon *you*)
SabaaH al-khayr (good morning)
SabaaH an-noor (good morning to *you*)
Kayf Haalak (how are you?)
Zayn al-hamdu lillah (well, thanks be to God) *wa anta?* (and you?)
Zayn al-hamdu lillah (well, thanks be to God)

And so it goes on, for as long as you wish, inquiring after the family, the in-laws, the goats, even the weather, until the essential topic is reached. Such an approach does create very lengthy meetings but ensures absolute tact and diplomacy at all times. By the time I had finished with the greetings I found it impossible to be argumentative when discussing the key subject. Thus, clutching my colloquial Arabic dictionary and a copy of *All Creatures Great and Small* as a veterinary textbook, I boarded the now beloved Hercules aircraft for our painfully slow flight to Koussi's Tafasset Airport.

The country is now a thriving, high-profile, very prosperous land. In 1981, the year of Globe Trotter, it was still struggling. When I reconnoitred the village of Haruj, our area of operations, I was horrified. There was nothing. Little more than a few ramshackle houses, a contaminated water supply, and goats and camels as far as the eye could see. The locals greeted our arrival, in a noisy Huey helicopter, as a gift from Heaven. Immediately we were surrounded by chattering men and women, each offering us dates and tea. Each wanting his or her own moment of discussion with these strange beings who had miraculously appeared from nowhere. It made an assessment difficult but superficially it seemed a good location from which we could work.

As I leapt from the helicopter, determined to make a good impression on our impromptu reception committee, I sank up to my knees in sand. I understood immediately why the helicopter pilot kept his engine running, maintaining a theoretical hover millimetres above the ground. I fell forwards on to my hands, instead of effecting the professional exit I had planned. I laughed. I had to, as for those present I must have looked like His Holiness the Pope, kissing Mother Earth on arrival. It was so like the story of one of the R A M C's model women doctors in Northern Ireland. Called in haste to the scene of a terrorist bombing, she had been landed by helicopter in a ploughed field. It was only as she stepped gracefully from the aircraft, medical pack in hand to rescue a mortally wounded comrade, that she realized her high-heeled shoes were still in place. Stranded in the field, skewered by her heels, her attempts at resuscitation had to be conducted barefoot. I had no high heels in the desert, but the sand's softness was just as good.

In Haruj, a small Portakabin dispensary already existed, manned by Ali and his two medical assistants. Ali was from Pakistan and not overly happy to have been banished to the wilds of the Middle East as a dispenser. His skills were good, but he was not medically trained and there were obvious limits to what he could achieve. However, I detected immediately that his heart was in the right place. He cared for his patients and wanted the best for them. He greeted me with open arms, showing me around the dispensary with great pride.

'We have two examination rooms, sir, *and* a big medical store,' he declared, his arms stretched wide and a sparkle in his eyes.

'Any laboratory facilities?' I inquired, knowing I would need to test blood and urine to help with diagnoses. Without some form of primitive testing facility, it would be impossible to make anything other than very basic decisions.

'Oh no, sir,' Ali replied, shaking his bowed head sorrowfully, his arms now by his side. 'We have to send specimens to Lanurte, a village one day's travel away. There they have a small medical centre, but the samples are usually destroyed by either the journey or the heat. We have to do the best we can.'

I nodded my understanding. It did not surprise me. This same story could be repeated in a thousand other locations around the world. If I had ever harboured doubts as to whether joining the SAS had been right for my career, the Regiment had by now totally dispelled them. My ambition to become an orthopaedic surgeon, and assist the Third World, still remained. I was at the bottom of the ladder, but now well off its first rung. The experience I was now amassing in Third World conditions was enormous. I had a lot to thank the SAS for.

Haruj, I decided, would be a good starting-point for our work in the Ramlaat Bawiti. Nothing was perfect, but with an existent dispensary, a crude water supply and Ali, things could be much worse. After ten minutes on the ground we clambered back into the Huey, shouting our promise to return, in incomprehensible

Arabic, over the noisy, classical clatter of the helicopter's rotors.

It was a short flight from Haruj to Greboun, little more than thirty minutes. It was as we landed that the search and rescue call came through. A Scandinavian tanker, some distance offshore, had a sailor in trouble following a broken thigh bone. They needed help, and they needed it fast. I was the only doctor within easy access, so the helicopter pilot asked if I would assist. I had been given strict instructions not to become overtly involved in the local armed forces' activities, before leaving the UK. Here I was, barely in the country twenty-four hours, being asked to disobey what I had been told. As a doctor, of course, there is no dilemma. If a patient is ill, whatever the cost to you, it is your task to deal with it. 'How can I help?' I inquired.

The ship was 160 kilometres south of Greboun, at the very limit of range for a Huey helicopter with extended fuel tanks. It was already 4 p.m., which meant we would have to land on the tanker after dark. While the Huey was fitted with long-range tanks, a Strikemaster jet was sent to find the ship and circle overhead. Meanwhile, so that SAS personnel would not be seen working openly alongside local armed forces, I was given the uniform of a Flight Lieutenant for the event. I strutted round Greboun airfield as we waited to leave, feeling most important. I even received a salute from an airman at one stage, though failed to respond. I was caught by surprise, as saluting protocol was not rigidly enforced within the Regiment. It was my first salute for more than a year.

Greboun airfield is an unremarkable place, but politically very sensitive. It was here the American Delta Force landed by C141 aircraft, before changing to their C130 Hercules during Operation Eagle Claw, their attempt to rescue the Teheran hostages. Many of us felt sorry for all parties involved in that Desert One tragedy. It appeared to me the event could be ascribed to the failure of several helicopters originating from the USS *Nimitz*. Rumour had it that those in the desert, despite the disaster unfolding, wanted to continue with the rescue attempt. The politicians in Washington, it was said, overruled them and cancelled. During the Iran/Iraq war, Greboun was also used as a base for disguised C130s in support of Iraq. Pressure from the UK's Lord Carrington stopped this. Greboun was evidently a very sensitive place. Even as I strutted around in my Arab uniform I could see a massive American transport plane offloading men and supplies. With thirty-four US warships offshore at that time, albeit just beneath the skyline, the area was extremely active.

We left Greboun at 5 p.m., heading south-west to the coastal settlement of Dilma. This was to be the Huey's final landfall before heading over the sea to the tanker. As we flew I could tell by the pilot's voice that all was not well. I have always hated flying and much prefer to jump out of aircraft than stay on board. It is, I suppose, a morbid fascination with air disasters. I always imagine the next crash will be the one to involve me. So when the pilot started talking over the intercom about fuel capacities, speeds, ranges and headwinds, I knew we had problems. His difficulty was the lack of room for error. The tanker was at the extreme limit of the Huey's range. With a strong headwind and a full load of personnel and medical supplies, the helicopter would be struggling to reach the ship. More than a few degrees off with his navigation, or a few litres out with his fuel calculations, and we would have to ditch in the sea. I had already seen vast numbers of sharks from the air during our earlier trip to Haruj. I had no desire to go swimming at night in the Arabian Sea.

As the sun was beginning to set, the pilot stationed the Huey on the very edge of the cliffs at Dilma, looking out over a vast expanse of ocean. I was beginning to feel helpless, being entirely in his hands. I knew I had to shut up and put up, whatever the decision he made. Anyway, I was damned if I was going to be the one to say yes or no. It was a beautiful view, I remember that as I write, but it did not detract from the terrible dilemma facing us.

We backed down in the end, for the sake of safety to all concerned. Before making that decision the pilot radioed the tanker's captain. By the time this conversation had finished I was not impressed. It transpired the thigh-bone fracture was already twenty-four hours old, and the ship's medics had been able to rig up some form of traction. Traction is the medical term for pulling on something. With a broken leg or broken arm, pulling on it is an excellent way of reducing pain and blood loss. If in doubt, when faced with a fracture, try pulling on it. You are unlikely to do great harm, though there are some exceptions. The injured sailor was also receiving painkillers by injection, so it appeared everything was in control until the tanker could reach harbour. There was certainly nothing extra we could do. Crash landing a Huey on to their helicopter landing pad would do no good at all. We abandoned the rescue, somewhat annoyed that the ship's captain had considered risking our lives for a casualty that was not an emergency. Scandinavia was not popular that night when we returned to Greboun to console ourselves in the bar.

My reconnoitre of Haruj had shown me one vital point. I could not do my job without a woman. Bedouin culture was strictly sexist. In public there were two societies, one for women and one for men. Behind closed doors, as in the rest of the world, the situation was different. Girls frequently ruled the roost. As a man, even as a doctor, I would not be allowed to do much with female patients. They were frequently covered from head to toe, two tiny eyeholes in a hood-like arrangement allowing them to see. The response to my simple request 'Can I examine your knee?' would be to expose a few square inches of the area and nothing else. Without a woman to help me it would be worse than veterinary medicine if I was to deal with females.

We were rescued by Rosie, a truly remarkable woman. Married to an ex-Royal Army Medical Corps officer, she was a London-trained nurse. I think she was somewhat overwhelmed by the idea of going into the desert with an all-male SAS Squadron, but in the event volunteered her services wholeheartedly. At the start the SAS operatives were doubtful. Taking women on Squadron activities was not something the Regiment normally entertained. By the end of our tour she had reversed this opinion. Rosie was worth far more than her weight in gold.

It is almost 300 kilometres from Koussi to Haruj. An easy journey by air, travelling overland is difficult. For most of the journey one is faced with endless miles of rolling sand dune. This is the land of Wilfred Thesiger who wandered the area with his camels and Arab friends. We did not have camels, but standard-issue Land Rovers. Dune driving, now a recognized adventure sport, was then almost unknown. The principle is to throw your vehicle forcibly at the things. Lowering the air pressure in your tyres to give improved grip, you drive as fast as you can go down the side of a dune. The process is electrifying – and terrifying – with slopes being slanted often at sixty degrees or more. Once at the bottom you must not stop, but maintain a low-ratio four-wheel drive to the summit of the next dune. If you stop at the bottom you are stuck. The Ramlaat Bawiti is not a place to call out roadside assistance. Dunes can sometimes be 100 metres high.

It took two days and several mechanical emergencies to reach Haruj. I realized then that desert navigation is a challenge. In Europe there is often a mountain peak, or a road junction, even a telephone box on which to base one's compass bearings. The Empty Quarter of this barren land offers no such luxuries. Largely uncharted, your navigation points are being continually blown and moved by the wind. Salt marshes appear and disappear, tracks exist when they should not. The fact we reached Haruj at all, without the luxury of Global Positioning Satellites, was a credit to our Squadron navigation team.

My impression of Haruj, having reached it overland, was very different to the opinion I had developed by air. Surrounded by rolling sand dunes, the village consisted of no more than twenty ramshackle huts. Twigs, corrugated iron, blankets, wire fencing were leant, one on top of the other, to make a bedouin house. Usually one-room, never more than two, these tiny dwellings would house an entire family. Animals, primarily goats, would be outside, their dry black droppings littering the sand. Our oven-like patrol base was in the centre of Haruj, though it was too hot to remain in for long. By nightfall, when the temperature declined to frequently chilly levels, it became more tolerable. We slept in small tents to one side of the base, away from prying bedouin eyes. On patrol, in the surrounding desert, there was no need for tents at all. A standard Army sleeping bag, fondly called the 'maggot' due to its bulging, transverse, down ridges, was all that was needed. Lay it on the ground, head on your escape kit, rifle in hand and off to sleep you went.

Sleeping at night under a desert sky is a magical experience. I wish I knew more about stars. They must have incredible stories to tell. You are not alone, of course. The sand can come alive. Once darkness falls, a host of God's creatures set about their respective tasks and most love the feeling of a warm body near by. Into your maggot will crawl all manner of beasts: scorpions, spiders, even the occasional snake. Like Jack in the Far Eastern jungle, it is important not to panic if this happens. You lie very still, breathe shallowly and regularly, and feel whatever crawls in crawl out again. Easier said than done, may I assure you.

Despite many creepy-crawlies, malaria was not a risk in the Ramlaat Bawiti — it was too dry. Mosquitoes need moisture to survive and water was in short supply. Sandstorms would occasionally whip up, particularly in the evenings. Sand gets everywhere when this happens. Eyes, nose, mouth, ears and, tragically, a Land Rover engine. You undertake mechanized desert travel without a mechanic at your peril.

Despite Haruj's initial appearance of being wild and uncivilized, its barren outer impression covered a warm, caring society within. Bedouin communities are ruled by the *waalee* — the head man. He is their direct contact with Government in Koussi. It is he you must woo and coax, in order to win the cooperation of his people. Haruj's *waalee* was a small man. Small in body perhaps, but huge in character. Outwardly quiet, a word from him and anything was possible. He was an important man to impress. I tried hard, perhaps too hard at one point, convinced my medical skills were all that was needed to ensure lifelong cooperation from the bedouin of Haruj. We had been there barely forty-eight hours when the *waalee* himself paid me a visit. Shuffling slowly through the hot sand, he knelt down outside my tent and put his head inside.

'*Tabib* [doctor],' he said. '*Tabib*, I have a problem.'

I was resting after a particularly chaotic clinic, though sat up immediately I heard his voice.

'Yes, what is it?' I asked. This conversation actually took place in awful Hereford Arabic.

'My son. Please come. He is not well.'

I sprang to my feet instantly. The *waalee*'s son was perhaps the most valuable member of the bedouin community next to the man himself. If the boy was sick, Doc Villar had to be on his best behaviour.

'I'll come right away,' I replied, grabbing my medical bag as I crawled from the tent. It was a very hot, stifling day.

As appeared usual in the Ramlaat Bawiti, all sick individuals were wrapped in several layers of blankets. The *waalee*'s son was no exception. Beneath a massive pile of at least eight of them, I found the terrified boy. He had already been half suffocated. Removing the blankets gave me an opportunity to look at him more closely. Certainly his temperature was high, well over 40 degrees Celsius, the normal being only 37 degrees. There were two sore lumps in his neck and two slightly red eyes, but nothing to explain such a high temperature and illness. No skin rashes, no enlarged liver and spleen, no infection of his waterworks. What the hell was going on? Through my mind raced a thousand tropical possibilities – impossible names like tsutsugamushi fever, onchocerciasis, toxoplasmosis. Then I thought to look in the boy's mouth, mainly to check his tonsils. The tonsils were normal, but on the inside of his cheeks I could see dozens of tiny white spots. No! Surely not? But yes, these were the so-called Köplik's spots of measles. An everyday occurrence in Hereford, but not something you would expect to see in a bedouin village. I was as likely to see measles in Haruj as malaria in Hereford, though when I thought about it, I had seen that too.

The *waalee*'s son represented the start of a massive measles epidemic throughout the region. In populations such as the bedouin, who have no inbuilt resistance to the disease, measles can represent a medical disaster. Over the next two months I was to see dozens of measles cases, some patients almost dying from the disease. More than 80 per cent of the adult population acquired it and I imagine some perished, even though I was never told.

There was little I could do for the *waalee*'s son, beyond reassuring his father that all would be fine. However, I felt that sedation would be reasonable, so produced my bottle of liquid sedative. It was marvellous stuff, perfect for quietening children and, I thought, ideal for the *waalee*'s son. I checked the instructions in my small reference book, administering the precise dosage to the child. The boy gulped it down enthusiastically. I then covered his tiny body with one blanket, not eight, and made sure he had enough air to breathe. The *waalee* was delighted with my treatment, producing his wife who lent support to his thanks. Happy with my administrations I returned to my tent, confident that I had secured the standing of the SAS in the Ramlaat Bawiti for the rest of time. Confident that was until the following morning. It must have been 4 a.m. Again, I was woken by the sound of a voice outside.

'*Tabib! Tabib!* Please come! My son. He is not well.' There was genuine terror in the *waalee*'s voice. I knew this was not the time to have a quiet discussion whether or not I should stay in my sleeping bag. You pick such things up very quickly as a doctor. I scrambled to my feet and walked briskly alongside the *waalee* to his house once more. There, reburied beneath the bottomless pile of blankets, was the little boy. He was stationary and barely breathing. His lips were a faint shade of blue and his pulse thready. He looked awful. I knew immediately what it was – the sedative. In my dose calculations I had not taken account of possible racial variation in response to the stuff. The quantities I had given were the same I would have prescribed an equivalent child at home. For the *waalee*'s son, never before exposed to the drug, the response had been extreme. It had flattened him out, making him unresponsive to anything his parents had tried. Effectively, I had overdosed him by at least three times. If I had known any Arabic swear words, I would have used them. The only way out now was to evacuate the child to Koussi, and evacuate him fast.

The evacuation went well, without any radio jamming by the Russians, and all ended happily. By the time the child reached

Koussi, the overdose was beginning to wear off and the boy starting to recover. By the time he reached his hospital bed he had returned to normal, without any long-term damage. I received the credit for the cure, having created the problem in the first place, and the *waalee* had been shown to be of sufficient standing to merit an official Skyvan to fly out his family. It was a narrow escape that I never wish to repeat.

Running a bedouin clinic is an experience for which any amount of training in the United Kingdom cannot prepare you. The numbers are enormous. It was not unusual to find a hundred people waiting outside the surgery door each morning, sitting patiently in the sand. Rosie would take the girls and I the boys, and between us we would struggle through. Patient identification was a challenge. Firstly, the women were fully covered, making recognition imposs-ible. Secondly, so many of the men had identical names. In one morning alone I treated eighteen called Hamed. I tried to solve the problem by asking a medical orderly to issue each new arrival with a left-luggage ticket. Instead of Abdullah, Ali or Ahmad, the patient simply became number 357 or whatever. This worked perfectly for several days, with patient records being kept by number rather than name. I then began to notice certain ticket numbers appearing more than once and not attached to the same patient. Apparently a thriving Black Market had developed outside the clinic, with luggage tickets being sold to see the foreign doctors. I abandoned the idea immediately.

While Rosie and I ploughed our way through the morass of sickly bedouin, SAS patrols throughout the area were doing the same. As well as treating patients they were doing their best to recruit young men to form a local *firquat*. They were doing well, with several tough young bedouin signing up for duty almost daily. Generally the Ramlaat Bawiti was a safe region, but the presence of opposition dhows offshore, combined with occasional reports of border incursions, did give an air of unease to the situation – no more so than early one evening as I was returning to Haruj from an outlying village.

I had gone to see for myself whether patrol reports of a measles outbreak had been correct. Measles in the bedouin had an unusual appearance and it was possible their diagnosis had been wrong. In fact they were correct. I should not have doubted it for a moment, but it was refreshing to escape the packed dispensary at Haruj if nothing else. It was getting dark as I drove the open-top Land Rover along a narrow rocky track, within a short, low gulley that briefly blinded me from the desert around. The track turned sharply to the left at the gulley's end. As I heaved on the steering wheel to negotiate the bend I saw before me two figures, one on either side of the track. I thought they were large boulders at first. The figure to my right raised his arm, indicating I should stop. The one to my left was lying prone and motionless behind a few scattered, low rocks. I could see the glint of an ancient machine-gun pointing at me. An ambush? Who the hell were these guys anyway?

I looked again at the figure to my right. Dressed as a typical bedouin, his face was cracked and weatherbeaten, his teeth chipped and broken. In his arms he held an AK47 rifle, partially levelled at my chest. He began to chatter loudly, and aggressively, in a dialect I could not understand. My sweating palms gripped the steering wheel tightly. I tried to stay calm by taking small, short breaths. I did not want the Arab to see how I really felt. As I could not comprehend him, I shrugged my shoulders and waited for his next move. I had no idea what he wanted. Then, suddenly, he stopped talking, took one step back and aimed his weapon directly at me. I braced for what I was sure would come next. There was nothing else I could do, stuck behind the steering wheel of the Land Rover.

For what felt an interminable period I sat very still, hands in full view on the steering wheel, waiting to be shot. In reality it was probably less than a minute. No shot came. Then, very slowly, the Arab lowered his weapon and started to talk incessantly again. He was still incomprehensible. Walking across to my Land Rover, he looked into the driver's compartment, still talking. As before, I remained motionless, not wishing in any way to upset either him or his companion, still lying prone to my left. I could tell I was being sized up, his gaze flicking from one side to the other of the compartment. As the Arab talked, his eye caught a paperback novel I had been reading, wedged on the narrow dashboard to my front – Jeffrey Archer's *Kane and Abel*. He raised his eyebrows quizzically, as if to say 'What's that?'

'Jeffrey Archer,' I replied. I could not think of an Arabic translation for his name.

The response, however, was instant. 'Jeffrey Archer?' replied the battered Arab, in an accent that made the name barely recognizable. I nodded, very slowly and very cautiously. Then stretching out one hand, the Arab indicated I should hand the book to him. Gingerly, holding it very obviously between finger and thumb, just like plastic explosive, I passed it over. No sooner had I done so than the Arab grabbed it, clutched it tightly to his chest and repeated the words 'Jeffrey Archer!' once more. Then with a flourish from his AK47 he waved me on.

To this day I have no idea who those two men were or what they had planned. Nor do I know if they had genuinely intended to harm me. All I do know is that Jeffrey Archer, now Lord Archer, did both the Arab and me a service that day.

As a doctor to the bedouin I had to turn my hand to many things. Human illness was only part of the task. Animals featured highly, in particular the local goats. I was glad I had guessed correctly before leaving UK, though my Melton Mowbray training was not a great help. Herriot's *All Creatures Great and Small* certainly was. It was one lunchtime, three weeks into Globe Trotter, that an elderly bedouin woman brought me her goat. Black, scraggy and becoming bald in places, it was obviously unwell. The story the woman gave was one of having insufficient water for the beast and feeding it a local form of Coca-Cola instead. I could well imagine it. There appeared to be an endless supply of a dark, sweet, fizzy liquid for all to drink. Genuine water supplies were frequently contaminated, as both animals and men drank from the same source. This was an open well, without any protection from the outside world, not a deep dark hole in the desert. I would frequently see camel droppings floating on the water's surface.

The goat was unable to walk and panting furiously. The only

abnormality I could find was a massively swollen abdomen, distended like a huge bass drum. There is a medical technique called percussion where you rest one finger face down, flat on the surface of any of the body's cavities, such as abdomen or chest, striking it sharply with a fingertip of the opposite hand. It allows you to hear whether the cavity is full of fluid, or air, or is perhaps a solid expanding tumour. The technique is used all the time. I tried it on the goat. Bang-bang-bang! Percussion confirmed the animal's belly was most likely distended with air, perhaps even bowel gases. I next listened to the abdomen with my stethoscope. Could I hear the gurgling sounds of bowel activity? With many human abdominal problems, the bowel sounds disappear altogether, particularly when a piece of intestine has burst, resulting in life-threatening peritonitis. But the goat did have bowel sounds, faint, tinkly ones – very high-pitched in nature. Such noises are, in the human, classically associated with bowel obstruction. For whatever reason, the intestines can occasionally become blocked. Perhaps they twist, or a tumour begins to grow, or even a lump of excrement fails to move on. This can cause massive distension of the guts upriver from the blockage. If the distension is not resolved, the guts can burst like a balloon. The pressure build-up can be enormous.

Once, when working for one of the UK's top bowel surgeons, I was helping in the operating theatre to relieve an elderly woman's blocked lower bowel. To do this the patient was anaesthetized and laid supine on the operating table with legs held elevated and to the side, out of the way. Deftly, my boss inserted the sigmoidoscope, a shiny steel cylinder about eighteen inches long, up the woman's tail end. As he did so there was an enormous explosion. I was sure it could be heard in the pub across the road. Faeces went everywhere, and certainly hit both my boss and the far wall of the operating theatre. The surgeon had simply, and skilfully, slipped the sigmoidoscope past the patient's lower bowel obstruction, releasing days of increasing pressure taking place higher up.

With my goat diagnosis made – intestinal obstruction – I had to act. Fascinated by my diagnostic methods, I had by now gathered a throng of bedouin onlookers, perhaps a hundred altogether. Nearest to me was the elderly woman, visibly distressed by her animal's plight. Goats are valuable assets to a bedouin. The animal panting before me would cost her a local fortune to replace.

I was stuck without any idea of what to do. I assumed my diagnosis was correct, though had no way of proving it. I certainly could not ask the animal and could barely understand the emotional outbursts from the owner that were becoming increasingly frequent. Gradually I could hear the low rumble of voices from the assembled crowd become louder. There was obviously intense discussion taking place between individuals, and an air of increasing dissatisfaction.

'You're going to have to do something, Doc', whispered Trooper B, one of our most capable Regimental medics. '**** knows what this lot will do if you don't.' He indicated the restless crowd behind me as I knelt on the sand beside the breathless animal, wondering what to do next. I nodded. Trooper B was right. I had to perform.

Before leaving the UK I recalled seeing a film, or perhaps a television series, where a vet thrust a large metal cannula, a form of surgical tube, into an animal with a swollen abdomen. I believe it was a cow. Well, I thought, if it is good enough for cows, and the BBC, it is certainly good enough for this goat. I knew also, for the restless bedouin crowd and the now hysterical owner, I would have to make a ceremony of what I did. I rose to my feet and turned to the crowd, trying to look each one of them in the eye as I spoke. 'I am now,' I shouted, 'going to save the life of this poor animal. It has suffered too long.'

For a brief moment the throng fell silent, then a few heads nodded their agreement as the voices began once more. With a flourish I slipped on a pair of surgical gloves from my medical bag, not an easy task when under stress, and produced a needle and cannula with a grand gesture. As I did so, I whispered out of the corner of my mouth to Trooper B, 'For God's sake help me! What the **** do I do next?'

'Stick it in, Doc. You know, just stuff it in. We've both seen it on the telly. The bloody animal's buggered if you don't.'

He was right. I was going to do it anyway but felt I needed moral support to help me with the task. Together the two of us knelt down beside the animal, the poor beast's abdomen swelling visibly by the second. It was in desperate straits. Eyes now closed, its mouth was open as it panted in agony. Trooper B held the goat steady while I made a great show of what I was about to do. The crowd fell silent. You could have heard a pin drop. Even the desert wind appeared to stop blowing for the occasion.

With the needle and cannula held in both hands I raised my arms well above my head. There was a gentle murmur of fascination from the crowd as I briefly glanced over my shoulder to see them still frozen to the sand. I looked back towards the animal, identified the most distended spot, and thrust the needle and cannula firmly downwards. I was like some ancient Aztec priest in the process of sacrificing his first human victim of the day. The needle and cannula thumped home with a resounding 'pop', followed by the steady hiss of a deflating balloon. As I struck, for a brief moment the animal opened its eyes, then gave a loud, agonized 'Baaaa!', and died. I was horrified. My theatrical performance had gone badly wrong. For perhaps a minute my bedouin audience remained silent, uncertain as to what had happened. Then, one by one, they realized Doc Villar had skewered their prize goat. The elderly owner fell to her knees, sobbing in the sand, while discontent in the voices of the crowd began to reappear. There was no way I could escape what I had just done.

After my disaster with the goat, the clinics became quieter for a while. I had made the cardinal error of any bush doctor – allowing a patient to die on my doorstep. The patient may only have been a goat, but there is an unwritten contract in Third World medicine. If you agree to take a case on you must get it right. What I should have done was to tell the animal's owner that the beast was going to die and not attempted to save it at all. Like many things in the SAS, they are often learned the hard way.

As well as general medicine and animals, teeth and eyes are common causes for local complaint. Though it would horrify an ophthalmologist, an excellent way of winning over the hearts of a population is to arrive laden with assorted pairs of spectacles. You do not need to be obsessive about the exact power of each lens. It is the elderly male population in particular that likes these things. Partly it is because it allows them to see better but, more importantly perhaps, it makes them appear dignified. If a tribal elder wishes to be seen as statesmanlike and wise, a pair of glasses goes a long way to help him. Spectacles are a simple way of ensuring the help of those who make the decisions in local society.

Teeth are a different matter. I had always wondered why it takes dentists so long to train when all they are dealing with are thirty-two tiny white structures crammed into the human mouth. Now I have tried basic dentistry myself, with all its associated hazards, I understand. The bedouins' teeth were terrible. Brushing them was a technique they had never heard of, while chewing and gnawing sickly sweet dates were commonplace. When I opened the average tribal bedouin mouth, I was faced with a sea of holes, stains and awful breath. Abscesses were two-a-penny. I exhausted tube after tube of temporary dental filling. Some mouths would need more than twelve holes filled at a time.

Lighting for dentistry – achieving illumination of the little nooks and crannies at the back of the mouth – was a problem. Without good lighting much of dentistry is impossible. My solution was to hold a pen torch in my own mouth so I could direct the light accurately into the patient's. This worked well unless the treatment was particularly lengthy. With the pen torch between my lips I was unable to swallow, which meant my own dribble ran down the pen torch into the patient. It was unpleasant for both of us, though fortunately not too many patients noticed.

Tooth extractions were great fun. If I had removed every rotten tooth I would have been clearing almost all bedouin mouths of anything within them. It was important to be selective as I had no way of making false teeth. The only extractions therefore I undertook were for the most decayed. The average tooth is locked in tight and special instruments are needed to remove it. Each type of tooth, be it canine, molar or whatever, has a specific design of grasper dedicated to its removal. The principle is to push rather than pull at first. By pushing *in* you break its tight connections to the bone. If you pull before the connections are broken there is a chance you will chip off a piece of root. With a root left behind, the patient is likely to develop an abscess around it. By the time I had finished in Haruj I had nevertheless performed more than 400 extractions. A few, I confess, had shattered roots, not a fact of which I am proud.

With the SAS hard at work in the Ramlaat Bawiti, there was intense interest within the country's Government as to what we were doing. No more so than from the Minister of Health. He was a pleasant, ambitious man, with whom I had liaised before leaving Koussi. When I had first asked him what the Government expected of us, he had replied that so little was known of the Ramlaat Bawiti that anything we could do would be fine. Once we had looked at fish smuggling and recruited a local *firquat*, of course. He did promise to visit us.

The day he arrived at Haruj we were four weeks into the job. I had gone totally bedouin, with a lightweight cotton pyjama suit, *shimaagh* Arab headdress, and moderately respectable beard. I would walk either barefoot, or in sandals. The SAS operatives were looking similarly tribal, although the occasional vestige of military uniform still remained, such as khaki shorts or battered suede desert boots. The latter, fondly called 'desert wellies' were favoured items in the Regiment and always in short supply. When worn in Hereford, in combination with civilian clothes, they represented a type of badge of action. A label that said 'I've been there and you haven't'. Anyone wearing desert wellies in Hereford, bearing in mind the strong desert associations of the Regiment, was definitely the bee's knees.

That morning it was, as usual, bright baking sunshine. The clinic had been uncontrollable and I was exhausted. Suddenly, at about 11 a.m., I heard the sound of a helicopter approaching. It was not a Huey, but was certainly white and spotlessly clean. I could see that, even as it descended from around two thousand feet. It was sparkling. Transfixed to the spot and wondering who this could be, I waited in the sand to greet the newcomers, hand to my forehead as I squinted into the sun. I had not noticed that my SAS operative colleagues had, to a man, disappeared.

It took another two minutes for the helicopter to land, by which time I could clearly see the Royal crest emblazoned on its side. As the Minister of Health stepped from the machine, closely followed by several aides, I began to feel exposed. I was filthy. So keen had I been to integrate myself completely into bedouin life that, to an outsider, I must have looked disgusting. Having not had a bath since we arrived, I also smelt revolting. As the Minister crossed the fifty metres of sand between me and the helicopter I could see confusion in his expression. Where were those famous soldiers about whom he had heard so much? At one stage I saw his gaze strike me and then move on. He even started to turn back. Then, after a brief hesitation, his expression brightened as he turned in my direction once more. This was associated with an obvious shuffling in the sand either side of me – my SAS colleagues. Each had dashed back to his tent, quickly donned a spotless uniform and was now standing in even rank to my left and right. Rigidly to attention and looking every bit the perfect British soldier, it had been like an actor's quick change at a Christmas pantomime. Of the entire base team, eight of us in all, I was the only one to look dishevelled, unkempt and dirty. The smartness of those beside me made my own appearance even worse. To the credit of the Health Minister, he ignored the insult, though what he would have told his masters in Koussi I do not know. With a brief handshake he looked me firmly in the eyes and asked, 'Would you kindly take me round?'

The visit lasted little more than ten minutes. I could tell he was in a hurry, so concentrated on showing him priority problems. In particular, the communal water well that was littered with camel droppings. A young bedouin girl also obliged by squatting in the sand to one side of the Ministerial party and opening her bowels, right in the centre of the tiny village. I could not have had a better display of poor hygiene if I had tried to set one up. Cat sanitation, defecating in the sand, was the only thing available to the bedouin.

In hot sunshine the fresh motion would sterilize and dehydrate quickly, but the flies loved it. They would hop from there to your food. It was a perfect way of transmitting disease.

During that short tour, every point I made was absorbed silently by the Minister, who then turned to his aides behind and snapped his fingers. As if using some hidden code, one of them would write furiously on a tiny clipboard. I realized rapidly that the Minister was actioning everything I asked. Within those ten minutes, the village had been promised a new well, proper sanitation, a new dispensary and a measles vaccination campaign. How I wish I had such direct Ministerial connections in my current employment in the UK. It would normally take years to negotiate such things.

With the Minister gone, life returned to its usual cycle of clinic and village visits. Slowly we built up the confidence of the Ramlaat Bawiti bedouin. It was a lonely job, though I had become accustomed to such feelings working full time with the SAS. However friendly one's military colleagues, as a doctor it is useful to have medical people available with whom you can discuss cases and treatments. Otherwise it is easy to make the same mistake repeatedly. Moreover, when working alone, no one can tell you whether or not you are doing a good job. I began to feel very lonely in Haruj, despite Rosie and my SAS colleagues. I started to find it difficult to get out of my sleeping bag in the morning or to go to the clinic, and noticed it was taking me longer to make medical decisions. I decided the only way out was to add an extra dimension to my life – marathon running. I cannot explain why as it is a singularly mad idea to dream up in the middle of a desert. Each day, however, and for sanity's sake alone, I would put on a pair of trainers and running shorts. Off I would go into the desert, up sand dunes and along gravelly tracks, training for the first marathon race I could find once I returned to the UK. It was my salvation. Every man needs his escape in life, whatever that may be. Marathon running was mine.

Physical prowess is important to a man, no more so than his abilities in bed with the opposite sex. The bedouin are a tough lot – sexual prowess is important to them, particularly as the men get older. In one clinic, towards the end of an interminable patient queue, I came to an elderly bedouin. His face was as weatherbeaten as they come, his hands knurled and wrinkled, his walking unsteady. Sitting on a stool facing me, his legs apart and his body supported by an irregular walking stick, he claimed his love life was at an all time low. Now, at the age of seventy-three years he was unable to satisfy any of his five women. Was there anything I could do?

I did not have the heart to explain that this was perhaps part of Nature's ageing process, or that a man fifty years his junior would have trouble satisfying so many women simultaneously. It seemed fairer to let him work it out for himself. However, he looked undernourished, so I gave him a multivitamin injection, a treatment I was sure would do no harm. Unfortunately, I had not reckoned on bedouin resilience.

The moment I injected him, surrounded by twenty onlookers, his face perked up, his stature broadened and the walking stick was left to gather dust in a dispensary corner. Out he strode, much to the delight of the surrounding throng, shoulders drawn back, an even pace to his walk.

For three weeks he barely emerged from his dwelling except to say, 'That injection was marvellous, *Tabib*.' Then, early one morning I saw him at the front of the queue, no longer his rejuvenated self. Back in his hand was the walking stick, his stature stooped, his head bowed. I took him to one side.

'What's the matter?' I asked, after the usual sequence of mumbled greetings.

'My wives, *Tabib*,' he said. 'Now they want your injection too.'

The old man and his impotence was an excellent example of maintaining the confidence of one's patients. The injection worked wonders and was something for which the patient will be for ever grateful. It did create one problem, however. After my success with the old man, my clinic became swamped by men of all ages seeking this instant sexual stimulant. I was so horrified at the prospect of dozens of rampant bedouin males, each trying out my new wonderdrug, that I called a halt to the idea immediately.

You can find yourself up against formidable local, medical opposition. Cupping, or branding, even bloodletting, were all practised by unqualified bedouin practitioners. Branding was the commonest. The principle is to take a hot stone, or glowing ember, and apply it to the painful area. Wherever there is pain, that is where you brand. I have seen it done. The smell of burning flesh is foul. If you have abdominal pain, then your belly is branded. If you have leg pain, so your legs are branded, and so on. Branding does sometimes appear to work, perhaps because the patient is so terrified of what is going to happen if he claims persistent discomfort that he tells lies to avoid further treatment.

Unfortunately branding may do little for what is called *referred* pain. For example, it is common to feel the pain of a heart attack in the left hand, or that from gallstones in the right shoulder. Sciatica, the pain from a slipped disc in the low back, is classically felt in one or other leg. Branding for these conditions is worthless. Nevertheless, irrespective of one's own feelings about such treatments, it is important not to belittle the local practitioners in the eyes of their own people. Wherever I go in the world I always put them on a medical pedestal, and keep them there. You gain their support and do everyone more good in the end.

As a Squadron we felt it was important to win over the locals. To do so meant entering into every aspect of their lives and showing respect for their customs and traditions. So we ate with our right hands, not our left, and always took time off to have tea and sickly dates before discussing business. We would never show the soles of our feet to anyone and would not look at their women, which was the most heinous crime. The result was that we became gradually accepted by the bedouin of the Ramlaat Bawiti, and were occasionally given presents. I remember one well – a huge, shark-like fish. We were very excited by this, having survived for weeks on military rations. Anything fresh was a Godsend. We cooked it immediately, spending most of that night around a fire telling each other stories as we digested the meal.

It was at 3 a.m. that it hit me. Acute, colicky, central abdominal pain. Not only was I smitten, but many of the others were as well.

One by one we succumbed to the most florid gut rot I have ever known. Within hours our supply of lavatory paper had been exhausted, the only paper left being paperback novels. By the time we had recovered there was barely any reading matter left in Haruj. Mixing with the locals had certainly taken its toll. We subsequently discovered that this particular fishmeat carried a high concentration of a chemical called ammonium. In our haste to celebrate the gift, we had not checked how it should be cooked. After we had recovered, the locals told us the meat should normally be buried in the sand for at least twenty-four hours before cooking, to allow ammonium to escape. The episode did not do my local reputation any good. In bedouin society, if a doctor is any use at his job he will not become sick himself.

One major reason for our base in Haruj was to prepare what the Army calls a 'medical appreciation'. This is a detailed medical report that allows a complete view of an environment and its medical problems. The SAS may be excellent at looking after itself for weeks on end in a disease-ridden land, but if larger numbers of more routine troops are to follow, particularly those without desert experience, the Army will need to be fully informed about possible medical risks beforehand.

In war, illness is the greatest cause of casualties. The second commonest cause is being shot by one's own side. The least common is being shot by the enemy. If you are shot by enemy action the chances of death are even smaller. Contrary to belief, the majority of soldiers are fairly safe in a war zone. Preparing an appreciation is a time-consuming task. It goes on for pages. The document, typed finger by finger on a manual typewriter, took seemingly for ever to complete. My only consolation was the knowledge that I was bound to be handsomely rewarded before I left. Everyone was. I was certain I would not be an exception.

The standard gift, for those who had pleased the local system, was a gold Rolex watch. All those at Hereford who had served in the Middle East sported a magnificent, sparkling timepiece. That, I thought, is unquestionably for me. Unfortunately I already owned a Rolex, though of stainless steel design, given to me by my parents on qualification as a doctor. Because of family loyalties I had no intention of displacing my stainless steel one, but having *two*, that would be wonderful. I knew my best chance of receiving the gift would be through the Minister of Health.

It came to my last day in the Middle East. The Squadron had been extracted from its various locations and I had completed my laborious medical appreciation. When he had visited Haruj, the Minister had insisted I report to him on my journey back through Koussi. On this occasion I did just that, sprucing myself up with an immaculately pressed uniform, clean shaven and desert boots as smart as they come. I looked the immaculate British soldier. I did not wear my winged dagger beret as this was felt to be politically unwise. Consequently, I dusted off my little used Medical Corps hat and presented myself to his staff and secretaries, appreciation tucked under my arm. I was, of course, bare wristed, my stainless steel Rolex hidden firmly away in my trouser pocket.

I was ushered into his massive office almost immediately. Rigidly I came to attention, cracking the most perfect military salute I can recall giving. The Minister, sat behind his desk, looked up and smiled. I could see confusion in his eyes as he struggled to recognize me. I appreciated his predicament.

'Yes, sir,' I said. 'I looked different when we last met.'

'You certainly did,' he replied, smiling. 'How have you done?'

'Our report is complete. I have a copy for you here. With full recommendations.' I handed the document over, feeling a huge weight lift from my shoulders as I did so. I was delighted to see it go but hoped my happiness was not too obvious. The Minister reached up to accept the buff folder, studying me intently.

'Thank you,' he said. 'I imagine a lot of work has gone into this document. I will read it with interest. Do you have the time by any chance?'

I could barely believe what I was hearing. This was it. This was how it was done. This was when I would receive my gold Rolex. My anticipation was almost uncontrollable. Taking a firm hold of myself, and the increasing, overexcited tremor in my hands, I slowly and obviously lifted my bare left wrist towards the Minister, pretending to look at an imaginary watch.

'I'm terribly sorry, Minister. I'm not wearing a watch. I can't help you I'm afraid.' My chest was bursting with anticipation. Any moment now, I thought, and the Rolex would be mine. Then I glanced at the Minister's face. For a brief moment I thought I sensed amusement in his eyes. Then came the smile and I knew he was aware of what I was up to.

'I do believe you were wearing a watch when we met in Haruj, Dr Villar,' he observed. 'You will not be needing one from us. If I need the time I shall ask those outside when you've gone. Thank you for your work. The country is very grateful.' His eyebrows lifted slightly, almost in challenge. I had been caught out, well and true, and now felt barely more than a few inches tall. Humbled, I saluted and left the room. The gold Rolex was not for me.

Much as I enjoyed and admired the Middle East, I was glad to return home to Hereford. It was important not to lose my civilian contacts. SAS service never lasts for ever and I knew that I would one day have to leave the Regiment. In some respects it was adventurous and attractive to undertake covert projects and operations in far-flung lands. In others it was a disadvantage. To ensure some chance of progressing up an orthopaedic career ladder, I had to maintain the support of those outside the Regiment who could help me. What I needed was a reason for staying in the UK for a while. I thought hard on the problem before realizing the obvious answer. Antiterrorism. Of course – that was it. Antiterrorism it would be.

CHAPTER 6

Do They Pay You By the Body?

'Go! Go! Go!' Instantly I heard the sharp reports of the stun grenades as the teams went in. Glass shattering, earth shaking, smoke billowing from the building in front. Staying motionless beside the team commander, I waited for the order to move. With luck my medical skills would not be needed at all. My hopes were ill-founded. Sixty seconds later the call came through my Pyephone's earpiece, 'Starlight. You're wanted. Come forward now.'

Antiterrorist assaults were dangerous things, large numbers of high-velocity bullets, and high explosive, being used within confined surroundings. To be successful required split-second timing, rigorous training and luck. Today luck was obviously in short supply.

I jogged forwards, breathing laboriously in my respirator. Already I could see one corner of the right-hand lens had begun to mist up. Damn! If it misted fully I would have to remove the thing. With the gaseous agents the teams had used, lack of a respirator would render me ineffective. The Kevlar body armour was heavy, particularly with the high-velocity protection plates worn front and back. My right arm felt wrenched out of its shoulder socket as I dragged the huge emergency medical pack towards the charred remains of the building's back door.

Steve, also in full antiterrorist kit, stood outside the door to greet me, his MP5 submachine gun still held ready. 'The stairs are first on your right, Doc. The lads will meet you there.' His voice sounded muffled and rubbery from within the respirator.

Inside was chaos. Glass everywhere, scorch marks on the walls, broken furniture scattered around. Two bodies lay near the foot of the stairs, motionless. They were no longer a threat. Through the smoke I could make out the broad stairway on my right as it curved upwards to the first floor. Three operatives stood on the stairs, hugging the wall, one at the top, one centre, one at the bottom. I could not recognize the one at the bottom of the stairs, but as soon as I turned to climb them, he put a hand on my shoulder. 'Wait,' came the rubbery instruction, 'they're coming down.' Immediately he spoke I knew it was Tom. Respirators and balaclavas made even good friends unfamiliar. All you could see was a large, threatening shadow. Then the shouting began. Loud, forceful shouts with screaming in the background, 'Go! Get out! Go! Downstairs fast! Go!'

I could see the stumbling shapes of several confused women being manhandled down the stairs, forcibly pushed from one operative to another. Finally, coughing and choking, they were expelled through the back door into the fresh air beyond. I could see how frightened they were. Though the siege had not been long they had begun to relax, trying hard to build an understanding with their captors. A desperate attempt to ensure their own safety. Then, unannounced, and with brutal aggression, the team had done its job. Within sixty seconds the task was complete, terrorists incapacitated, hostages secure. We had one casualty, not a major wound, whom I persuaded to limp out once the hostages were clear.

I never understood how the SAS developed its skills in antiterrorist warfare. It is such a contrast to its original role, sneaking behind the lines in North Africa. It probably dates from the Aden conflict, where urban terrorism first appeared, both enemy and SAS operating in civilian clothes. The Regiment, its eye always on the future, realized this was the way of things to come. By the time of the 1972 Munich massacre, an event sending politicians leaping for answers, the SAS was well placed to offer one. The 'team' was created, one Squadron being permanently stood by as the country's final solution, whether the crisis was at home or overseas.

Planning had to start from basics. As the concept expanded so its technology also increased. Special weapons, communications systems, gaseous agents, tactics, transport and so on. Medicine, in the early days, was left behind. I think it was assumed that SAS medical training would be sufficient or that local hospitals would muddle through on the day. It was rather forgotten that actions often take place in major conurbations and were likely to expose civilian medical services to injuries they had never seen before. Casualties would most likely be contaminated with incapacitating gaseous agents – CS gas, for example – that could in turn contaminate civilian casualty departments as they attempted to resuscitate the wounded. This was certainly a problem after the Iranian Embassy siege of 1980.

Until the 1980 siege, basic antiterrorist medical advice given to the Regiment had probably come from high-level Ministry of Defence sources. 22 SAS's Regimental Medical Officer was barely consulted. Medical plans and tactics were often prepared by those without firsthand experience of SAS activities. Consequently, in my day, if you wanted to play a part in events, you had to invite yourself. My participation was based on keeping an ear to the ground and learning when the teams were summoned. I would make sure I was there, uninvited but medical pack in hand, insisting I should look after my patients.

After the Iranian Embassy assault the situation changed. That year Delta had experienced a high-profile failure in Iran, while we had shown high-profile success at home. Political attention was unquestionably focused on antiterrorist warfare. 'Doc,' I remember the CO saying, 'I want you to sort out the medical side.' And so I did. From that moment I ensured the teams had their own, closely attached, medical support. I felt our role was clear. We were there for SAS casualties primarily – instant assistance at an operative's side.

Beyond the close support provided by SAS medical personnel, such as me, there also existed SMTs – Specialist Medical Teams. Officially they were not meant to exist, being tightly controlled from the Ministry of Defence. They were designed to work independently, and not alongside civilians. This would have been regarded as a security risk. The role of SMTs, in the eyes of the hierarchy, was to keep VIPs alive. Imagine, for example, the Prime Minister is taken hostage. After days of negotiation the SAS goes in, narrowly saving the day but wounding the Premier accidentally. These things can happen. For such people to die en route to hospital is not acceptable, so immediate on-site medical cover is required. These would offer consultant-level medical assistance at or near the action. Teams would come from all three Services, their equipment being on permanent standby in Hereford. The staff involved would go about their normal jobs, but would be ready to move at a moment's notice from wherever they happened to be. I had strong doubts about SMTs. Some were excellent, while others had no real idea of what was expected of them. It is one thing to be working in a comfortable Service hospital each day. It is another to be thrust into the back of a C130 Hercules at one hour's notice, flown to a farflung land and asked to perform medical miracles under fire. You need to be physically and psychologically prepared for such things. Many of the SMTs were not. Nevertheless, those involved did take their job very seriously.

Being on the receiving end of an SAS antiterrorist assault is not something I would advise. I have been through it on numerous occasions during training exercises. Such events are as real as they can get. The assault always happens when you least expect it. After all, the antiterrorist forces often have plenty of time to make their plans. The more a negotiator can slow talks down, the better prepared are the troops when the time comes. They can pick and choose their moment and have relays of freshly fed and slept individuals to do the task. The terrorist is surrounded by hostile forces and is unlikely to have slept or fed normally for a long time. Teams can get in anywhere. Through doors, walls, roofs or windows. You can be sure they will have been watching and listening to you intently by whatever means possible before committing themselves to an attack. By the time you realize an assault is under way it is too late to do anything about it. In come the flash bangs, the unofficial description of stun grenades, plus CS gas. Out go the lights and the next I know was that I lay flat on my face, a large boot on top of me. It was a position I was forced to adopt on many different occasions with the Regiment. I was completely disorientated. I had no idea who was attacking, how many were attacking or from which direction they were coming. I was always utterly surprised, even though I was in the trade. With antiterrorist tactics being so finely honed worldwide, it astonishes me that terrorist groups still try hostage-taking at all.

Most major powers, and many minor ones, now have their own antiterrorist teams. Many have been trained by the SAS. These were the so-called 'team jobs' where small groups of SAS antiterrorist experts would spend three months in a distant land, teaching local forces how to deal with siege situations. Buildings, boats, buses, trains, airplanes – they were all fair game. Medical training would form a significant part of a team job. It was not all about how to inflict injury, but how to treat it as well.

The secret of antiterrorist medical cover lies in good preparation. Though it may be exciting to think of hooded operatives blazing their way daily through doors and windows of embassies, real life is different. The requirement for antiterrorist troops is infrequent. A lot of time is spent training for that very rare operational requirement. A man may rehearse for several years for sometimes less than one minute of antiterrorist action. That action may be politically very sensitive, with the eyes of the world focused on the event. There is no room for error as both lives, and careers, depend on a successful outcome. Training is therefore taken seriously. This applies as much to the medical support as it does to the operatives. Antiterrorism gave me very little medical work throughout my time with the SAS, but occupied many hours in planning, negotiation and preparation. Terrorist events anywhere in the world are closely followed by all antiterrorist teams, wherever they may be, so that everyone concerned may gain maximum value from the experiences of a few.

Medical problems are diverse. Gunshot wounds, GSW, are a possibility. If the teams have performed their task efficiently, it is likely the wounds will only involve terrorists and are most probably fatal. For a doctor there is little to do except ensure a reasonable supply of body bags. Operatives train both by day and night to ensure they can reflexly distinguish a terrorist from a hostage so that only the bad guys suffer. It is not easy.

Burns and smoke inhalation are more likely. A hostage may not be able to escape, either due to terror or being forcefully immobilized by his captors. As soon as the action is complete, it is therefore vital that all innocent parties are evacuated speedily, taking care that no terrorist tries to mingle with escaping hostages. This occurred at the Iranian Embassy siege. Medically, one needs oxygen near by and a good supply of sterile dressings to cover burned areas. Severe burns will also need an intravenous drip erected as the exposed raw flesh exudes large amounts of serum, causing shock and a fairly rapid death.

In the early days of antiterrorism, the psychiatric side was largely ignored, teams concentrating on the practical aspects of winkling out terrorists from awkward locations. However, everyone is affected in some way at a terrorist incident – hostages, terrorists and antiterrorist forces. Most civilians have never been in a position where they fear for their own life and will be unfamiliar with the terror such a feeling can create. It comes as a rude shock to many with possible profound psychiatric difficulties subsequently.

Before any assault goes in, it is natural the security forces would wish to build up a picture of what is going on between hostage and terrorist. This is where the whizz kids are needed. The intelligence services would provide technical assistance. All manner of gadget would appear – cameras in walls, listening devices, thermal imaging cameras. The flaw in the system was the military skill of the technicians themselves. However fancy the gadget, if you cannot position it silently and effectively, then it is no use. The terrorist will detect it and your lack of tactical skill may bring the situation to a head sooner than is safe. Whatever the technology, there is no substitute for basic military skills. Stealth, camouflage, weapon recognition, are all time-honoured techniques, but just as vital to the outcome of a siege as the most modern, whizz-bang device.

Clearing a building of hostages and terrorists is a noisy event. It can be deafening. Not only are you completely disorientated but you cannot hear for minutes afterwards as a result. Hearing loss is something the Army now takes particularly seriously, though for years the effect of loud bangs on the human ear was not fully understood. They have been forced to comprehend by the large payouts made to sufferers. Generations of soldiers have been exposed, unprotected, to high-volume noises. In my early years of training, ear-defender devices barely existed. Now they are commonplace and insisted upon. There is one major flaw – you cannot use ear defenders happily on true active service. The same applies to realistic, live training. It is impossible to hear the enemy creep up on you when your ears are covered. Particularly at night, a soldier relies heavily on his hearing. Because of this, many will leave their ears unprotected in every scenario except a range. It is difficult to connect any one incident with deafness as its appearance is usually delayed, rather than being a major problem at the time. It is a terrible handicap.

On one occasion, I was practising close-quarter battle at an urban range on Salisbury Plain. The Army had rigged a complete town to look like a street in Northern Ireland. As I dashed up the main staircase of one building, Browning pistol in hand, but wearing neither respirator nor ear defenders, someone lobbed both stun and smoke grenades in through an open window. I did not know what hit me. Not only was the noise truly painful, but the smoke totally penetrating. I could not breathe. Stuck in the building, disorientated, I realized I had problems. It would be so easy to choke to death. I could not see where I was, the smoke was so thick. All I could do was lie on the floor, mouth wrapped in a grimy handkerchief, coughing and spluttering until the air cleared. I remember the smoke being gritty, full of particles I could almost chew. It took a week for my hearing to recover and two months for breathing to return to normal. If I become a deaf, respiratory cripple in years to come, I know exactly who I shall blame.

The Army, and the SAS, have designed many ways to remove unwilling opponents from buildings. Gas is particularly effective, provided those you are fighting do not have a respirator. There are different types of gas, some designed to kill, others to incapacitate.

Because of the genuine threat from certain overseas powers, not counting the antiterrorist requirement, how to behave in a gas-contaminated environment is widely practised in the Services. Called 'NBC' – Nuclear, Biological and Chemical – you must be able to function in all ways while fully kitted out in respirator and protective clothing, the noddy suit.

There are various ways in which a gaseous agent can penetrate your body. For most antiterrorist and riot situations, the agent is either inhaled or irritates exposed areas such as the eye conjunctiva and open mouth. The instant feeling when CS gas affects you is of burning eyes, tight throat and copious dribbling. It is most uncivilized and totally incapacitating. It is worth remembering that CS deaths have been suggested. In previous wars, though not with antiterrorism, blister agents have been used. These can be delivered in droplet form, causing blistering of any living tissue the tiny droplets touch. When inhaled, blistering can irreversibly damage the lungs. Sometimes it can strip a soldier completely of his skin. The use of mustard gas in the First World War is a good example. The cruelty of man to man never ceases to horrify me. John Parker's *Killing Factory* is a remarkable review of NBC methods should your stomach be strong enough to read it.

Nerve agents are different again. These paralyse the nervous system, with only tiny quantities being required for devastating effects. They were discovered by accident during efforts to find a chemical to kill lice. Tabun gas was the first, followed by sarin. Injections exist to reverse or prevent the lethal damage they cause, but you must act very quickly if in contact with the poison. The necessary antidote must be into your system within seconds. Biological warfare, such as cholera, anthrax or typhus, is also a major threat to the Armed Services, but of no use to antiterrorist agencies. These, or nerve agents, would kill everyone, not only the bad guys. Incapacitating, irritating vapours are therefore employed. To ensure all involved know how to handle such things, you are occasionally required to practise in a gas chamber. To me, this was a horrific, claustrophobic experience.

Positioned in some out of the way location, a gas chamber is little more than a concrete building, perhaps ten metres square. A single metal door, unmarked, leads into the one room. Each wall contains a window, properly sealable to prevent gas escape – or soldier escape if you are me. In the big Army, several of you are marched into these things, though in the SAS you stroll. However you enter, you must be fully togged up in noddy suit and respirator. Once inside, the door is shut tight and your small group stood to one end of the room. An instructor does remain with you, in the very likely event that someone panics. Then the action starts. Like one overcast Wednesday morning, late in March.

'OK lads?' said the instructor confidently from within his respirator. 'Ready?'

'Mmmm . . . mmmm . . . mmmm,' came the faint, rubbery, mumbling replies in unison, from behind a handful of gas masks. Heads nodded consent as they mumbled. No one was enthusiastic.

'Villar, you can go first. OK? Villar? Villar! Come on man! Wake up! Pay attention!'

My mind was full of questions. Couldn't someone else go first this time? I was first last year. What had *I* done to deserve it?

At this point the instructor produced the small white tablet, ignited it and threw it on the floor. I saw the white vapour, like stage smoke, begin to stream from it. Oh damn, I thought. Here we go.

'OK, Villar,' ordered the instructor, our heads now surrounded by gaseous fronds, visibility reduced to a few feet. 'Off you go.'

I hesitated for a brief moment. The instructor allowed no quarter. 'Come on, Villar! Get on with it!'

With a trembling, irregular effort I took a deep breath through my respirator and ripped the thing off. Its green, elastic strap caught my right ear as I did so. Never mind, I'm committed now, I thought. As soon as the mask was removed I felt the tearing, scratchy sensation in my eyes, my nose, my throat. God this is awful! I struggled to spit out the required words in the short time left.

'241984 . . .' I choked. '241984 . . . (cough) . . . Trooper . . .' I choked again. '241984 . . .' I gave up as the searing pain attacked my throat. I must get out! I had to escape! I could not speak. It was too painful.

As I dashed for the closed door in my panic, the instructor's firm hands grabbed me by each shoulder. 'Come on man! Speak! Name! Rank! Number!'

It was too late. Nothing would stop me. With superhuman effort I threw the instructor to one side, regardless of later consequences. I watched him thud forcibly against the far wall as I lunged for the sealed door. With a click it was open and I stumbled into the fresh, clear air beyond. I coughed, I vomited, my eyes streamed.

As I wheezed towards recovery, lying on my back on the damp, grassy ground, I began to feel angry. Each year I had to do this. Familiarization they called it. Building confidence in your equipment. Seemed bloody stupid to me.

Northern Ireland is as big a centre for terrorism as one gets. It is here that the UK has earned its justified reputation as the antiterrorist expert of the world. On whichever side of the political argument you lie, the province offers immense counter-revolutionary challenges. My first visit was by accident, one bitterly cold Hereford morning. Barely a month into my job as RMO, I had decided the covert, long-haired look was not for me. Before reaching Hereford I had been terrified to be recognized as SAS, so had initially grown lanky hair and respectable stubble. I was assured that SAS medical cover in Northern Ireland was not my responsibility. The routine, big Army would deal with it. Once I started my RMO post, I realized I did not have to resemble a drug-addicted dropout to disguise the nature of my job. Consequently, and being sure I would not be asked to visit Northern Ireland at all, I decided to have my hair cut short again. I felt the image I portrayed was not in keeping with a hygienic medic. Literally as I returned from the barber, crewcutted almost to skin, I was summoned to the Kremlin, Regimental HQ. 'Doc,' said the second-in-command, 'I think it would be a good idea if you went over the water. We need to be sure the guys' medical cover is as good as possible. How about the end of the week?'

Having agreed to go, I walked away from the Kremlin kicking

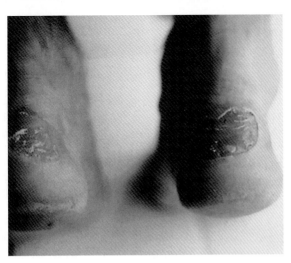

SAS Selection – sometimes you just walk too far

Mount McKinley's West Buttress – I am at 5000 metres and climbing

Treating a goat in the Middle East. The poor animal died shortly after this photograph was taken

Examining a Bedouin's mouth with an improvised light source. It was impossible to avoid dribbling down the torch into the patient

The holding area for our highly secret operation during the Falklands War. I lay in this tent for seventeen days, convinced I would die

Hard at work cooking an inedible meal at Everest's Roadhead Camp

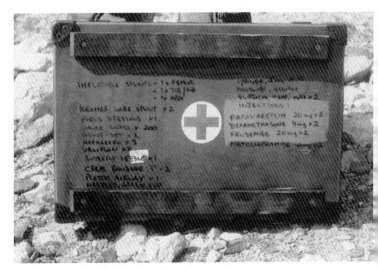

Everest's major wobbler kit. Something for every emergency

Everest's North Face. All I see is Tony when I look at this view

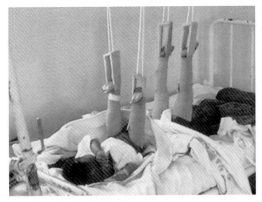

Pushed for bed space in the Third World – sometimes you just have to share. Two small children recover from their broken legs

Hundreds queue to see me in central India. Each case more insoluble than the one before

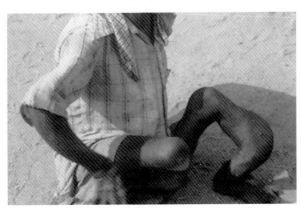

You'll have your work cut out to straighten this one. Gross bowing of the shin bone present since birth

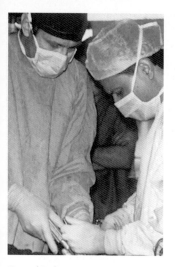

Central India – operating on polio victim. I assist Vincent (*right*) in major tendon surgery

Photograph by Nicola Townley

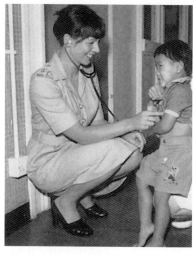

Louise, the paediatrician, at work in the Far East. No wonder I love her

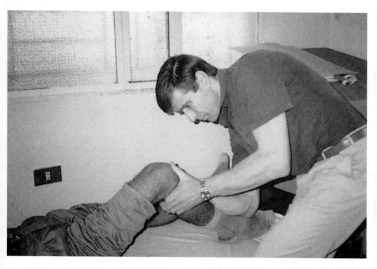

Examining a Palestinian knee in southern Lebanon. Only minutes before there had been a gunfight outside the consulting room

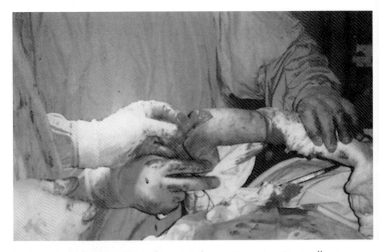

Trying to undo the after-effects of war in Lebanon. Reconstructing an elbow damaged by shrapnel

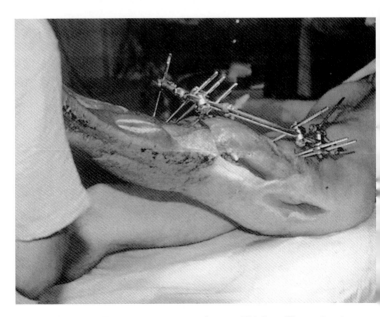

One high velocity bullet can cause immense damage. This leg will never bend fully again

Sarajevo's Swiss Cheese Hospital. In genocidal war, even hospitals become so-called legitimate targets

Photograph by Roop Tandon

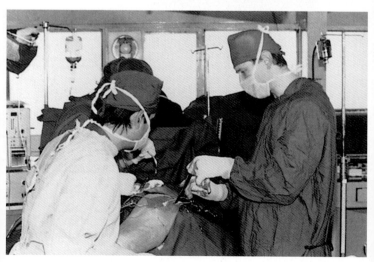

Teheran – I (*right*) operate under the close scrutiny of local surgeons

myself. How stupid I'd been to get my hair cut so short. I could not have looked more Army if I had tried. The second-in-command had allowed me three days' training before I went. Though familiar with traditional SAS techniques, this new world of covert operations seemed very strange. Entirely in civilian clothes, I was taught the basics of personal security in the province, how to avoid or detect a follower, and how to follow someone oneself. I was struck by the recommendation I should be able to change my appearance instantly to confuse those who would wish to do me harm. A reversible jacket was an excellent method, plus an assortment of hats of varying design.

Immediately, I went into Hereford town to buy a reversible, corduroy bomber jacket. It was blue on the outside, but cream on the inside. I was delighted with the transforming effects it allowed. Delighted that was until I received my close-quarter battle training in the killing house. There the experts showed me every conceivable way of inflicting injury on others with a 9mm Browning automatic pistol. I am hopeless with the weapon but managed to master the 'double-tap', two bullets fired in quick succession, reasonably well. My problem came when I was taught to shoot and roll. The principle is to double-tap one target, roll and double-tap another. Your pistol sits in a holster inside the waistband of your trousers. I had not noticed my new, reversible jacket not only had different colours inside and out, but also pockets on both sides. Thus, the moment I tried the quick draw needed to set off the shoot and roll sequence, the inner pocket caught on the butt of my pistol. Physically I could not remove the weapon from its holster, nearly shot my own left foot and the instructor, and finished in a laughing heap on the floor. IRA, I thought, as I lay in hysterics before two untouched targets, you are unquestionably safe in my hands. I resolved then that such things were best left for the professionals. I could probably inflict greater harm with my scalpel than a Browning.

Whether or not to carry a weapon can be a difficult decision for a doctor. Regulations state you should carry one, for use in the defence of your patients. This may be good in theory, but the situation is different in practice. There is a great contrast between being an excellent shot on a peaceful range and surviving a close-quarter shootout with an enemy. Often the best range shot will not be the best during close contact. You are also surrounded by professional soldiers, be they SAS or otherwise. They can knock spots off you when it comes to shooting. They do it all the time. I had to sympathize with the woman RAMC doctor, so famed in Northern Ireland, for her refusal to carry a pistol. First, she loved tight skirts, making it impossible to hide the bulk of her Browning if she wished to carry one. Secondly, she felt no match for an IRA man if confronted. This was despite her classification as an accurate pistol shot on a military range. Native wit was her weapon and with it she would drive alone through the province's most danger-ous areas. Her Scottish roots were also her protection. It is not so much the British the IRA dislike. It is the *English*. Her bloodline was on her side – a formidable creature.

I was collected from the Officers' Mess early one Friday morning for my journey to Northern Ireland. Scheduled to fly by civilian airliner from Birmingham airport, the young man tasked to drive me had no idea who I was. He had simply been asked to pick up one male passenger and drive to the airport, or so I thought. The car was unmarked, with civilian number plates. I was beginning to feel more confident. Apart from my haircut, which made me look as if I had recently undergone brain surgery, I felt well-prepared. It was as we drove towards Birmingham that I developed the first inklings of the dangers that could face me.

The driver had only been attached to the Regiment for a matter of weeks. Barely twenty-one years old, he was obviously overcome by the male passenger he had been asked to chauffeur. I am not a small man and was fairly fit, so I looked the part of the killer, even if in reality I could not untangle my jacket from a Browning.

'Are you going to . . . well you know?' said the young man with a quizzical wink. I was in the death seat, immediately to his left.

'Yes,' I grunted. 'I'm off to . . . you know.' I noticed the car's speed pick up slowly as the young man questioned me further.

'I mean it's pretty dangerous over there, isn't it? With the IRA 'n all.'

'I guess that's true,' I replied, trying to sound relaxed as the speedometer inched steadily towards 160 kilometres per hour. Instinctively I could feel my foot pressing hard on the passenger well, forcing my body against the near-vertical seat back. I tightened my seat belt for extra security.

'How many deaths have you seen?' pursued the driver. 'You must be dealing with it all the time in your game.' The statement took me slightly aback. I had not realized the young man knew I was a doctor. Still, it made no difference.

'Plenty, I'm afraid,' I replied. 'Must be well over a hundred by now. It's my trade in a way.'

'Cor! That's great!' exclaimed the driver. By now his accelerator pedal was as far down as it could go, our speed hovering at around 210 kilometres per hour. He was out to impress and speed was his way of doing so. I began to pray silently that a flashing blue light would appear and stop us. My prayers were not answered.

As the car vibrated at terminal velocity, the driver spoke again. 'If you don't mind me asking, do they pay you by the body or by the job?'

'What?' I exclaimed, suddenly realizing what this was about. The driver thought I was a professional hit man. Someone in the transport section had wound him up. He was most disappointed when I confessed to my medical training and that I could not kill a man however hard I tried. His speed also came down to legal levels.

I have always felt Birmingham has one of the better airports. It was no exception that day. As with Heathrow, Northern Ireland passengers were channelled into a separate area, rather like carriers of the pox. One particularly disreputable fellow was wedged into a plastic seat opposite me as we waited to board. He looked most unsavoury. Unkempt, unshaven, filthy jeans and battered shoes with frayed laces. Terrorists come in many forms. They, too, have to travel between Northern Ireland and the mainland. It would be just my luck, I thought, to be on a flight the IRA chose to bomb.

Meanwhile, standing to one side, was a small group of obvious servicemen returning to the province, looking totally relaxed.

From time to time I saw the unkempt one cast me a glance, as if he was wondering who or what I was. I was tempted to stop a passing security officer – there were plenty of them – to ask that the man be checked out. Something held me back, perhaps a fear that I was being unnecessarily alarmist, so I resolved instead to keep a careful eye on him throughout the flight. He had been ahead of me in the check-in queue, so I knew he was slightly in front, and to the left, of my own seat once on board. For a moment I thought hard, going through the various techniques I would need to incapacitate him if it came to it. I had done karate for years and in my mind considered the alternatives open to me. By the time we had boarded I had decided what to do. A direct blow to the top of his right collar bone would paralyse the nerves to his right hand, followed by a stranglehold from behind. In my mind the job was as good as done.

Throughout the short flight to Belfast I stayed poised on the edge of my aisle seat, two rows behind the unsavoury fellow. I watched his every move. When he twitched, I twitched. When he breathed, I breathed. Meanwhile the servicemen were chatting away, blissfully unaware of my worries. Then, glancing furtively around him, I saw the man stand up and reach towards the overhead locker. I had to get him! I bounded from my seat, raising my right hand in knife-like form to crash it down hard on the man's collar bone. From the corner of one eye I could see the open mouth of an astonished stewardess as I barged past her drinks trolley, thumping it hard against an adjacent seat. To break a collar bone you have to strike very forcibly, starting with your hand almost behind your head to create the power. It was a fraction of a second before I struck that I saw it. The unsavoury fellow fumbled with the zip to one end of his black, plastic holdall and produced the device. My heart sank as I watched. It was not a bomb or weapon at all. A paperback. A bloody paperback novel. Villar, you are unquestionably a prat, I thought. I stood there, stranded, hand raised, wondering what to do. I must have looked a fool. Then, quickly, I realized the answer. Bringing my raised hand downwards I clutched my bladder in simulated agony and rushed past, cheeks glowing in embarrassment. For some reason I could not understand, I saw a tiny smile on my target's face as I strode my way forwards.

Needless to say, the unsavoury chap did no harm at all. We arrived at Belfast airport in fine fettle without hijacks, bombings, gassings or even surface-to-air missiles fired from the ground. The man highlighted the very nature of terrorism – a lot of it is in the mind. Because their actions are so unannounced and seemingly below the belt, terrorist groups exert much of their effect by keeping society on permanent edge. In reality, whoever you are, the chances of being bombed, shot or disembowelled in Northern Ireland are small. In your mind, however, such things are happening all the time. Every street corner has a lurking terrorist, every car is following you and each pair of sunglasses hides a murderer in disguise.

In practice, however tense it makes you, suspecting everyone and everything is still essential. I remember having a drink in a local pub one rare, sunny Hereford afternoon with a very good SAS officer friend. He had just returned from the province after three months of covert operations and was one of the best operatives I knew – highly admired by everyone, irrespective of rank or social status. A car backfired in the distance, at least 200 metres away. Immediately and instinctively, he reached for his imaginary pistol and started to roll off his seat into a firing position before holding himself in check. Northern Ireland had made it impossible for the man to relax.

Walking through the main exit doors of Belfast airport, I saw my unsavoury target being welcomed by the most voluptuous, leggy blonde I had seen in a long time. It was a passionate embrace that almost led to other things before the couple had reached their car. As I stood transfixed, feeling like a voyeur, a rattly voice disturbed me from behind. It was slightly high-pitched. 'Are you the Doc?' it said. I turned to see an enormous creature leaning over me. The man must have been at least six foot four. Huge, broad shoulders, wide enough to land an airplane on, stood above a chest as large as three beer kegs. The chest tapered to a tiny waist from which two massive thighs extended. The whole frame was squeezed into a tight, ill-fitting, grey suit. The face was smooth-shaven and the hair close cut, even shorter than mine. The shoes were black patent leather, slightly scuffed, covering two massive feet seeking to burst out. This fellow, whoever he was, came as near to the children's Desperate Dan as one can get.

'Who are *you*?' I asked the man suspiciously, every nerve, every muscle, braced for a cunning IRA trap.

'Transport, Doc. I've come to take you to your location.'

'ID? Have you got any?'

'It's in the palm of my hand, Doc. Don't look down too obviously, but you'll see it there.'

I glanced down. In the palm of Desperate Dan's right hand I could see the pink outline of his service identification card, the MOD 90. The picture looked identical to the huge brute standing before me. However powerful he looked, I had to admire his slickness in producing the card. With the two of us standing outside a civilian airport it would be unwise to display publicly our service occupations. Palming of ID cards was a common way of making it past searches in civilian clothes without showing everything to those around you. I nodded once I saw the card and followed Dan to a large, silver-grey Ford parked near by. In the front passenger seat was another man, though of more normal size and shape than Dan. He turned and smiled as I climbed into the seat behind. A hundred yards away, in the same car park, I saw the other servicemen with whom I had flown entering a computer company's minivan. Wrong again, I thought. They were not servicemen at all, but businessmen. It was part of a long education by the SAS that no one is who they appear to be from the outside.

It was my first time in a covert car. Outwardly normal, it was in reality heavily armoured. As we pulled away from the car park, from beneath his tight grey suit jacket Dan produced his Browning automatic pistol, placing it under his right thigh for instant access in the event of trouble. I had been taught that in Hereford. At his feet was an open holdall containing a fully loaded, and cocked, MP5 submachine gun.

'How about you, Doc?' he asked. 'I've got a short for you if you want.'

'No thanks,' I replied. 'I'll be more of a hazard than anything else if we get into a shootout. I'll leave it to you if I may. With my tangled experience on the floor of the killing house I felt it would be safer to avoid a weapon altogether. I could see that Dan understood and was probably relieved.

Though there was little conversation between the car's occupants as we made our way through the tortuous roads of Northern Ireland, there was still much chit-chat. Dan would continually use his covert radio, reporting his position at all times. I did not understand the language he spoke, full of Tangos, Bravos and Zulus. There was obviously an effective, secure, voice-procedure system used by Northern Ireland's covert forces. Occasionally we would pass cars going in the opposite direction, usually driven by single males. If the other car made a hand signal in acknowledgement, Dan would return with an identical signal. Sometimes he would lift his whole hand in a form of wave, at others he would simply raise a finger. Whatever he did, he would ensure his response was identical to the sign he received.

Two hours' drive from Belfast, I paid my first visit to a Northern Ireland military camp. Surrounded by high fencing, the SAS operatives were billeted in prefabricated bungalow-type buildings. Each building was covered by suspended wire netting to catch mortar bombs the other side might fire. I was astounded at how bored many of the operatives looked. For much of their time they were waiting for the next military operation. Life was not a continuous cycle of undercover activities deep inside enemy territory. That is not to say they were unwilling. Each was highly enthusiastic. They were simply victims of the political system. Time and again senior SAS officers would develop astonishing ideas to counter terrorist activities. Time and again they were turned down by the politicians for overstepping the mark. Fighting a war in a civilian, urban environment, surrounded by the media, is very different from all-out conflict in open countryside. Being kept in check by politicians can be immensely frustrating. It showed.

Restriction by protocol does not come easily to an SAS operative. He is trained to act promptly, when the time is right, and is frequently seen as the final solution to many problems. Hence my amazement when operatives were arrested and tried for murder. It is most likely, should an SAS operative have a shootout with the other side, that the opposition will come off worse. Hence the Dunloy graveyard shooting, or for that matter Gibraltar. Both of these were operations following which SAS operatives were either tried for murder or questioned in bitter detail about their actions on the day. I cannot understand this, as the senior hierarchy tasking the SAS know exactly the nature of the beast involved. If you have a weapon in your hand and pose any threat whatsoever to an SAS operative, be it real or imagined, the chances are you will perish. I do not wish to enter the rights and wrongs of these episodes as I feel desperately sorry for everyone concerned. It is usually a waste of young life and a worrying time for the soldier involved, who is never sure of being cleared until the day. Trials drag on for months, if not years, during which time the operative would be less than human if he did not worry. Such emotions can affect his performance with other Regimental activities and can be a hazard to both himself and others.

Added to the SAS, the people I admired were those of 14 Intelligence Company, whom we would call 'the Det', short for detachment. The Det was originally an offshoot of the SAS, being trained and selected by them in the early Belfast days. They are the covert operatives, out and about day and night, in full-time service on the streets of Northern Ireland. On two-year attachments, the majority come from a Service background. Very few now come from the SAS itself. Their selection is well described in *The Operators* by James Rennie and is something with which I would occasionally help. In particular the milling.

Milling is a somewhat pointless exercise invented, I believe, by the Parachute Regiment. Two candidates are placed in a boxing ring, suitably gloved. They are then told to beat each other as hard as they can in the face for two minutes. No holds are barred and defending yourself is forbidden. When I tried it my opponent happened to be a flyweight boxing champion. This did not worry me greatly as my karate free-fighting had prepared me well, so I started both to block his punches and use my bare feet. Within seconds the bell was rung and I was publicly disciplined for defending myself and for striking my opponent everywhere except his face. Thereafter the two of us had to slog each other about the head for a two-minute period, simply to prove our aggression. Milling is mad, bad and unnecessary.

The Det caters for both men and women. Most look very ordinary and try hard to look plain. Blending with one's surroundings is not only a matter of what you wear, but how you behave – your mannerisms, your walking style, your general shape. You may, for example, be a muscly sort of person. Striding down Belfast's Falls Road with shoulders drawn back is a certain way of attracting attention. Slouch a bit, scuff your feet and look a little overcome by the events of the day. Everybody else does and so should you. Security is naturally paramount. During their selection, Det candidates are referred to by number rather than name. That number follows them from beginning to end. This can create problems if you happen to know the person concerned. I remember Mike L, an excellent friend and capable soldier, applying to join the Det as number 124. As I was then Medical Officer to 22 SAS, our paths crossed on a number of occasions. It required enormous self-control on my part to avoid shouting out 'Mike!' at the top of my voice whenever I saw him. Saying 'Good morning, 124,' seemed most unnatural.

It was Dan's job to take me round Northern Ireland, so I could talk to SAS and Det operatives in their various locations. I soon realized that there was little requirement for my medical skills in the province. Surrounded by first-class civilian hospitals, any injuries are normally taken directly to them, whether military or otherwise. One major problem, however, is trench foot. This is a condition created by prolonged immersion of the feet in cold water. It was particularly common during the Great War. Hence the name. Gradually the water softens the skin, making it spongy, like blotting paper. Then it blisters and peels off, exposing the bare flesh beneath. Permanent damage is created to the tiny blood vessels in the skin, making it impossible for the victim to withstand prolonged water immersion for many years to follow. SAS and Det operatives are particularly vulnerable as they must remain motionless in their various observation posts, often for days at a time. Particularly in a rural environment, such as the southern border, a favoured hiding place such as a ditch can fill with water in no time. For fear of detection the operative cannot move, with trench foot the consequence. The only treatment is careful drying of the feet, antibiotics if the skin has exposed underlying flesh, and time.

For some operatives, the condition meant they could never go on Northern Ireland OP duty again. Trench foot is one form of what is called 'cold injury'. Other conditions in this family include frostbite and frostnip. Frostbite is the most serious, with extremities eventually turning black. Frostnip is between the two, with the extremities turning deathly pale but eventually recovering. In all three – trench foot, frostnip, frostbite – the result is often lifelong sensitivity to cold. For a covert operative this is, understandably, a catastrophe.

As part of Dan's Northern Ireland tour I was fully briefed on many aspects of counterterrorist activities in the province. Sometimes I was faced with unexpected surprises. On one occasion I was visiting a remote location, talking with some Det operatives about what they were doing. I was fascinated, becoming so engrossed by the detail that I did not notice the figure positioning itself at my side. Slowly, I became aware someone was there. I looked to my right.

'Hi, Doc!' came the smiling voice. 'Remember me?'

For a moment I frowned, struggling to hide my lack of recognition. I remember hips, knees and the occasional backside in clear detail. With names and faces I am hopeless. Then, with a flash, even I remembered.

'You! But . . . what are *you* doing here? I don't believe it!'

The smiling face nodded, and then put its thin arm around my shoulders, head inclined slightly towards me. 'Yes, Doc. It's me.

The airplane – do you remember? You were going to thump me, you bastard, weren't you?'

I nodded. I had to. It was him – the unsavoury fellow. I was dumbfounded. There, behind, was the voluptuous, leggy blonde busily cleaning her small pistol. Once again, I thought, no one in life is who they appear.

Love them or hate them, the Det operatives are immensely brave. Exposed, often isolated, and occasionally unsupported, they must find it hard to fit into normal life when they return to the mainland. This was certainly the situation for many SOE operatives after the Second World War. The Det was involved with one tragedy that hit me particularly hard – the death of James R. Having listened to his comments on the effects of lignocaine when I had first arrived in Hereford's Officers' Mess, our old friendship had been rekindled. In a combined SAS/Det operation he was killed trying to assault a terrorist gun team. His SAS group was advised to assault through the wrong front door during the attack, the one next to the terrorists' house rather than the house itself. James, last out of the covert civilian car, was shot dead. The sad photograph of his body lying covered on a Northern Ireland pavement appears frequently in newspapers and books to this day. I feel awful whenever I see it. It highlights the waste of life these things create. After the tragedy, I remember one SAS officer saying to me that James had died 'because he wasn't quick enough'. I realize the remark was a soldier's effort at justifying death, something that is in fact impossible, but I nearly hit him at the time. The reality was death was unavoidable. At least he died quickly.

As a member of the security services in Northern Ireland, one must accept a percentage of the population hates you. However nice you are, whatever you do to help, to them you represent something they truly dislike. It is what you stand for, not what you are, that is the trouble. Driving round the harder areas of Belfast, regions that look similar to a city in the aftermath of nuclear war, you can detect real hatred in some people's eyes. Once, I was performing the simple task of carrying a ladder from one building to another. It was not a covert operation. All I was doing was adjusting guttering on the front of a house in which I was billeted, a very non-SAS activity. I was outside a military base, unarmed and looked outwardly like any member of the Northern Ireland civilian community. I would have done credit to the Det. As I walked along the pavement, the short distance to the building, a car pulled up to ask directions. Inside were four young men. None would have been over twenty years of age. Four youths in a Belfast car spells trouble, but my mind was on other things. I was stupid.

'Can yer tell me where the hospital is?' said the driver, in a broad Belfast accent, winding down his window as he spoke.

'Of course,' I replied, sounding terribly English. It is one of the perils of a public-school education. As I spoke I kicked myself. I would usually revert to Scottish when communicating with the locals as my attempts at mimicking an Irish accent are normally disastrous.

The moment I opened my mouth I saw the eyes of each of the car's occupants glaze over. Immediately they realized where I was from. No use my telling them I had operated on at least twenty of their countrymen in a local hospital during the past week. It would have made no difference. The driver looked me hard in the eye, then spat on the ground out of the window, his gaze never once faltering. 'Don't bother, yer monarchist bastard,' he said as he drove off, loathing in every syllable. 'We'll get yer all in the end.'

An unpleasant, but fortunately rare, duty of an SAS doctor is the handling of death and its aftermath. Though this is officially the task of a Commanding Officer, in reality it may be delegated to others. I hated it. I was dealing with some of the nation's fittest people and yet had to tell their nearest and dearest they had died. Furthermore, the dead men had frequently been friends. I therefore had my own grief reaction to contend with, as well as a job to do. James R highlighted this particularly well. Deaths could occur at any time, and usually when you least expected it. Even the Det was not exempt.

Late one evening, a particularly dark and damp one as I recall, I received a telephone call from Regimental HQ. A rising star in the covert world, no more than twenty-five years old, had been shot in the head by a high-velocity bullet. Despite an appalling injury, he had managed to survive the initial impact. Local medics had struggled to revive him, being sufficiently successful to evacuate him to a neurosurgical unit in Scotland. It was there I first saw him, surrounded by his family, later that night. We did not have a padre, so with me came a highly respected Regimental Welfare Officer, Robert P. The operative was connected to all manner of tubes and bleeping electronic devices to keep him alive. Despite these, a brief word with the neurosurgeons told me his chances of survival were almost zero. He would most likely die soon. Should he survive, brain damage was too severe to allow him to be in anything other than a vegetative state for the rest of his days.

Breaking news like this to a family is one of the hardest things a doctor can do. Some choose to get on with it directly, calling a spade a spade. Others work up to it more slowly, fencing around the subject until the topic of death is eventually reached. Worse still, the young man's family had no idea of the type of work in which he was involved and we were not allowed to tell them. As so often happens on these occasions, the father controlled his distress by asking questions about the incident and telling us of the outstanding abilities and ambitions of his son. The mother, quite naturally, was horrorstruck by the affair and could barely speak. Human distress presents in so many different ways. Medical training cannot prepare you for scenes like this. You must simply do the best you can. I often end up crying myself. Certainly neither civilian teaching hospital, nor Army, had given me any training in such counselling at all. When faced with a bereaved family, staying in control, and yet remaining supportive, is immensely difficult. You must be prepared for anything, including being blamed for the event yourself. It was during our discussions with the family that I realized how much a general experience of life helps. Robert P was many years my senior and medically untrained. What he had was an undefinable, enviable ability to reach into the hearts of those with whom he talked. I learned a lot from him that night. He handled the situation beautifully, allowing the family to talk as they wished, prompting them when they fell silent, holding a hand when needed. It was a brilliant display of counselling, unrivalled by anything I have seen either before or since. His manner permitted us to leave the family settled and content, though naturally still distressed.

My time in antiterrorism was ideal for my planned surgical career. Though much of what I did was preparation and negotiation, it put me in touch with civilian medicine once more. I needed to know which hospitals in the land could cater for casualties we might create, what facilities they had and whether their staff were suitably trained. Much of this took place in the UK, so that I was in continuous contact with civilian colleagues. I needed this, for the break I would have to make one day from under the Army's broad umbrella. So far, the training and experience I had received was excellent, particularly for medical organization and experience in the Third World. My SAS patients had exposed me to a wealth of conditions, many of which would never be seen by a civilian practitioner. Clinics were frequently stuffed full of patients with minor orthopaedic problems – torn knee cartilages, broken wrists, funny hips or ankles. However, as a doctor, working singlehanded from a basic medical centre, there were limits to the depth of treatment I could offer. If the situation became too complex, I would have to refer the patient to others. I realized it was time to move on. Flattered by the CO's offer that I should extend my SAS service, I declined. He, too, was a hard-core professional and subsequently reached even dizzier heights in the Army. Nevertheless, he understood my reasoning. Thus it was I turned my back on Hereford's Bradbury Lines, thinking I would never be involved in SAS activities again. I was desperately sad. With 21 and 22 SAS combined, I already had seven years of Special Forces' activities to my credit. The Regiment was a second family. Something I had eaten, breathed and slept for so long.

It is difficult to settle into normal routine once you leave the SAS. The Army posted me to a military hospital in London, where I began work as a junior orthopaedic surgeon. I found it both fun and professionally rewarding, but missed the unpredictability of

Special Forces life. No longer was I required to be on thirty minutes' standby to move, nor asked to dine with leading politicians. I was now just any old surgeon, in an ordinary hospital, struggling to climb the orthopaedic ladder. At least that is what I thought until I was asked by the RAMC to command an SMT. Having fiercely criticized such teams when RMO to the SAS I now did a complete about-face. Suddenly, to hear me speak, SMTs became the most indispensable items in the land.

There were four of us, each based in my hospital, attached to our commitment by a long-range bleep. Though the Army had offered personnel for SMT service, it had not thought through how we were to reach the scene of the action physically. After much discussion, the hospital's Commanding Officer, a kindly brigadier, offered his official car. If summoned, we would have first call on it, irrespective of his commitments.

It was important to establish whether such a loose arrangement would work in practice. Late one night I decided to experiment. Gathering my three SMT colleagues together, I created an imaginary terrorist incident somewhere in north London. The system ran like clockwork. The team assembled in the hospital reception area and the CO's driver appeared, somewhat overcome by events. He was quite convinced he was off on his first secret mission. Very quietly, and not daring to ask what we were doing, he drove us to a prearranged location thirty minutes away. I had dreamt the spot out of thin air, as I used to pass it on my daily jog. Good, I thought, once we reached our objective, no more than a dogpee-stained lamppost near an Underground station. At least the transport works, even if my SMT had yet to be tested in action. Satisfied my worries about SMT transport were ill-founded, I asked him to turn round and drive us back to the hospital again. All credit to him, confused though he was, he never asked the purpose of such an apparently pointless exercise.

We returned to our beds, for a brief two hours' sleep prior to the morning's duties. Even so, the driver was not to be deterred. While we snoozed, he sat firmly in his car, for the rest of the day, refusing all orders to go elsewhere. The CO, with an important meeting in central London that morning, could not budge him and had to travel by tube. 'I'm sorry, sir. I have a priority engagement,' was all the driver would say. It was my fault, of course, failing to stand the man down when we returned to the hospital. As a true soldier he was not going to move until I told him so. Villar was not a popular name with the hierarchy that day. It is the story of my life.

Not long afterwards my SMT was called out for real. An African airliner had been hijacked and was sitting at a provincial airport. The call came from the hospital switchboard early one evening. 'Captain Villar?' it said.

'Yes?'

'I'm to say the words "Spanish Galleon" to you, sir.'

'Spanish Galleon?' I asked, having no idea what the man meant.

'Yes, sir. Spanish Galleon.'

'Sorry,' I said. 'Can't help you. I haven't a clue what you're getting at. Got to go. Bye.' I hung up. The hospital switchboard must be off its rocker, I thought. It was a frenetic day as I had at least eight young men with cancer to treat, all of whom required chemotherapy. As soon as I put the telephone down it rang again. Exasperated, and sighing loudly, I picked up the receiver. 'Yes?' I shouted.

'Spanish Galleon, Captain Villar. Spanish Galleon is what I've been told to say.' The switchboard operator's voice was now somewhat hesitant.

I was furious. I was well behind with my work and knew that cancer chemotherapy was not something you could rush. Spanish Galleon indeed! Then, in my anger, a brief thought flashed through my mind. Blast! Of course! A sick realization welled up in my stomach as I suddenly recognized the codeword for emergency SMT call-out. Spanish Galleon it would be.

Despite all our plans, and dress rehearsal, the CO's car was unavailable that evening. It was getting dark and I had trouble enough finding my three colleagues. Bleeps are not a guaranteed method of communication. Three hours later, we bundled ourselves and our mass of equipment into my tiny, gold Renault 5, setting off towards the airport. I knew the SAS would already be there, guided by police escort along hard shoulders, between crash barriers and the wrong way up many one-way streets. The waters would have parted for them. For their SMT medical support the situation was different. We jerked our way from London in my car, aided only by an Automobile Association *Book of the Road*. None of us had been there before, so we had no idea where to go.

Two hours later, in the vague vicinity of the airport, I pulled to the side of the road to check the map. It was dark, very quiet and with barely any traffic to see. As we discussed which way to go next, each of us similarly confused, none of us noticed the flashing blue light of the police car draw up behind. It was only when the police officer leaned through my window that I realized he was there.

'Evening all,' he said in classic Dixon of Dock Green fashion. Apart from nearly jumping out of my skin at the shock, I had to kick one of my colleagues to stop him from laughing out loud.

'Um . . . hello. We're a little lost,' I said.

'Oh, are you, sir,' came the reply. 'And where might you be wanting to go?'

'Um . . .' I had no idea what to say. I knew SMTs were meant to be highly classified and did not know whether the policeman was aware the SAS were at the airport at all. I could see lines on his forehead as the poor fellow tried to work out what was going on. Then, suddenly, it dawned on him.

'You're SAS, aren't you? That's who you are, isn't it?'

'Um . . .'

'Come on, gents,' added the policeman. 'You've got it written all over you. You're bleeding SAS. You must be.'

'Um . . .'

'Look, you silly buggers. Stop mucking me about. Just tell me. Are you SAS or aren't you?'

I decided to give in at that point. It was obvious the policeman knew what was happening, though I was not certain that four large men sitting in a battered Renault 5 was a recognized mode of S A S transport. 'O K. Yes, we are,' I said, not wishing to explain that I was the only one of the group who had had the opportunity to take S A S Selection. The remainder were sturdy fellows, but not truly badged. It did not matter in any event. It was much easier that we each adopted the same mantle.

'Well, why didn't you say so? Stupid bastards,' said the policeman, now thoroughly exasperated. 'Follow me. I'll take you in.'

The airport was busy. The main passenger terminal had been shut off, with television cameras placed as far away as possible. Even so, you had to walk directly in front of them to reach the holding area – not a good introduction to antiterrorist security. One of the team whispered in my ear as we walked immediately in front of a large telephoto lens, 'Hey, Doc! What say you and I turn round on the count of three and shout "Hey Mum, it's me!"' I had to elbow him in the ribs, a well-known method of military control, to stop him doing it.

By the time we had arrived, the airplane had been on the ground for several hours. S A S assault teams were busy making plans in case they were needed, their Regimental Medical Officer, Captain L, being with them. The S M Ts were relegated to the main terminal area where we set about organizing a casualty evacuation chain. A chain involves the organization of several steps along which a casualty will travel after injury, treatment being available at every stage. At the time of wounding, the 'buddy buddy' system applies. The injured man will be cared for immediately by his military partner, assuming safety allows it. At this stage the object is basic life-saving manoeuvres – shell dressings to wounds, morphine injections, maintenance of breathing. The soldier is next treated by his Regimental Medical Officer. Either the R M O will go forward to the casualty or the casualty will be brought back to him. Either way, it is the R M O's job to ensure basic life-saving manoeuvres are as good as they can be, before sending the injured man to the next stage in evacuation – the S M T. The S M T provided a further level of treatment sophistication. If we had to, we were in position to open a belly, split a chest, or apply electric-shock therapy to a failing heart. Once a casualty was stabilized, he would be evacuated to the nearest hospital, civilian or military. There he would stay until recovered.

The object of this step-by-step evacuation was to ensure an increasing level of medical sophistication at each stage. Ideally, you would want the complete facilities of a major teaching hospital within 100 metres of an SAS assault. This was obviously impossible. A casualty evacuation chain was the next best thing.

Successful evacuation is based on a procedure known as *triage*. Triage describes the separation of casualties into groups of differing priorities. It is the job of the most senior medical person present to run triage. He, or she, stands at the receiving door and immediately divides casualties into one of four categories: Priority 1 (treat as urgent), Priority 2 (treat as fast as reasonable), Priority 3 (take your time), Priority 4 (don't bother). Senior people are needed for the task as they will generally have the breadth of experience needed to make rapid, accurate assessments. Just because a casualty looks badly injured does not mean he is classified as Priority 1. A gunshot wound to the head, for example, if it does not immediately kill the soldier, may still be classified as Priority 4. As the man is likely to die anyway, medical efforts are best aimed at those with some chance of survival.

We planned that casualties should be brought to us from the aircraft, in whichever order they emerged, directly to the triage point. From there the triage officer would direct the casualty to one of a number of resuscitation stations. Ambulance crews would take the wounded thereafter to the nearest civilian hospital. I telephoned their casualty department to warn them of the likelihood of heavy casualties and left them to their own arrangements. I had to be careful what I said. If an assault went in, it depended upon an element of surprise. Telling a civilian hospital they could be overwhelmed within the next few hours is the type of information the media love. From there, to the terrorists being given advance warning of an SAS assault, is not a huge step.

To our astonishment we discovered we were not the only medical team at the airport that evening. In the terminal with us was a civilian team, already setting up shop. I believe it was their first hijack. As we were not supposed to exist, and yet were physically in the presence of civilian medics, our cover was blown. This breach of security did get me into trouble afterwards. An irate telephone call from the Ministry of Defence challenged my organization at the scene, particularly when the civilians later requested joint training with us. However, during the hijack we had to cope with the security implications as they stood. It had been the police who had positioned us. They had also summoned the civilian teams without talking to us first. There was nothing we could do.

The other SMT members rapidly set up our resuscitation station while I went to find out what was happening aboard the aircraft. As is usual with these situations, it appeared there would be no sudden solution. Antiterrorist forces were busy establishing ways of best gaining the intelligence they needed, while the SAS already had their immediate action in place. The immediate action, or IA, is prepared from the moment troops arrive. It is the instant response to anything that might go wrong while more formal, effective plans are made. It is a high-risk option and best avoided.

I learned the terrorists on board the aircraft had already shot the co-pilot, or claimed to have done so. Quite what their demands were I did not know. During such events the requirements of the terrorists are not a major issue to you. You do not enter into the politics of the situation. You assume that troops *will* assault and make preparations accordingly. It is better to waste effort than to be surprised by developments, creating unnecessary casualties on both sides as a result. On the one hand, such sieges will have police and negotiating teams trying hard to bring the thing to a peaceful end. On the other will be the SAS, ready and raring to go from the moment it arrives. Control and use of these two extremes is the key to successful siege handling.

Within thirty minutes of arrival we were fully set up and ready to receive casualties. I knew that numbers could vary from nothing to a full plane load. Everything had to be be ready for an instant response. Haemaccel drips were prepared, artificial airways laid out, shell dressings arranged in perfect order for easy access. I could see the civilians looking at us slightly perplexed, dressed in our black overalls and working well as a team. Two of our number, having set up their part of the resuscitation kit, had already climbed into their sleeping bags and curled up on the floor. In the Services you have to sleep when you can. On SAS operations anywhere in the world, a clear eight-hour snooze is unlikely.

Seeing their inquisitiveness, I went over to the civilians and talked with them, introducing myself but leaving out details I knew would make security worry. It was when I asked them, in the event of an assault, to deal with SAS casualties as well as civilians that I could see I was on icy ground. 'If we do get casualties,' I said, 'it would be good to see anyone in a black suit and respirator being treated rapidly.' There was a slight double take at that by the civilians, but to their credit they accepted the concept. Whether they would do it was another matter.

With such events there are highs and lows. One moment you are being stood to, expecting an assault at any minute. The next you are feeling interminably bored. The airliner hijack was largely one of boredom – until our first casualty appeared. There had been no gunfire, so I was surprised to be disturbed from my sleeping-bag slumbers by a tap on my shoulder.

'Are you the doctor?' came a voice I could hear through a rapidly resolving sleeper's fog. I looked up to see the huge frame of a policeman, clad in fluorescent jacket, leaning over me.

'Yes,' I answered, hand on my forehead to ward off the bright lights. 'That's me. Are we on?' As I spoke I could feel an instant adrenalin rush to my chest and leaped out of my sleeping bag. The things are designed for a rapid exit with a long, freemoving zip fastener from top to bottom at the front. I could feel the policeman's hand on my shoulder gently restrain me, but by then I was into overdrive. With a loud shout of 'Stand to!' I kicked the sleeping bodies of my SMT colleagues, each tucked away in his own peace and solitude. Instantly each man sat upright and then leaped from his sleeping bag, ready for action. I was delighted with their response. Within less than three seconds my SMT had changed from a dozing outfit to one prepared for anything. I could see the policeman looking concerned.

'It's OK. It's OK. Don't worry,' he said.

'What do you mean, don't worry?'

'There's no assault yet. It's just me. Have you got an aspirin for my headache?'

'No assault? Aspirin?' I stuttered. My heart sank. Here we stood, ready for anything terrorism could throw at us and all the man wanted was an aspirin. Sheepishly I turned to my colleagues. 'Sorry gents,' I said. 'My fault. Stand down.' Worse still, we had no aspirin. The equipment stood prepared to receive anything from full thickness burns to massive blast injuries. But an aspirin? Not a hope.

The hijack fizzled out in the end. Within twelve hours of our arrival the terrorists had given in. The so-called gunshot wound to the co-pilot turned out to be a knife attack. He was lucky, as the blade had passed perilously close to his spine. I recall how quiet and controlled he was when I examined him. You would not have imagined he had been in a hijack at all. One very brave man, I thought. The same applied to the passengers, all of whom came off the aircraft in perfect control. No one was hysterical.

Several hours later we had returned to London and were tucked safely away in our beds. Though nothing dramatic had occurred, preparation and anticipation can be more exhausting than action itself. The hijack had highlighted basic faults with the SMT system. Call-out was unpredictable, transport unreliable and function at the scene ill-prepared. I sent my comments upwards to the RAMC hierarchy, but imagine they have been lost without trace in the bowels of the MOD.

Terrorism, and hence antiterrorism, should be taken very seriously. It invariably catches you by surprise. One major problem is that it follows you everywhere. You are unable to leave it behind. Even though I cannot imagine why any group would be interested in a doctor, the fact is one never knows. Special operations in far-flung lands do not expose the operative to risk once he has left the area, apart from any diseases he brings home. The same does not apply to terrorism. The other side, whatever cause they believe in, are frequently a passionate lot and aim to achieve their end in large part irrespective of the consequences. You cannot assume, simply because you carry a red cross or are in a caring profession, that you are exempt from being targeted. Admittedly the risks are low, but they are nevertheless there. For many years after leaving full-time SAS service I would receive strange telephone calls, sometimes two or three a day. Threats would be made to send my details and full identity to Heaven knows who. Who it was I do not know, except to say, for the moment at least, such things have ceased. Whoever you are, and I imagine Special Branch now know you, please be sure you had the desired effect. I was at times very worried and even now answer the telephone with caution.

Back in London I worked hard at my orthopaedic training. It was a strange world, this life of hip replacements, keyhole operations and broken bones. Though orthopaedic surgery was my ambition, I still yearned for the SAS and their adventurous, outdoor existence. Their strange, unpronounceable illnesses; the singlehanded responsibility; the ability to pick up the telephone and talk to whoever I wished in the land. My colleagues saw me daydream as I began to feel frustrated and, to a degree, disregarded. Surely there was more to life than this? I need not have worried. The Regiment had not forgotten me. Within months, Argentina invaded the Falkland Islands.

CHAPTER 7

The Month I Should Have Died

It is difficult to tell this story. Difficult because I have never been so scared. I think about it even now, more than a decade later. When I read what others have to say about the Falklands War, it is a conflict I do not recognize. Either I was somewhere different or they are unable to feel fear.

The story behind the war is clear. Argentina felt passionately the Malvinas were theirs – the British Government, and hence us, felt differently. On the 2 April 1982 the Falkland Islands were invaded, South Georgia suffering the same fate the following day. By 5 April, 22 SAS was on its way south, throughout the campaign conducting its operations both vigorously and professionally. However, with every war there is much classified activity behind the scenes of which the public, and many senior Service personnel, are unaware. One such operation involved the Regiment. In retrospect I was privileged to be part of it. I learnt more about myself than I thought possible. We are alive, I believe, thanks to the merciful indecision of the nation's politicians. As a soldier you consider the politics of the situation at your peril. Your job is to undertake the task you are contracted to do. You can pass comment on how a job is to be done, but not on why it should be performed. The reasons are for the politicians. You can only pray that your military superiors have sufficient leverage on Government to influence the final conclusions.

When the task force set sail, amidst all manner of tub-thumping and media hype, I was certain nothing would happen. I felt Argentina was sure to see reason and withdraw. Nothing of the sort. Slowly it became apparent they would have to be pushed off. Their politicians had too much to lose by capitulating.

While Britain hovered on the brink of war, I was hard at work as a trainee orthopaedic surgeon. Supervising my somewhat inept attempts at what surgeons call 'cutting' were two of the finest practitioners I have met. I shall call them Colonels Jack and Graham. Both had that enviable skill that so few surgeons have. When they used a scalpel to cut the skin, a patient would barely bleed. It cannot be learned and most certainly cannot be taught. My immediate superior was Martin. In civilian life he would hold the rank of Senior Registrar, an experienced surgeon shortly to become a consultant. Martin is, and was, one of life's great characters. Once a medical officer to the Parachute Regiment, he is a man of action, decision and firm convictions. Together we would sit in the surgeons' coffee room between operations, bemoaning the fact we had been left behind as the task force sailed south.

'It's easy, Richard,' he would say.

'How?' I would ask.

'Just bomb the bastards. Drop a nuc. That'll sort 'em out.'

Our fanciful conversations would become ever more wide-ranging. By the time the ships had reached Ascension Island, the halfway stage, Martin and I had hatched dozens of different plots and secret missions. Galtieri was to be assassinated and the entire Parachute Regiment would be dropped over Port Stanley in a full frontal assault. President Reagan, meanwhile, was to be black-mailed to ensure American participation. Of course, in reality, none of these ever happened. Colonels Jack and Graham tolerated our manic discussions as only wise men can, while Martin and I resigned ourselves to the role of armchair warriors. True REMFs, as the Americans call them: Rear Echelon Mother Fuckers. Several of the guys from stores were whisked away to the South Atlantic at short notice. For the rest of us life continued at its weary, somewhat tedious pace. My role had been established as one of caring for casualties once they returned to the United Kingdom. The South Atlantic medal was not one for me.

It was at half past midnight in mid May that my life for ever changed. I had been out at a stag night and was feeling terrible. I had had far too much to drink. The telephone rang in my central

London flat. It was the Ministry of Defence – Major N, who had been trying to find me for three hours. The bleep system had let him down at every turn. I was summoned to an urgent meeting at the hospital and was given thirty minutes to attend. Major N did not explain the reasons over the telephone.

I met him in a small room in the building's administration wing. Across a bare mahogany table the two of us sat. There was no one else present. Considering a war was in progress, his briefing was remarkably limited. In retrospect it was probable that he, too, had been told very little. The operation was highly sensitive. That night he had been asked to find two surgical teams for an SAS operation. My name had been given as a starting-point. There was no time to lose. He could not say what the operation involved, but it would mean working in the back of an aircraft. There would be no facility for fancy surgery. Our task would be to keep operatives alive as long as possible, until they could reach established medical care.

I asked several questions about the background to the request, and more specific detail of what was involved. He could not answer them. In the end I gave up asking and concentrated on bringing the teams together. Though SMTs were available, nothing existed for this new scenario. I imagine the RAMC had never considered such a situation would arise. Whatever the reason, everything created that night came from thin air.

At 2 a.m., forming two three-man medical teams by dawn is a difficult task. I had a free hand. Naturally, and immediately, I thought of Martin. We had both already imagined a multitude of situations in which the war could involve us. Here was our chance, whatever that might be.

To his eternal credit, the moment I telephoned, he offered his services immediately. When Martin says he will do something, you can be sure it will happen. Together we set about finding the other four we needed. There was no purpose in having six surgeons. Though a surgeon may be a good, practical person with his hands, he requires much support. We decided the others should be nurses and operating theatre assistants.

By 4.30 a.m. the MOD had its teams. I was astonished how

readily everyone agreed to help, particularly when I could tell them so little about the operation. One assistant was due to move house that very morning. As he lived in a married quarter near the hospital, I went to his house. The assistant, his wife and I sat on the various packing cases that littered his living room to discuss taking the man of the house to war. I could see how torn he was. I was unmarried then, without children. It never crossed my mind he could have loyalties anywhere other than active service. I can still see his wife's distressed face as, after initial hesitance, he agreed to come.

During war, RAF, Navy and Army have different agendas and varying ambitions. The senior hierarchy may speak with one another and cooperate, or so one hopes, but at ground level the situation is far from satisfactory. Interservice rivalry may sometimes be frankly hostile. The Falklands War, known to us all as Operation Corporate, was my first experience of a major, triservice, conflict. One might imagine that all involved are kept fully updated and briefed. The reality is different. You are a small cog in a very large wheel. Whether by accident or design, you are well-informed in your one, specific, tiny area of activity but rarely privy to the big picture. The Army calls it 'need to know'. What you don't need to know cannot hurt you. The SAS is better off than most. Even then information can be lacking. No surprise therefore that the CO learned of the original invasion from the BBC. No surprise also that all of us were glued to every World Service bulletin to hear how the war progressed. The BBC has a style, an accuracy, a relaxed manner, with which few can compete.

Whatever the reasons, the true hazards of the operation were never made clear at the initial briefing. I was subsequently to learn that I had been selected, and selected others, for a mission with an optimistic 30 per cent chance of survival for those involved. I knew that for normal troops the risk of dying in war was small. This operation, whatever it was, was something very different. Given a choice, I imagine my *Boys' Own* approach to life would have ensured my involvement. However, I would have thought very carefully about taking married men if I had known.

You know things are bad when the military top brass have to get out of bed to agree things. I should have guessed the Director-General being woken at 4 a.m. by Major N's telephone call spelt trouble, but I did not. With his blessing, we were told to be ready to move to a tiny airfield in central England by 1.30 that afternoon. I still had no idea what to expect. Even the destination after the airfield was kept from us.

Major N had asked that I should also collect the equipment needed for the job. As I had no idea what the task was, this was an impossible order.

'Where are we going?' I asked.

'Dunno,' came the reply.

'How many casualties can we expect?'

'Dunno.'

'OK then. How long will we have to keep them alive?'

'Dunno.'

I got the message quickly. We were on our own. Eventually Major N contacted me with a very vague casualty estimate, saying we should be prepared to keep them alive for twelve hours. I knew that, somewhere in the bowels of Hereford, there were several sets of antiterrorist medical kit for the SMTs. As there was no time to design and prepare equipment specially for this task, I asked that two complete sets be sent to meet us at the airfield. The equipment was mainly designed for use in a friendly country, where hospital facilities were close by. It could not cope with the large numbers likely on this occasion. I therefore instructed that extra surgical items be obtained from the Army's main supply depot. They, too, pulled out all stops that morning.

The final hours before one goes to war can be immensely confusing. There is certainly no time to worry. From all corners come strange items of equipment the Quartermaster hotly denied existed during peacetime. Suddenly they miraculously appear from hidden shelf, somewhere in a backroom. Everything for this operation was spanking new.

The administration must also have their say. You cannot go to war without every form being signed and fully completed. I must have put my signature to a hundred that day. My favourite was the FIdent107, with its two brilliant red crosses at each top corner. Safely protected in its plastic cover, and carrying an appalling photograph and fingerprint of its immature owner on the reverse, it proudly proclaimed I was a doctor. 'The bearer of this card is protected by the Geneva Convention of 12 August 1949,' it said. Some hope, I thought, knowing what the average Argentinian would do to an SAS doctor captured in the field.

The identity card was supported by the FIdent189, specially designed with a tear-off portion to be handed to the opposition in the event of capture. As well as name, rank and number, it also proclaims, 'If you are captured you are required, under the provisions of Article 17 of the Prisoner of War Convention, 1949, to give your captors the information set out below so that your capture may be reported to your next-of-kin. When you are interrogated, but not before, tear off the duplicate portion and give it to the interrogators. GIVE NO OTHER INFORMATION.' War was coming frighteningly close.

That morning, before leaving London, I made one vital telephone call. To my mother. I could not tell her where I was going, even if I had known. With a husband in Intelligence, and a son in the SAS, she had become highly skilled at the art of veiled conversation. I suppose this was one more episode to add to the already lengthy list of worries I had given her since leaving home.

'I've got to go away for a while, Mum,' I said. 'I'm not sure for how long.' I tried to sound as jolly as I could. Mum picked it up immediately. I could sense her distress even though she would never admit it. Dad, the voice of reason, came on after her. Having been sunk himself three times in the Second World War, I was sure he knew what faced me. Neither asked any detailed questions, just calmly wished me well. Mum whispered, 'Be careful,' and hung up. While I was away she listened to almost every news bulletin, at least twelve in a day. She had also faithfully stuck pins into a model of Galtieri daily.

It took three and a half hours to reach the airfield, lurching our way in the hospital minibus, crammed together with our kit:

Bergens, waterproofs, mess tins, Red Cross armbands. Everything was there.

Running a war is a massive logistic exercise. Running one 13,000 kilometres away is a challenge most will fail to meet. I can see now why the RAF's palette-packers were awarded South Atlantic medals. They must have worked twenty-four hours a day to keep the likes of ourselves supported. With so much kit available, there is a risk you can lose your own. It must be instantly recognizable by day or night, indoors or outdoors, rain or shine, from the many other items going in the same direction. Therefore mark it you must, though without any sign of rank, name, unit or location. Nothing to give you away when caught or if your equipment is found abandoned. After heated debate we decided on a team logo. A small, fluorescent orange mushroom. It was not my idea.

'Mushrooms are fed on shit and kept in the dark, aren't they, boss?' an assistant observed as we forced down a suspect meal at the airfield. From that moment the mushroom became our sign and we set about cutting dozens of small fungi from a large sheet of adhesive orange plastic, sticking them as markers on every item of equipment we possessed. At least our recently formed team had an identity, even if its mission was still unclear. I was willing to stake my life an Argentinian interrogator would have no idea of a mushroom's significance. Indeed I might have to.

At 3 a.m. the following morning we left for a tiny location in the middle of nowhere. The six of us were squeezed, like sardines in a tin, into the tiny recesses a Hercules' huge freightload would allow. The C130 is a wonderful machine. You cannot escape that feeling of real flying. Shaking, vibrating, rattling one's way around the world, she seems able to cope with anything. She is also unbearably slow. It took twenty hours of juddering to reach our destination.

This was to be our holding area. A volcanic region, full of rough, jagged promontories and spurs. In its centre stood a faded green hillock, unjustifiably called a mountain by the locals. The tiny airfield on which we landed was packed with aircraft, though this time they were bombers rather than Hercules transports. I had never seen a Vulcan bomber close up before, but they are *huge* – absolutely massive – guaranteed to reinforce that now established feeling I had developed: the tiny cog in an enormous wheel.

As I stumbled from the tailgate of the C130 I was greeted by numerous, smiling, familiar faces. Men I had known well while I had been RMO in Hereford. Their greeting was so warm it was as if I had never been away. 22 SAS was here in force and had been stood by to act for three weeks already. What was strange was why Major A was there, acting as Squadron Commander. As far as I was aware, Major D was in charge, and yet nowhere was he to be seen. Major A was very senior to be in such a post. A likeable man, he had the most impenetrable, rockhard façade I have seen – a truly professional soldier. He ushered me in the direction of his Land Rover, as he wanted to brief me, which meant there was probably little time to spare. His first words, spoken as soon as I had slammed shut the Land Rover door, set the scene. 'Doc, it's great to see you,' he said. 'I wondered whether it would be you who volunteered for this.'

Who the hell had said anything about volunteering? At no stage had anyone in the UK said there might be an opt out. Now at the operational holding area, nothing would be gained by pointing this out. Unless I wanted to look a complete fool, or worse still be accused of cowardice, I was stuck with the situation. Major A started his briefing as we lurched towards the holding area.

The operation was enormously risky, depending almost exclusively on surprise. Scheduled to strike many miles from the front line, the SAS would be stranded, or even annihilated, if events went wrong. The Argentinian forces were not a placid enemy. They were well-trained, and very well equipped. This was not the Third World, whatever the news bulletins had suggested. Furthermore, intelligence sources had warned the enemy we might attack and they were upgrading their defences as a precaution. It was as if they were waiting for the SAS to arrive.

A number of senior Regiment personnel had already made their feelings known before leaving Hereford that the operation represented a needless risk to Squadron life. Simpler alternatives were suggested. When experienced SAS operatives start to worry, you can be sure there are likely to be problems. Major A had been brought in to shore things up. He was an excellent choice. It would have been difficult for the Squadron to have done better. For sure, he was the type who would see the operation through to its conclusion, whatever the risks involved. You had to admire him, however terrified you felt.

Major A's briefing had been very matter-of-fact – a man with no doubts. I decided an identical surgical team should be present on each of the two aircraft to be used, in case one was shot down. Martin would command one and I the other. Unless fate smiled on us, there was little chance we would be going home.

It is difficult not to mope when you are told you are going to die, especially if it is unexpected. What impressed me was the self-control of the operatives. They knew the exact nature of the operation and the risks involved. Most had families and loved ones at home. For three weeks they had been stood by to kill themselves for Queen and country. At first appearance they seemed remarkably relaxed and accepting. 'That's why we're here, Doc,' one old hand remarked. But behind the façade, many were deeply and significantly affected. As the days passed I was to become intro-duced to their worries on frequent occasions.

The camp was small, stranded in the centre of an area of black, volcanic rubble. We were put with the signallers, in a large green tent away from prying eyes. When live operations are under way, the principle of quarantine is important. It stops awkward ques-tions at the wrong moment. The political repercussions, had the operation leaked out, would have been vast. Barely forty-eight hours after completing a comfortable, peaceful, operating list in London, I was now lying in a canvas tent waiting to die. That has a profound impact, however tough you may think you are. My main worry, as well as for my own safety, was what to tell the others. Each had agreed to come at short notice. None realized he might never see England again.

I decided not to tell them the full story, a decision that rests on my mind even today. It was easier that way. Perhaps it was a reflection of my inability to face reality. My whole approach, every innermost feeling, is best shown by the letter I wrote to a friend in the UK a short while after arriving in the holding area. It was kept deliberately vague, without mention of unit or location, in the interests of security at the time. My request it should be published in a leading medical journal immediately following the conflict was rejected by the Army. I should add that, by nature, I am not a depressive.

By the time you read this the Falklands conflict will be over and I shall be dead, though if I manage to survive then the words I am writing now will no longer carry the same meaning.

It was only forty-eight hours ago that a faceless gentleman from the Ministry called me from my comfortable bed and asked me to take part in a particular military operation. There is no one I know who would turn such an offer down and it is only as I sit here now that I realize the full horror of what I am about to do. This is no exercise, no war game, but the real, very frightening thing. I have brought with me five other medical men, some far more qualified than I shall ever be. Somehow I cannot bring myself to tell them the full facts of what tomorrow holds, for how can you tell good friends they may become national heroes but their chances of returning home are almost nil? I think we all realize how important is the task that lies ahead, for the lives of countless Servicemen and Falkland Islanders may depend upon it. But to me, my life is precious and the prospect of imminent death something I find hard to accept. I cannot pretend I am a stranger to war, but always I have had the upper hand and never have I seen it on the scale I see it now. Friends have died, comrades have been burned, but still the fighting goes on.

Fear is a peculiar sensation and each time I feel it I convince myself I shall conquer it next time. I remember the first parachute jump when I could hardly breathe in my panic, or standing outside the viva room at my primary Fellowship when it seemed that every five minutes I wanted to go to the loo. Now things are different for I can see no way I can make it out of this operation alive.

I haven't made a will as I have very few possessions, though a good friend has just written to his brother to make certain everything is left to his wife. I thought I had better write to my parents before things get under way and am surprised how cheerful I sounded though I know my mother is frantic with concern. Families and friends are so important at times like these. I feel rather guilty that I need to be so close to death to appreciate their full value. My sheer existence is dependent on the orders of a person I have never met.

I sometimes curse my medical education, for I am sure it makes my mind dwell on unpleasant thoughts longer than most. I can spend an entire day reading a paperback and yet find I have only read one page as my concentration has been elsewhere. Food is no longer attractive and sex something I haven't thought about since I left the UK. I visited a small local church today and spent most of the time sitting at the back praying that peace would be declared and we could all go home. Every World News bulletin has me transfixed for signs that the inevitable might be postponed, but all I ever hear is another ship has been sunk and no end is in sight. Such a strange contrast from the aggressive individual I was in London who reckoned that no holds should be barred and total war declared. It's a different matter when you become involved yourself.

Someone once said that war was long periods of boredom interspersed with brief periods of terror. How right they were, though it does not explain that permanent sickness I have inside me now. I feel, though, that I have come to terms with what is in store for me and writing this has certainly helped. Should I survive I shall be classed as a nobody, but if I die I shall be a hero and perhaps not forgotten.

Those words were written from the heart at the time, a time when I genuinely felt I would die. I read them often. A reminder that each day is a bonus and any problems I may have now pale into insignificance.

That first night in the holding area sleeping was understandably difficult. At 3 a.m. I was woken by the shout of 'Fire!'. A Land Rover was ablaze, whether by sabotage or accident I do not know. By the time I reached the spot, medical kit in hand, the situation was firmly under control. No one was injured, so I returned to our tent, settling again into a disturbed sleep.

We were up at dawn. The operation could be on at any time and it was important the aircraft were rigged for casualties. The Hercules C130 is a highly adaptable machine and can carry, or do, almost anything. Though I had travelled many miles in them, I had never had to deal with casualties on board. Rigging the inside for stretchers, and a makeshift operating table, was difficult but possible. By lunchtime the two medical teams had an accurate idea of what they would have to do, though were still unaware of the true spectre hanging over them. I decided to leave things that way.

That afternoon I was given a full briefing on Regimental activities throughout the Falklands campaign. It was good to hear the men were doing well, though so many had died when a Sea King helicopter plunged into the sea. Two of my former medics had managed to escape. Both always had a generous helping of luck and skill. Though it is a tragedy for anyone to perish, I was particularly saddened by Ray's death. I had got to know him over the years and well remember running a mountain marathon alongside him. He was tall, seemingly immortal and immensely confident. Whether it is worth a life I do not know, but it was his troop that destroyed the Pebble Island aircraft. The SAS, as ground troops, destroyed more Argentinian aircraft than any other Service during the campaign.

The Sea King disaster was in a class of its own, the reaction it produced from friends and colleagues similarly inexplicable. It was a simple transfer between *Hermes* and *Intrepid* late one evening, in a moderate sea. Whether the helicopter collided with a large bird, perhaps a petrel or an albatross, will never be known. The result was the biggest loss of Regimental life, in one episode, since the Second World War. Worse still, it was not an accident that could be blamed on any one person. Even the hardiest, most callous colleague was forced to admit the event was beyond control. Not surprisingly, the crash affected many Regimental operatives in a profound way. Nothing could be blamed except bad fortune. Bad fortune was something that could affect anyone, at any time. Suddenly, each of us became human and vulnerable, even without the threat of our own operation lurking near by.

From a medical viewpoint, the response of a soldier to the death of comrades is fascinating. Usually, if a man is killed in battle, or on the streets of Northern Ireland, his friends will find a way of blaming death on some military misdeed. 'He wasn't quick enough, Doc', 'It was his fault anyway,' were said to me more times than I care to remember. This is not a criticism of the dead individual, it is simply a way in which survivors deal with the horror of what can so easily happen to them. It is important to feel in control of one's destiny, even if in reality one is not. A soldier cannot afford the luxury of being morose and dwelling on the prospect of death. The fact that death might have been inevitable is an explanation most seek to avoid.

By the end of May it was becoming apparent, to my mind anyway, that Downing Street could not decide about us. At times we stood by to move at thirty minutes' notice, at others the operation was altered to two hours' standby. Once we even climbed on the buses to take us to the aircraft before being told of a further postponement. Each time you prepare yourself physically, and psychologically, for what you are certain is imminent death. Each time, your emotions having been raised to fever pitch, the rug is yet again pulled from under you. This happened thirty times or more. It must be similar sitting on a US Death Row waiting for that last-minute reprieve.

As a doctor you are everyone's confidant. I do not intend to characterize such confidences here, as that goes against everything I stand for in medicine. However independent and aggressive a soldier may be, he does need someone in whom to confide, someone who can listen to his innermost concerns. I remember one operative taking me to one side to say he was sleeping terribly, plagued by recurring dreams of an aircraft crashing in flames. What was he to do? It was an impossible question, particularly as his dream was an accurate reflection of what might occur. At such times I found it best to own up to my own fears and weaknesses. No one expects a doctor to be gung-ho, running around with a dagger between his teeth. Soldiers regard you with immense suspicion if you do. Honesty was best. I simply admitted to being terrified myself, reassuring all concerned there was no dishonour in fear. It was how one controlled it that mattered. The soldier with the bad dreams was reassured once he realized he was the eleventh person to consult me with worries that day. He had a wife and children in Hereford, a family I was careful not to mention. It was dangerous to remind him of his family or friends back home. I did not want to weaken his resolve. However aggressive or courageous a soldier may appear on the outside, he needs enormous self-control to cope with what is asked of him. The SAS is no exception.

Another operative took me aside, asking if I would put an intravenous drip into each man *before* they went into battle. In the trade we call it 'keeping a vein open'. A small plastic tube, or cannula, is placed in an arm vein and a plug inserted into its outer end. If the individual starts to bleed, for whatever reason, it is a simple matter to remove the outer plug and insert blood, or saline or a plasma expander. It is the best way of minimizing the chance of shock due to blood loss. I found his request difficult to answer. Rather than dismissing the idea out of hand, I promised to discuss it with other members of the medical team.

When we did talk it over, we decided against the idea. Though keeping a vein open is part of routine hospital practice, for example to allow immediate resuscitation of a heart-attack victim, it would be dangerous in the field. What would happen, we debated, if the outer plug became dislodged in the heat of battle? Quite possibly an operative could bleed to death without even being shot. When I told the operative, he was not surprised, but I could sense he was now happier that someone had taken his worries seriously. I took Major A to one side at that stage, as I felt someone should highlight the troops' concern. How hopeless they felt their situation was. In retrospect I was stating the obvious. We stood in an open patch of volcanic ground to avoid prying eyes and ears, be they friend or foe. He was, as always, very understanding, listening carefully to what I said. His reply was typical. That is why I like him.

'I know the lads are worried, Doc,' he replied. 'But it's got to be done.' The conversation was over.

At midday I was summoned to Squadron orders. This is the daily update of what has been happening, and what is expected in future. I had not slept well that night. My diary tells all:

Awful night's sleep worrying about what is in store for us. It's funny – you don't tend to think of anything specific to worry about. It's just a sense of permanent sickness with occasional bouts of palpitations. Woke up by 0430 hours and couldn't get back to sleep again. Had a breakfast that was very difficult to swallow and hung around with the boys most of the morning.

I could not give specific details in the diary in case it fell into the wrong hands. Names, units, taskings, I had to omit.

At the midday orders we were informed the operation had been postponed. Instead, I was told to be ready for immediate departure by passenger aircraft, destination to be advised. The plane was scheduled to leave two hours' later, so there was no time to spare. The remaining members of the medical team would return home to the UK. After many years with the SAS one learns an ability to move anywhere, at any time, without notice. Anything you do not immediately need is packed away in your Bergen. No sooner had I prepared myself than the plans were changed again. Something had happened to the main fighting forces, though the exact reasons were never made clear, and the original operation had been reinstated.

With such toing, froing and unpredictability, it was difficult to keep everyone suitably occupied. The medical teams had by now gleaned snippets of information from a variety of sources and were clearly concerned. One man was particularly upset by his lack of Red Cross identification card, the F Ident107. Somehow the R A M C had lost it, the hasty departure from the UK giving insufficient time to prepare a substitute. Trying to obtain one in our holding area was impossible, so the poor man was stuck without medical identity at all. I doubt it would have been of any use to him in any event. Though the Geneva Convention is a wonderful thing, you cannot expect to receive the best of treatment when involved in secret S A S operations. The S A S have a habit of upsetting the other side.

Red Cross identification is a mixed blessing. Through an opponent's telescopic sight, everyone should look the same. Around your neck you wear two metal identity discs, wrapped tightly in black masking tape to ensure they do not clash noisily together. On the discs are embossed your name and number. Red Cross armbands, good in theory, are out in practice. They can be seen for miles and can help identify the lines of communication for the fighting troops. In Bosnia, more recently, the Red Cross on the side of Sarajevo's military hospital was used as an aiming point for Serb gunners. At times I was tempted to secrete my armband and rank epaulettes in a tunic pocket, to be miraculously produced in the event of capture. The temptation was strong, but military training took over. Nothing suggested I was a doctor.

Once it became obvious the operation could happen any time between the next five minutes and the next five months it was important all concerned were kept busy. Physical training was our way, with frequent runs up and down the area's tiny mountain extremely effective at keeping us fit. After all, we reasoned, if we had to keep pace with the S A S operatives, the medics could not be outdone.

When alone, each would occupy himself in his own way. For me, it was revising for my next surgery examination, scheduled for later that year. I am sure the author of *Lecture Notes in Surgery* had no idea his book was being so avidly read on such a covert mission. Admittedly, memorizing facts was impossible, particularly when disturbed by yet another thirty-minute standby to hell.

Writing to Forces' penfriends was another activity, and strangely attractive it was. You would not believe the quantity of mail the Services receive, totally blind, from young ladies and young men in times of war. Tons of it. It is extremely welcome. Not every soldier has a loved one at home to whom he can write. Particularly so the SAS, which appears to have an unfair percentage of single, independently minded individuals. I cannot remember to whom I wrote, but the Doc is always regarded as fair game for such things. The operatives would line me up with the most provocative, suggestive missives and insist I replied. I enjoyed the challenge.

By now it was becoming clear that life was still not going well for the fleet. Despite the main troops landing on East Falkland, the Naval casualty list was becoming longer by the day: *Ardent, Argonaut, Antelope, Sir Galahad, Sir Lancelot, Coventry.* These names do not include those struck by unexploded bombs, UXBs. There appeared a great disparity between what the media now reported and what was truly happening on the ground. Downing Street had to be sweating.

Furthermore, our own operational security was now becoming a problem. A leak had been discovered in a nearby conurbation and our tasking was apparently being discussed openly. Occasional reports would also appear in various UK newspapers of likely SAS options. Most were wildly inaccurate, but a few, if they had but known, were perilously close to the mark.

At this point I felt we were as close as we would ever be to the operation being launched. Again, we were on short standby to move. As if to emphasize the situation further, I was asked to update myself on a variety of weapons. 'Just in case, Doc,' I was told. I spent the best part of a day on a makeshift range firing an assortment of death-delivering devices. I loved the grenade launcher. It was a tubelike 'lob and hope' affair, attached to the underside of a rifle. You get quite good at it in the end, but I found accurate aiming an impossible task. The cartridges, however, do make excellent egg cups. With the upgraded training, and horrifying reports from the task force, all of us were convinced Downing

Street was a hair's breadth from letting us on our way. The operation must surely be launched?

It never was and the reasons not explained. I imagine you feel as let down as us when you learn this. Probably, the sensitivities and the risks were too great. For those of us poised to strike, we had lived and relived the operation for weeks. My mind had pondered all manner of grizzly ends. Our masters, for most likely very good reason, had developed cold feet.

By early June we returned to the UK, happy in some respects, disgruntled in others. My first port of call was to Major N. I told him my mind, even though tact, rank and diplomacy might have suggested otherwise. How could the Army, I asked, send its people on a projected suicide operation without warning them beforehand? Why were we not properly briefed? Why was I not stopped from taking married men with me? Of course, now the operation had been cancelled, I had no argument. It was as if it had never happened, that the idea had never occurred. Major N was shaken and there was not much he could say. My objections were passed up the line, though I do not know who received them.

As for myself, this is the first time I have written this story. I always swore I would not. In many respects I still feel ashamed that I reacted as I did. That I felt such immense, sometimes uncontrollable fear. For years I avoided the subject of the Falklands completely. For those who knew I had been involved, I preferred to talk as if I had been part of more traditional activities. My true role is an aspect of life I wish to forget. Much has been said in closed Regimental circles about the operation that never was. Emotions do run very high. I have seen brief, partially accurate mention in the press of what we were supposed to be doing. I have seen outlines presented in several books. None effectively describe the terror and hopelessness felt by many involved. You do not need to be shot at to be scared.

The Army left me little time for pondering when I returned. In my absence, a number of other hospital staff had been sent to the South Atlantic, doubling the duties I was normally required to perform. More on-call, more clinics and more surgery. I did not object. It felt good to take my mind away from what had been asked of me only days previously. In early June the landing and supply ships *Sir Galahad* and *Sir Tristram* were hit by Argentine air attack. The result was fifty-three dead and forty-six injured, many of whom passed through the military hospital where I was based. The majority were burns victims, some severe, some minor. Burns are awful injuries as they scar for life, however well you treat them. Your chances of survival diminish as the area burned increases. The main problem is infection. Once the skin has been burned away, underneath is revealed a raw, unprotected surface. At the scene of the incident, the best thing is to cover the burned area with something clean. Burned clothing is left where it is as the initial heat has probably rendered it sterile. The casualties from the Falklands returned to London, by sea and air, with their burned hands in antibiotic-lined plastic bags. The troops were also very fortunate as they had with them an exceptionally skilled plastic surgeon. It was thanks to his advice that complications were kept to a minimum.

My task in London was to help perform countless skin grafting operations – hands, feet, faces, bellies – nowhere was exempt. The operation is called 'tangential excision', the burned region being gently cut away with a long, razor-sharp knife, until healthy tissue is found beneath. Skin graft is then taken from an undamaged area, usually a thigh, and transferred to the burn. It takes a week to ten days for the graft to join to the patient. It does not always join fully, so there may be a need to repeat the performance several times, over many weeks, until skin cover is complete. Sometimes burns can be so severe that the victim does not have enough undamaged skin available. This can be a major problem for plastic surgeons and a life-threatening issue to the patient.

As well as burns victims, the Falklands conflict created many casualties due to gunshot and blast injury. Two in particular stick in my mind. The first was a bomb-disposal man, tasked to go on board a ship to defuse a UXB. Two of them had entered, only one surviving when the UXB had exploded unexpectedly. The survivor lost his arm, clean through the middle of its upper bone, the humerus. The injury, though horrific, was not what impressed me. For an orthopaedic surgeon, the traumatically amputated arm was relatively easy to solve. It was the man's approach to life that astonished me. Only days earlier he had been staring death in the face, far closer than I had ever got, and yet he appeared completely relaxed and in total control. He had lost a good friend, had been maimed for life, but was as emotionally sound as one gets. I cannot define the word 'hero' but he would be near to it if I could. I am unable to say whether he was decorated for his efforts – it would be a travesty if he was not.

My other memory is of a young Scotsman who was the victim of a negligent discharge. This is what happens when a weapon is fired by mistake. The Services take great pains to ensure such events are kept to a minimum and make an 'ND' a punishable offence. Even so, NDs still remain one of the commoner ways of being injured in action. Twenty-five per cent of American injuries in the Gulf War, for example, were due to friendly fire. It nearly happened to me on one occasion, in the Far Eastern jungle. I had joined the SAS troops on a jungle range, as they practised skirmishing skills. We were using live ammunition from high-velocity Armalites with a lot of fire being put down. Perhaps one thousand rounds per minute were cracking through the air around me. Anyone who thinks bullets whine or whizz has simply never been under fire. At one point I dived to one side, taking cover at the foot of a flimsy tree, preparing to put down fire myself to allow my skirmishing partner to move forward. As I dived, splinters flew from the base of the tree, inches from my head, as several Armalite rounds punched home. It was my fault, as I had run directly in front of a colleague's rifle without thinking. It is thanks to his quick reactions that I am here to tell this tale today.

The Scotsman had suffered an ND in style. Not a rifle, not a grenade, but a missile from a jet. He was fortunate to survive. It had blasted away much of his shin bone and part of his foot. The shin bone – tibia – is not a good one to break. In its central portion the blood supply is poor, so damage in this area can be slow to heal. In fact, healing sometimes never occurs. The missile had removed at least a third of the bone, depositing it in a thousand pieces on the runway at Port Stanley. When we took an X-ray, there was a massive gap where the bone should have been. The Scotsman, like the bomb disposer, bore his injuries with immense strength. Our initial advice had been to amputate the leg as none of us could envisage the tibia healing. At times, however, it is good that patients prove you wrong. This was one such occasion. The Scotsman refused amputation and struggled onwards for months in a plaster cast. 'Let's see what Nature does,' he would say.

He was right. Six months later, with youth and Nature on his side, the bone started to recover, the massive gap in the tibia slowly reducing. Within a year the bone had healed. He walks today with his own leg, albeit with a limp. I would hope he is delighted to have proved the medical profession wrong. All credit to him.

Once the last Falklands casualty had been discharged from hospital I had more time to reflect on life. I was still suffering badly from the shock of being asked to kill myself so overtly for Queen and Country. I decided to leave the Army as soon as the opportunity presented itself. Aware of my decision, the RAMC decided to post me to Aldershot, deep within the heart of the British Army. Aldershot, too, changed my life – in a most dramatic way.

I was on the children's ward. A young baby, no more than a year old, had been born with dislocated hips. I had surgically placed them back in socket, where God intended them to be. After surgery, the baby could not eat or drink. It sometimes happens after big operations, though only lasts a few days. During that period you feed the mites by drip, but their tiny bodies need minute attention to detail. You can so easily administer too much drip fluid and bump them off as a result. Exhausted from the operation, I sat at the nurses' table towards one end of the huge, open ward, performing interminable long-hand calculations on how much fluid to give. I was struggling – perhaps due to tiredness, or perhaps due to a congenital inability to add two and two.

As I tore up the twentieth piece of scrap paper, covered in illegible, inaccurate, mathematical jottings, a forceful, feminine voice disturbed me from behind. There was a trace of Scottish about it.

'Why don't you ask a paediatrician?' it said. 'We do it all the time.'

I turned to greet the voice, ready to defend the rights of orthopaedic surgeons worldwide to solve their own problems. How dare she. I'll show her, I thought. She wouldn't know a hip joint if you hit her with one. What did she know anyway? There is a traditional, longstanding war between surgeons and physicians that has existed since the beginning of time.

Then I saw her and knew instantly I could not argue. She was brunette and beautiful, with a smile as broad as they come. Her tight Army uniform covered an immaculate body, a major's crown decorating each shoulder. 'Hi!' she said, before I could gather myself. 'I'm Louise. Who on earth are you?'

You never believe in love at first sight until it happens. It did for me. That very second I knew I was smitten. You sit in a pleasant, isolated tunnel, oblivious of the world outside. You forget everything that has gone before, sometimes cruelly so, and the future appears irrelevant. It is a most intense disease. One day I shall invent a tablet as cure, so deeply physical are the feelings.

Over the next few weeks Louise and I saw each other regularly. The more I learned about her, the more involved I became. She was a living legend in the R A M C. The five simultaneous boyfriends in Hong Kong? That was her. Refusal to carry a pistol despite being a crack shot? That was her too. Wearing high-heeled shoes on active service, combined with her encyclopaedic knowledge of all things medical, made me realize what a formidable creature I had met. Asking her to marry me – and thank God her acceptance – was the most natural act of my life.

Since that day we have stayed as tight as tight can be, which is something of a record in modern society. We have had differences by the dozen, and misdeeds when we should not. Even so, Louise is, and was, the girl for me.

My remaining months in the Army passed in a haze. The girls take over once they agree to marry you. I still had residual duties to perform with the SAS and would somehow have to fit them into my now very changed life. For the first time I had to think of someone else, not just my self-important ego. The duties on this occasion were not concerned with armed conflict, so the chances of being shot were nil. They were nevertheless very hazardous. High mountains, my next port of call, can be the most vicious opponents on earth.

CHAPTER 8

Great Heights

The damned knee would not come straight. I had tried everything I knew, but it was still locked tight, bent in its agonizing position. Mark was one of our best climbers and had been doing well on the approach to Alaska's Mount McKinley. Disaster had struck suddenly when he had unexpectedly twisted his knee.

'Come on Doc! Pull the bastard!' he shouted as I struggled to manipulate his knee in the tiny tent. As I heaved hard I could tell I was hurting him, pain written on his face. It was a simple condition, a torn ligament. Split in two it had displaced into the centre of the joint itself, locking it from any movement. Why here, I thought? Stranded in the middle of McKinley's Kahiltna glacier.

Though I had ketamine anaesthetic with me, I was frightened to use it. Fearful what would happen if Mark lost control of his breathing, something anaesthetics were prone to cause. I needed him to relax, to eliminate the power of his huge thigh muscles, which were preventing me from applying the necessary force on his joint. My eventual compromise had been a mixture of rum and sedative. I had hoped this would overcome his impressive muscle tone, but it did not. Mark simply insisted I drank some too. He was a social type of man. The result had been an intoxicated doctor trying desperately to unlock the knee of an unanaesthetized SAS operative. Needless to say I had failed.

'I'm sorry, Mark,' I eventually confessed. 'There's not a hope. We're going to have to evacuate you from the mountain. You're no use to anyone like this.' I could tell he was disappointed despite his acceptant nod. Mount McKinley, at 6200 metres, is America's highest peak. Reaching the summit was vital for those of us who wished to try Everest's North Face the following year. I was partly to blame for Mark's predicament, making me feel even more guilty. I had known about the ligament tear before we had left Hereford but had taken a gamble it would not displace. I had been wrong. My friendship with the popular SAS man had overridden medical considerations. I resolved to be more self-disciplined should the same happen again.

It had started with a simple question from Bronco two years earlier. I had been coming to the end of my time in full SAS service. 'How about Everest?' he had asked. Bronco was a remarkable individual. You would be forgiven for thinking he was the SAS. He had been everywhere, done everything and knew everyone. The wealth of experience he had amassed after many years in the Regiment was impressive. In 1976 he and Brummie had slept the night out near Everest's summit, surviving perilous temperatures with the loss of several fingers and toes. Despite this, they both wished to return, though on this occasion with a team drawn entirely from the SAS.

I was astonished to be asked, knowing almost nothing about climbing and being terrified of heights. I was well able to experience vertigo on top of a bunk bed. Everest? No way. That was stupid. I think Bronco noticed my initial hesitation. 'Have a think on it,' he added. 'Let me know.'

As he walked away I had to smile. He knew very well I would eventually accept. From my first day with the Regiment I had resolved always to say 'Yes', whatever was asked of me. Saying 'No' might mean I would miss an important part of life. Within hours I had decided to support the 1984 SAS Everest attempt, irrespective of the fact I could not distinguish a karabiner from a kettle, nor a rope from a rucksack. I had several years to learn.

One advantage of medical examinations, for whichever qualification, is that they demand instant recollection of long factual lists. How many of the 234 causes of bloody diarrhoea do you know? Tell me the forty-six ways appendicitis can kill? I applied this acquired skill to climbing. I went on courses, talked to instructors and read every book written on the subject since time began. Within two years I was theoretically sound, though practically very inexperienced.

The first stop was not Everest, but McKinley. Our visit there was to sort the wheat from the chaff. Climbing is not everyone's forte. Masquerading as a military exercise, Exercise 'Top Slap', it was to be my first experience of high-altitude snow and ice climbing. McKinley was well known to be one of the world's fiercest peaks, especially when the weather turned sour. Twenty-nine of us went to Alaska. The subsequent Everest attempt only required fourteen.

By the time we left for McKinley, my climbing knowledge was well-ordered, but my personal life in chaos. Being in love does that to you. Louise and I had decided to live together before we were married, though we had set the wedding date for soon after my return from Alaska. This was a difficult situation for the RAMC, which did not know how to handle two officers, in the same Mess, falling in love. Even the Queen's Regulations – Queen's Regs – had no advice to offer. The Army is run on the Queen's Regs. If you perform an act that lies outside the text in those massive tomes, all manner of disciplinary horrors can befall you. It has opinions on homosexuality, rape and other assorted deeds, but nothing covered Louise and me cohabiting in Farnham. It was to our advantage. We simply did it and in no time it became accepted as normal.

Alaska is a long way from Hereford and Hercules aircraft very slow. The first stop after leaving the UK was a Royal Air Force base in Newfoundland. It must be the loneliest place on earth. I felt desperately sorry for the RAF ground crew stationed there. There was nothing to do. Nothing except fantasize about life elsewhere in an attempt to enjoy one's own company. My memories of the base are now limited, but I do remember lots of snow, miles of forestry and an endless supply of pornographic videos. For most of our twenty-four-hour stay we saw nothing of our hosts. They remained locked away in a darkened room looking at assorted views of the same act of procreation.

Staging through Vancouver, we arrived eventually in Anchorage and were transported from the airfield to the US Army base of Fort Richardson. It was an interesting introduction to the eating habits of our American partners. I cannot recall seeing so much high-fat food being squeezed on to a plate before. Having queued, you would eventually be confronted by a massive, overweight chef, frying pan in each hand, furiously cooking omelettes. Not one- or two-egg omelettes, but six- or seven-egg ones. He was surrounded by rows of stainless steel pots and containers filled to the brim with dietary extras: hash browns, syrup, waffles, cream. The temptation was too great. I was in Fort Richardson for two meals and put on half a stone. I knew then I would have to climb to great heights, simply to expend the calories I had gained.

My impression of Alaska was like something from the great Wild West. The area surrounding McKinley, the Denali National Park, is home to many wild, fully bearded trappers. Moose are their favoured prey. 'One that got away' stories abound and bars really do have chest-high saloon doors. Town names, and local behaviour, are wonderfully traditional, as shown by the near shoot-out in Moose Creek. One night, almost at closing time and before we had gone anywhere near the mountain, I was sat at a small round table in a bar being interviewed by a journalist for a climbing magazine. He was becoming quite intense, quizzing me in minute detail on the various tablets available to deter mountain sickness. Scattered around were similar tables of SAS climbers, each deep in discussion. The atmosphere seemed friendly. Suddenly I heard a female voice shout, 'Get the hell out of here or you'll regret it!' It was the bartender.

'I'm going for my gun!' came the swift reply from a well-oiled trapper. Two men, both trappers, had been arguing furiously, in subdued tones, for some time. I had not realized: it seemed the only solution, if you were Alaskan, was a shoot-out.

At the mention of the word 'gun' the bar emptied instantly. People dashed everywhere. Being somewhat slow about these things it took me a while to realize why the journalist was now under the table. By the time I had thought to join him, one trapper had already charged from the bar into the street outside to get his gun.

From beyond the saloon doors I heard a whispered voice, as I cowered, trembling, beneath the table, hugging the journalist for extra security.

'Doc! Come over here. We need you.' I looked around me and tiptoed out through the doors. The only person left standing in the bar was the other trapper, lounging against the counter in an astonished, alcoholic way. Outside, I was greeted by a number of smiling SAS faces. Fifty metres away I could see the trapper in his four-wheel drive wagon, scrabbling through assorted bags to find his weapon. I was immediately grasped by a dozen hands and pushed to the front of the group. 'Go on, you walk first. We'll follow behind,' I was urged. Our accommodation was the far side of the intoxicated trapper in his vehicle. Despite the distance, I could see the satisfied smile on his face as a large Magnum revolver appeared from the depths of a light brown holdall. So much for not getting shot on the mountains, I thought.

'What's this about?' I asked. 'You're the professionals. You've done this sort of thing before.'

'That's the point,' one SAS operative replied. 'He knows you're a doctor. He won't shoot *you*. With one of us out in front he's bound to have a go.'

So I was frogmarched past the trapper, as a form of friendly hostage. The gun-toting drunk barely spared me, or my SAS colleagues, a second glance. For the first, and perhaps only time of my life, I could claim to have saved the SAS.

There are many routes to McKinley's summit. Our chosen one, the West Buttress, is perhaps the simplest of them all. A long, winding glacier, the Kahiltna, finishes at the base of an almost vertical ice Headwall. Once up the Headwall it is a long, dangerous trudge to the top. We flew in to our base camp on the Kahiltna glacier, a paltry 2150 metres above sea level. Bumping through the sky in a tiny, single-engined Cessna we negotiated the fearsome One Shot Pass, whose name speaks for itself, before landing smoothly on skis.

My first feeling was wonder. Clear blue sky, perfectly white snow and the overpowering image of the summit, miles away, leaning over us. My second feeling was terror. Avalanches. Fresh snowfalls had covered all slopes with a thick layer of unstable snow. By midday, our time of arrival, the sun had warmed the area and the snow began to slide. Avalanches were everywhere. Wherever I looked I could see another one – dozens of them. From a distance an avalanche is a beautiful thing. Near by, the impression is different. It starts as a feeling of the mountainside moving. Then comes a high-pitched rattle as the smaller ice blocks and snow particles begin to move. The rattle is followed by a rumble, becoming louder and louder as, quite possibly, a whole mountainface gives way. As the avalanche picks up speed it can push before it a great wave of air, well able to pick up a man and throw him down again. Then follow the larger ice blocks and mass of snow, covering everything in their path. After I counted twelve avalanches in the first hour, I realized what a dangerous game high-altitude climbing was. The advance climbing party, highly experienced in such things, had sited our base camp well out of harm's way. With luck the experts would see me through.

Snow and ice are not the only hazards of altitude climbing. The environment is a major problem – a medical nightmare. As you ascend, so the pressure of oxygen in the air gets less. At the top of Mont Blanc (4807 metres) the pressure of oxygen is half that found at sea level. On the summit of Everest (8848 metres) it reduces to a third. It is this reduced oxygen pressure that causes so many of the problems climbers can suffer. Red blood cells, responsible for carrying oxygen around the body, simply do not have enough of it available to do their job properly. Brain and lungs swell, the so-called high-altitude oedema, blood thickens in the legs and clots, while blood vessels in the eyes can burst. The process of acclimatization is therefore vital. This long word describes the body's adjustment to the strange high-altitude environment. In principle, the more rapidly a climber ascends, the more likely it is that medical disaster will follow. It is worthwhile climbing slowly at altitude.

Up to 2500 metres above sea level, given enough time, it is possible to acclimatize almost fully. Upwards of forty million people worldwide live at or above this height. Once over 3500 metres full acclimatization is impossible. You may not feel too bad, but the body is not fully efficient. Over 5500 metres deterioration is significant. Slowly the body's cells become damaged by reduced pressure of oxygen, however gradually one chooses to climb. If you stay there long enough you can quite possibly die. McKinley's summit was 6200 metres above sea level and high-altitude problems were assured.

From the air a glacier looks very innocent. On the ground the situation is different. It can be full of crevasses – small, big, enormous. Crevasses really can be covered with snow bridges that give way when you least expect it. The cause of death, should you fall through one, is very rarely the impact on striking the bottom, as crevasses can be quite shallow. It is more likely to be the effects of cold – hypothermia – in a climber who is unable to gain purchase on the crevasse's slippery walls and thereby escape. The body's functions are gradually slowed until the heart stops, at which time you are almost dead. I say *almost* because resuscitation is sometimes possible even then. By immersing itself in one of Nature's deep freezers, the body is maintained, for a few minutes at least, in a form of suspended animation. This particularly applies to children. It is always worthwhile resuscitating a patient with hypothermia, however dead they look.

Having reluctantly accepted my fears of being avalanched, dying from brain oedema, or hypothermia, I now had to cope with the worry of crevasses. The experienced climbers would play havoc with my imagination by regaling me with stories of past accidents, near misses and tortuous deaths. 'You do know how to Prussik, don't you?' asked Peter, a wicked schoolboy smile on his face. Peter was a leading light in climbing circles and virtually assured a place on Everest the following year.

'Prussik? Prussik? What the hell's Prussik mean?'

Peter laughed, knowing he had me at his mercy. I had no idea what he was talking about. Certainly the low-key rock-climbing course I had attended in the UK had not even mentioned the word. So Peter set about teaching me to Prussik, a means of climbing out of a crevasse should you have the misfortune to fall into one. Despite his teasing he looked after me well and before long I could Prussik in and out of anything.

To reduce the chances of falling into a crevasse you need something on your feet to spread the weight. The choice is either skis or snowshoes. I hated snowshoes. They are incredibly hard work. Skis were simpler for me and I was pleased to find many others on the mountain felt the same. To go up major slopes on skis requires skins, now often synthetic, to be attached to their bases. If applied correctly, the skin hairs act as tightly gripping barbs on the way up but allow gliding on the way down. Skis and skins attached, and provision sledge behind me, I set off up the Kahiltna glacier.

There is plenty of time to think, as you trudge up a glacier's gentle incline. McKinley was being kind with her weather, so mostly gave us clear blue skies. I thought of home a lot, terrified what arrangements for our wedding were being made in my absence. Already Louise's plans to have a simple, quiet, cheap ceremony had turned into something costing a fortune. At current rates I would have to lock myself in the operating theatre, and not come out for a decade, to pay the bills. My wife does have one minuscule fault, however. She hates writing letters. All around me sat fellow climbers reading their missives from home. Some were Dear Johns, others full of emotion, still others torrid pornography. I received nothing. I understand the situation now, but it was unfamiliar then. Had she changed her mind? My colleagues detected my worries immediately. Expecting sympathy was a forlorn hope.

'Forget her,' encouraged Tim.

'She's got another bloke,' added Peter. 'Go and find someone else.' The banter of all-male SAS life was predictable. How I wished a letter, just one, would arrive.

My job, and inclination, was to hold well back in order to pick up casualties that might occur. Mark's knee was an example. By the time you have dealt with stragglers, the lead climbers have already gained the top and are coming down with their own injuries. It is therefore easy to miss out on reaching the summit altogether.

As we went higher, so injuries and altitude sickness became more common. Wind and sun, in particular, took their toll. Steve, fiercely committed to the idea of Everest, spoiled his chances by sustaining full thickness sunburn of his lips. Full thickness means what it says. The skin covering is burnt away, exposing the raw flesh beneath. It is incredibly painful, making eating and drinking almost impossible. The thick white glacier cream worn by climbers, and seen so often in mountain-adventure photographs, is vital. Snow being highly reflective, it is possible to be burned under the chin, behind the ears and, worse still, up your nose. It pays to take care. In Steve's case, his sunburn meant he would be unable to demonstrate his true skills on this Everest preparatory expedition.

At 4400 metres, and at the top of the Kahiltna glacier, was the Headwall, the crux of the climb, the part that separates men from boys. At the bottom of the Headwall the Americans had placed a research station for high-altitude medicine, doctors watching in bemused interest as climbers went past in either direction and in various stages of disrepair. By the time I reached the Headwall I had dealt with Mark's knee, the sunburnt lips, a number of more minor injuries, plus a case of life-threatening lung swelling – pulmonary oedema. The lead climbers had already returned from the summit, some with their own injuries, leaving me little time to make an attempt myself. Competition was fierce. Everyone knew that barely half those climbing McKinley would be selected for Everest the following year.

I set off up the Headwall early one morning, accompanied by Steve and his sunburnt lips. All credit to him. Despite awful cosmetic injuries, and barely able to speak, let alone eat, he wanted to try. SAS determination, I suppose. He was glad to have me around, and I him, as he was a technically excellent climber. I do not think even he realized the depth of my inexperience. Three-quarters of the way up McKinley you do not expect to find someone who has never donned crampons before. We decided to climb unroped. Should you fall, you would only injure yourself, not your climbing partner. Behind us, only fifty feet below, came an American team.

Up I went. Ice hammer in, crampon in, ice hammer in, crampon in, slowly working my way up the Headwall. I was petrified and did not dare look down. I must have been doing a reasonable job as an American below me shouted up, 'Hey! You're looking good! Where did you learn to climb? I thought you Brits didn't have any big mountains back home.'

I shouted back, staring directly at the Headwall to my front. 'Thanks very much. It's my first climb actually. I'm ****ing scared if it's any consolation.'

'Your first time? Jesus Christ!' came up from below.

Tentatively I looked down to see the disbelieving, open mouth of my unknown American companion. The entire American team, seven in all, were moving sideways across the Headwall rather than upwards behind me. I knew why. If I fell unroped, anyone directly beneath would be pushed off the face. They were moving out of the way to allow me a clear solo descent should I fall. I'll show the bastards, I thought.

After much muttering, blaspheming and cajoling from others, I made it to the top of the Headwall. Steve was a major asset. 'Come on, Doc, you can do it!' he would shout, whenever I showed signs of flagging. From the Headwall it was an easy climb, barely more than a stroll, to the base of the final summit ascent, an area called the Igloopex. By this stage I was beginning to feel unwell. I was out of breath and disorientated. Steve was still supporting me well, confidently saying it was entirely normal to feel like death at altitude and I should not worry about it. Given time, it would settle. I did not believe him, but was damned if I was going back down the Headwall again without having a shot at the summit. It had taken every ounce of courage I possessed to get up it.

My night in a tent at the Igloopex was a lesson in high-altitude sickness. I had lectured about it, read about it, knew about it, but never experienced it. Every movement was in slow motion. Even unzipping my duvet jacket made me breathless and exhausted, while my head throbbed so hard I thought it would burst. When I tried to cook a high-altitude meal, my trembling hands spilled the entire contents of the container on to the tent's floor. So cold was the temperature outside, below minus 50 degrees Celsius, that the lumpy liquid set solid the moment it hit the groundsheet. I did not have the energy to clear it up. Instead, I lay there all night, half asleep and half awake. I was feeling terrible – completely helpless. If I had seen one of my patients looking as bad I would have evacuated him instantly, combined with a hefty dose of diuretics to help him pee off the excess fluid. The nature of high-altitude sickness, however, is that it makes you feel listless and acceptant of anything fate throws at you. I could not have cared less at the time whether I was alive or dead.

By morning I was worse. Steve was also looking bad, huge purulent scabs appearing round his mouth. Between the two of us we were not a good S A S advertisement. It seemed best that Steve should keep out of the sun as much as possible, so I decided to try for the summit alone. During my approach to it, it was necessary to cross a massive, steep, snow slope that seemed to drop away for ever to my left. For an expert climber such things are probably routine. For me they were horrifying. I made my way slowly across the slope. I knew if I fell I would die for sure, particularly as I was unroped. With an ice axe in my uphill hand, I dug its pointed shaft firmly into the snow as I walked, gripping it tightly. The fingers of my right hand felt very warm, despite the desperately low temperatures around me. It was a strange, tingling impression at first, at my very fingertips. What I was feeling was not warmth but the early burning of frostbite. So confused was my high-altitude brain that I did not recognize what was happening. The metal head of my ice axe was frozen. I had failed to insulate it properly with tape before leaving Fort Richardson and even a triple layer of gloves was insufficient to protect me. When I eventually descended the mountain I took off my gloves to view the damage. The middle three fingers of both hands were white throughout their length. They had not yet turned black – that would come later. It was certainly going to cause problems for my operating abilities, though I did know of one surgeon who still operated having lost a finger.

Ill-prepared, I had climbed the mountain and not paid attention to the cardinal signs of altitude sickness. I had gone on alone, leaving my climbing partner to suffer in silence. I had paid the price.

In retrospect it is a worthwhile experience to be on the receiving end occasionally, though I would not recommend frostbite. I was evacuated from McKinley with several other injured climbers and treated by medical staff at Fort Richardson. Thanks to their expertise, antibiotics and a pair of protective gloves, my fingers gradually recovered. The tips eventually turned black, and the nails dropped off, giving me three months away from practical surgery. I am left now with fingers that turn pale at the least hint of chill, but their full length still remains. I was lucky. Fingers have a remarkable ability to recover from quite significant insults. Even if a digit blackens, this does not mean it is destined to fall off. In earlier days, the presence of a black finger would lead to a formal surgical amputation the moment a patient reached established medical care. The situation has now changed, as it is possible for significant recovery to take place. Even if amputation is eventually required it is worth waiting as long as possible, as some length can probably be saved. I could see the bloodthirsty look in my surgical colleagues' eyes when I returned to the United Kingdom. I made sure I kept my distance. I learned a lot on McKinley, my first high climb – an excellent preparation for Everest.

I was a worried man on my return, having heard nothing from my future wife since I had left. I was certain she would by now be surrounded by dozens of other male admirers. Richard Villar would no longer be her agenda. I was wrong and delighted to be so.

The wedding went well, if one can ever remember much about such events. Mostly they pass you by in a mist. Squeezed into an ill-fitting, sweltering dress uniform and S A S beret, I married Louise in London within days of my arrival from Alaska. Fortunately dress uniform comes with white gloves, so I did not have to explain my black fingertips.

With McKinley conquered it was time now for the SAS to turn its attention eastwards, tackling Everest via its North Face. Logistically this was an enormous task as the Nepal–Tibet border was closed. Those wishing to climb the mountain's northern routes had to pass through China, and Lhasa, the capital of Tibet. The Chinese are not known for their administrative simplicity, so preparations made by Bronco and Brummie for this attempt were nothing short of miraculous.

For myself, having been caught out by Mark's knee in Alaska, I was going to make certain the same did not happen again. I resolved that any illness or handicap, however minor, must be completely settled before departure. I arranged to perform detailed, pre-expedition medical examinations, bringing the chosen fourteen climbers, of whom I was one, together one afternoon in Bradbury Lines. Due to their continuous and varied overseas commitments, it is a difficult task accumulating thirteen SAS operatives from different Squadrons in one location simultaneously. Somehow we managed it.

Louise volunteered to help perform the examinations. By then she had left the Army, though was aware of the dangers involved in high-altitude climbing. From my viewpoint, her participation in the expedition workup was both valuable and essential. I was about to abandon my lovely wife for months on end. Not only did she have the required medical skills, but it was important she was involved with events. However strong emotional ties may be, prolonged separations are asking for marital trouble. You must do what you can to avoid them.

In remote regions, mild toothache can become a raging abscess, a grumbling stomach can turn into appendicitis and so on. Louise and I were rigorous with the Everest medicals. Every lump was removed, every tooth cavity filled, every ache investigated. One climber mentioned occasional headaches. Nothing worrying, but an unusual story from a tough man who would normally claim fitness in every respect. As the pain was in the forehead, and behind his eyes, I sent him for an opinion from an eye specialist. Normally I would never have gone so far, but it paid to be safe. The eye man declared him normal. I also sought specialist opinions on a climber with mild asthma, a man with piles and another with varicose veins. All were dealt with, so that by 27 February, our day of departure, everyone was as fit as could be.

It does not matter where or how high you climb in the world, Everest is in a league of its own. Everest doctors began to appear from everywhere, each with an emotional tale to tell. I talked to young and old alike, gathering what information I could, soon realizing I was being gradually welcomed into a form of medical secret society. I was shortly to become an 'Everester'. That does not make me unique, but there are still not large numbers of us, however routine the media may make the mountain appear.

Civilian life is less sympathetic to strange habits such as climbing than the military. By now I had moved my orthopaedic practice from Aldershot to Southampton, a civilian job, though still with part-time connections to the SAS. I had also become a 'Mister'. It is a strange habit of UK surgeons. They work for years to call themselves 'Doctor' and then work even harder to relinquish the title. Surgeons in other parts of the world think it is very odd. Odd or not, *Mr* Villar was now my name. The Army will frequently provide fully paid leave for its soldiers to take part in so-called 'adventure training'. It is seen as an essential part of the job. The National Health Service is not always so supportive. Permanently strapped for cash, allowing its key players to disappear without trace, however honourable the intent, is not something it easily permits. To climb Everest I had to resign from orthopaedic surgery and turn my back on the profession I knew. There was no guarantee I would be employed again when, or if, I returned.

Much of the time the role of an expedition doctor is a mundane one. You are dealing with a largely fit group of individuals who are unlikely to let minor ailments stand in their way. Mostly you will not be told if a climber is ill. They are terrified you will stop them from climbing. There is intense, unspoken competition on these trips to be the first to the top. Final decisions as to who will form the summiteers are often left until late in the expedition. He who appears strongest at the time is normally selected. There is rarely an opportunity for many to make the top. Windows in the weather are few, so an expedition will put in a great deal of work, simply to place one or two climbers on the summit. Everest's casualty list, a Who's Who of mountaineering, speaks for itself. Not everyone makes it up and fewer make it down. The North Face is a particularly difficult choice.

All climbing arrangements in China had to be handled through the Chinese Mountaineering Association, the CMA. This formed a significant part of expedition expense, but at least ensured we were in the hands of local people. It was the CMA who negotiated such things as yaks, sherpas and the transit of stores. So it was that the 1984 SAS Everest expedition, Exercise Pilgrims Return, landed with a thump at Peking airport. Chinese Airways had sent a dilapidated Boeing 707 to collect us from our transit stop in Hong Kong. It was barely able to taxi, let alone fly. Probably the aircraft posed a far greater threat to expedition safety than Everest ever could.

It was in Peking we met our CMA companions, attached to the expedition for its duration. There were three, with wonderful Chinese names: Mr Chen, Mr Chow and Mr Lin. Lin was our interpreter and Chow a so-called 'life manager'. I never did establish what this was. All three were excellent company, though it was Chen who was the climber, or so it appeared. Much of his face was missing, his ears and nose being grossly scarred due to earlier frostbite. Stories flew round the expedition like wildfire as to how this had happened, though no one dared ask the man himself. Whatever the truth, he made Everest appear terrifying.

Food is a vital part of any expedition. Proper selection, and reasonable diversity, will do much to raise people's flagging spirits. In the middle of nowhere, miles from the nearest shop, fresh food is an impracticality. Everything must therefore be taken with you, in vast quantities. We had trialled a high-altitude ration on McKinley, but had made it so comprehensive it was physically impossible to eat everything. The only way of finishing a daily ration pack, whose contents were based on scientific calculations of energy expenditure, was to stay in your tent, cooking and eating all day. The rations were trimmed down for Everest, providing approximately 4000 calories per man per day. Even so, the quantities required were enormous: 1728 pepperoni sausages, 5184 tea bags, 6912 sachets of milk powder. Jim our ration man, and Larry his assistant, had done well.

From Peking we flew to Lhasa, a city 3700 metres above sea level. Consequently, on arrival by airplane, you experience instant high-altitude sickness. You notice it the moment the aircraft doors are opened, a feeling you have consumed a whole bottle of gin. Having suffered so badly on McKinley, I was accustomed to the problem and did not worry. Acclimatization cannot be hurried. You simply wait until Nature does the job for you. Occasionally drugs can be used to help the body adjust. One called acetazolamide is particularly common. Various local remedies are also said to exist, but there is no better substitute than gradual, steady ascent.

It was fascinating to see the climbers' reactions to altitude sickness. It was fair game for me to tell everyone how awful I felt. No one expects the doctor to be a summiteer, and feeling sympathetic to you often makes them feel better themselves. Every man was experiencing the effects of altitude. Sleepiness, breathlessness, reduced appetite and so on. No one would admit to it as if this was a sign of weakness. I could see the same again as we drove by coach from Lhasa towards Everest. Travelling through the smaller towns of Xgazi and Xgur, the road ascends mountain passes as high as 5300 metres. As we went up so the volume of conversation by all present reduced. As we descended so the volume resumed.

Everest's northern roadhead, from where it is impossible to drive further, is traditionally positioned by the Rongbuk Monastery named after the valley in which it lies. Once a thriving institution it was where famous names such as Mallory or Irvine, in the 1920s, would stop to be blessed before moving onwards to climb extraordinary heights. Those were days when protective clothing amounted to a tweed jacket and smoking was considered a good way of avoiding altitude sickness. The Rongbuk is now a dilapidated place, with a few local Tibetans, but little else to its name.

The noise in the Rongbuk Valley, and our adjacent Roadhead Camp, was incredible. Wind was continuous – a distant, persistent, low rumble overhead. I dictated a diary during our Everest attempt. Throughout it you can hear a fearsome, overpowering noise. The Everest range is continually battered by astonishing winds. It is no wonder that rock, ice and snow blocks can be occasionally shaken loose.

That day we did not arrive at the Rongbuk until late. Exhausted, and feeling weak due to altitude, the team went to sleep, paired in tiny mountain tents. For the first time in my career, an SAS team closed its eyes without posting a guard against enemy attack. Our enemy on this occasion was Mount Everest, unarmed, but more vicious than any terrorist or foreign power could ever be.

Sleeping at altitude is not easy, however exhausted you may feel. Insomnia is a classic feature of high-level climbing. Consequently many of the team took tablets, temazepam, to help them snooze. They appeared to have a remarkable side effect, one you can happily enjoy – the erotic dream. I have never seen it reported in the medical literature. The combination of Everest and temazepam allowed us to pass the night away smiling from ear to ear. Lie awake at night and you could hear satisfied grunting from tents all around.

Unfortunately, you will also hear Cheyne–Stokes breathing. Classically seen by hospitals in patients suffering from severe head injuries, the low pressure of oxygen at altitude can cause the same effect. It is an irregularity of breathing where the climber gradually breathes faster and deeper over a period of about a minute. Then, suddenly, he stops altogether. He stops, and stops, and stops. It can appear he will never start again. Just as you feel you should do something to help the climber breathe, he begins spontaneously once more. The number of times I reached for the emergency oxygen to resuscitate my tent companion was countless. No sooner had I turned on the cylinder, resuscitation mask firmly in hand, than he would begin to breathe under his own steam.

Panic attacks, attacks of breathlessness at night, are also common at altitude. You scrabble furiously to escape your sleeping bag and tent, desperate for air. In fact they represent the very end of the breathholding phase of Cheyne–Stokes breathing. You get used to them eventually. A double dose of temazepam, with a supererotic dream, is a perfect cure.

'Please sir, how do you go to the toilet?' is the commonest question I am asked whenever I lecture to schoolchildren about Everest. The answer is 'With difficulty, and with pain.' I did not realize this until one morning, after breakfast. The air was pierced by an agonizing scream.

Immediately my mind went into overdrive. Where was the emergency kit? Airways? Drips? Shell dressings? Good – I had everything ready. Then from behind our latrine boulder, a short distance away, staggered one of our climbers looking much the worse for wear. I went over to him. 'Jesus, Doc,' he said. 'That was ****ing painful. I don't want to go through that again. It's got to be worse than delivering a baby.' I knew immediately what he was describing. Fissure-in-ano, one of the commonest climbing problems you can find.

Low-fibre rations, due to lack of fresh food, make a climber's motions hard and solid. The human tail end, however floppy it may be, simply cannot stretch enough to let the stuff out. As with childbirth, if it won't stretch, it splits. When it splits, it bleeds. I can promise you it is genuine agony. It makes you terrified to open your bowels, so your motions get even larger and more solid, until you have a veritable explosion with which to deal. Local anaesthetic ointment for the tail end is a vital part of any expedition doctor's kit. On one occasion I had to use it on a yak. Fresh food, or liquid paraffin laxative, are alternatives.

As to how you do it? That is easy. The 'crap flap' reveals all. This is a form of Velcro-fastened rear fly that can be ripped open in desperation. It is largely impractical, and often unwise, to remove your trousers altogether at altitude. Your most precious parts can freeze solid if you do. I changed neither underwear nor trousers for the entire duration of our Everest stay, more than two months. When you all smell as badly as each other, nobody notices.

Each evening, when at the Roadhead Camp, the team would meet to discuss its various problems and difficulties of the day. It was great for keeping up morale. A vital part of this meeting was the rum. Military rum, fresh from Jamaica – what wonderful nectar. Each man was issued his ration, faithfully placing it in a white, screwtop plastic container. Glass bottles would have shattered due to cold. Unfortunately, white screwtop plastic containers were also used at night as urine bottles, to avoid the hazard of urinating outdoors in temperatures of thirty or forty below. Rum can be brown, so is concentrated urine. I made the mistake only once. At medical school I had been taught how Hippocrates had tasted a patient's urine in order to make the diagnosis of sugar diabetes. I had never thought I would use the same technique myself. I found urine-tasting foul.

Keeping the locals on our side was important. With the twenty yaks came an assortment of handlers. They, with Chen, Chow and Lin, would join us in the communal tent. In keeping with tradition, when a soldier made a mug of tea he would take a sip himself and then pass it round all others present. I could cope with my colleagues, even if this tradition of 'sippers' was an excellent way of transmitting disease. When the man next to you is a partially-toothed Tibetan yak handler, who has just coughed a large dollop of green, blood-stained phlegm on the ground, accepting a sipper from him requires immense self-discipline. I felt it was taking hearts and minds slightly too far. How I avoided tuberculosis, and other assorted Tibetan lurgies, I shall never know.

Yakhandlers can be temperamental. It was my management of them one day that nearly caused a general strike and risked bringing the expedition to a halt. The principle of any large climb such as Everest is to move stores and provisions forwards, a step at a time, camp by camp. Roadhead Camp to Base Camp, Base Camp to Advance Base Camp, Advance Base to Camp 1 and so on. You might require five or six camps to reach the top. At the lower levels the carrying is largely undertaken by yaks. Higher, over about 5500 metres, yaks do not perform well and all carrying is by man, be it sherpa or climber. I had not realized a standard yak load had been negotiated by the Chinese. Thinking the yakhandlers would be as enthusiastic as me to see the expedition succeed, I squeezed in an extra kilo of provisions here or there when asked to prepare loads for carriage, completely unaware of the festering sore I was creating. One morning, I heard loud voices babbling furiously near the yak-loading area. The handlers were discontented. Lin translated.

'Men not happy,' he said, throwing up his arms in Oriental exasperation.

'I can see that,' I replied. 'Why not?'

'Loads too heavy. Money not good. Problem.' As he spoke, the entire yak herd wandered off, driven by their apparently irate handlers. A yak can carry approximately three times as much as a climber. Without animals the expedition would most likely fail. I tried hard to grab the lead yak and prevent it from leaving, but it was a futile task. Yaks may be hairy, flea-ridden animals, but they are immensely powerful. I was simply dragged along in its wake. The first all-out industrial yak action, for all I know the only one in history, was in progress.

It was Chen who came to our rescue. A master of arbitration, by the day's end a modified yak load had been agreed. This was approximately fifteen per cent lighter than we had anticipated, so more animals would be required. With loads lighter, and secret money changing hands, the yak herd performed miraculously. Thereafter we had no problems – beyond their fleas of course.

It is often said that doctors on climbing expeditions do not need to know much medicine. Your patients are either fit, in which case they pose no trouble, or dead, in which case they can be left where they lie. Complex injuries and diseases that need detailed treatment are supposedly rare. At the Rongbuk I had a constant flow of minor ailments: laryngitis, bronchitis, burns, blisters and boils. There was even one case of housemaid's knee, and a broken dental filling, even though in your mind are assorted horrors such as broken bones, fractured skulls and the need to perform gut surgery in a tent. A doctor friend – a remarkable man – had to open a belly on Everest once. I do not envy him the experience. Nevertheless, despite the simplicity of most conditions seen on the mountains, there is an inexplicable fascination with all things medical at altitude. It is not unknown for expeditions to visit the mountain purely for the purpose of scientific research. There was certainly an American team on Everest 500 metres from our Roadhead Camp, comprising a large number of doctors, well-equipped and undertaking advanced scientific experiments at altitude.

A persistent memory of Everest is the intensity of the friendships created. Our team was strongly bonded before we ever arrived, by virtue of being SAS. Once on the mountain, and living in the confines of small tents, confidences exchanged can be deeply personal. I developed a soft spot for everyone and count myself lucky to have known them. They all had hidden strengths and, to a lesser extent, hidden weaknesses. I got to know Tony particularly well. He was an excellent climber. The two of us would carry loads together, go yeti hunting (we were, surprisingly, always unsuccessful), and discuss any aspect of life one might care to imagine. Frequently he would tell me how he missed his family at home, and how worried he was about climbing, even though he realized he was skilled at it. 'I want to be sure I get back alive for them,' he said to me quietly, one sunny Everest morning.

Peter was also a good friend, particularly after his valiant attempts to teach me Prussiking on McKinley. A strong man, he had persistently vomited and felt unwell when we first arrived at the Rongbuk. So bad was it that I asked that he be evacuated to a lower altitude for a few days. Tony, having developed persistent headaches and intolerance to bright lights, accompanied him. This is 'photophobia', a feature of mild brain swelling that may occur at altitude. It can turn into more serious things if prompt action is not taken. Dropping altitude was the required treatment. After three days at a lower height, Peter and Tony returned, fully recovered.

By early April the team was moving confidently. Equipment and climbers had gone forward from Roadhead to Base Camp, and from there to Advance Base. All was going well, with the lead climbers already at nearly 7000 metres – less than 2000 metres to go. The Regiment was set for a record ascent of Everest. All around were climbers from other teams struggling to cope. The SAS was clearly ahead.

It was at dawn that chaos happened. It had been a terrible night. High winds battered the sides of our tents, snow being whipped horizontally at colossal speeds. I thought nothing of it at the time but realize now it was the winds that probably loosened the massive ice serac on the North Col. A serac is a huge, overhanging ledge of ice, frequently found at altitude. At the Advance Base Camp one of the lead climbers, Merv, was standing outside his tent preparing for the day's climb. It was he who first witnessed the 400-metre length of serac break loose and fall freely to the bottom of the North Face, setting off a major avalanche as it did so. Brummie, in his book *Soldiers and Sherpas* describes the event admirably:

'. . . I heard Merv scream a warning, but it came too late. A chunk of ice whistled through the tent in front of my face and the whole world went crazy. The tent, with me inside it, was picked up and thrown down the mountainside by what I took at the time to be a big wind. I felt myself being lifted from the ground and rolled around the small blue capsule [*his tent*] as it was flung down the hill, all my kit tossing and tangling around me as we went. I was screaming with panic, convinced I was going to die without seeing anyone ever again.'

I escaped the avalanche, being one camp down the mountain from the scene, but was fully involved in the casualties it created. Tony had been killed instantly, only forty-eight hours after he had said how desperately he wished to return alive to his family. Brummie had strong evidence of a broken neck with pins and needles in his left hand, which implied injury was perilously close to his spinal cord. Full paralysis could be only millimetres away.

Two climbers had more minor injuries, though one had somehow survived a two-ton ice block ramming into his back. He had also developed frostbite on most of his fingers and one big toe.

The major issue was Peter. It had taken the survivors some time to remove the snow and ice blocks covering his head once the avalanche had come to rest. When an avalanche stops its slide you have little time with which to play. The snow sets solid, entombing those caught within it. All equipment had been scattered and destroyed, the camp being shifted half a mile down the mountain. Little more than a spoon survived with which to dig out a casualty. The result was the climber had a serious head injury, a broken collar bone, several broken ribs and was disorientated. With such injuries, his chances of survival at that altitude were small. Anything that reduced his ability to breathe, such as broken ribs, could easily tip him over the edge. The moment I saw him, I knew I had problems. Suddenly my quiet, organized existence had turned into uncontrolled medical chaos. The majority of my medical equipment, poised at the bottom of the North Face ready for the final ascent, had been destroyed. This included my mountain-rescue stretcher that I had so lovingly cared for during our journey from Hereford.

Brummie and the two more minor injured were able to walk down the mountain to Base Camp without assistance, though I knew Brummie ran a risk of paralysing himself. It is part of basic first-aid training that you do not move a patient with a broken neck, except with the utmost caution. A bone fragment has only to shift a few millimetres for full paralysis to be the result. There was little I could do about it, except quietly hope his well-recognized strength would see him through. We decided the best thing would be to place the injured in a tent at lower altitude. For those injured who wished it, I gave an injection of a drug called chlorpromazine. This is a strong sedative, allowing the patient to gather his thoughts and strength. The Americans used it widely in Vietnam for battle stress. It works wonderfully.

It took most of the day to settle the injured in their tents at Base Camp. It was already beginning to get dark. My major worry was

Peter. He had been half-dragged, half-pulled down the mountain to Base Camp and could barely speak. He was in a very bad way. One eye pupil was bigger than the other, implying significant brain damage, and he was Cheyne–Stokes breathing furiously. With the other casualties settled, each being cared for by an uninjured climber, I could concentrate more specifically on him. That first night with Peter is etched on my brain.

As I lay beside him in the tent, his breathing irregular, I noticed his colour. Instead of pink, it was blue, particularly his lips and fingernails. This is called cyanosis and is a feature of insufficient oxygen reaching the body's tissues. When he did breathe, I could tell he was struggling for air. Then, without warning, he lapsed into unconsciousness, grunted loudly and stopped breathing altogether. This time it was not Cheyne–Stokes breathing but airway obstruction. Lack of muscle control allows the tongue to flop backwards in the mouth, blocking the air passages. You have about ninety seconds to correct the situation before the patient dies. With trembling hands, I struggled to retrieve an airway tube from my rapidly depleting medical pack, forced open the climber's clenched mouth and pushed down the tube. The cramped environment did not allow me to see where the tube ended up, be it in the food passages or the airways, but immediately the man brightened up. I had been lucky. Putting a breathing tube down the wrong passageway is a sure way of killing a patient. I blew down the tube first, as a form of artificial respiration, before attaching an oxygen cylinder and hand-operated air pump to make him breathe.

Peter did not breathe independently for several hours. During that time I lay beside him, working the air pump by hand, to keep him going. Thank God he still had a pulse, I remember thinking. I had no wish for him to have a cardiac arrest in addition to his breathing problem. We were still at 5500 metres, well above the Rongbuk Monastery. Somehow Peter had to reach the Roadhead Camp.

Having put a tube down his throat, the process of intubation, I removed it three hours later when he appeared to breathe by himself. By lying him on the uninjured side, and keeping the head well back, his breathing was clear. By morning, having lain awake all night worrying, I was pleased to see my patient was partially recovered. He could remember nothing of the avalanche, nor of my frantic attempts to keep him alive. Beyond a headache and chest pain, Peter felt reasonable. He had improved so much it seemed possible he could walk down the mountain to the Roadhead Camp with little more than simple assistance. I, naturally, would accompany him. The other injured climbers also set off to the Roadhead that morning, Brummie with a primitive surgical collar to ensure his broken neck did not shift further.

The decision to walk Peter was a mistake, though heavily influenced by the knowledge of what it would take to carry him down. He was a big man, powerful and enormously muscular. Carrying would take at least six of us, and we did not have the men to spare. Having walked with him only 300 metres downhill from the camp, I realized he would not make it, his broad frame buckling at the knees. Any physical effort, however minor, made his lips and fingers turn blue. Cyanosis had returned. I tried carrying him, in a form of fireman's lift. It seems so easy in the books and films. In real life it is a struggle. On Everest I found it impossible. Furthermore, lying him across my shoulder compressed the injured chest, making it harder for him to breathe. His cyanosis became worse. We could go no further. If the man was to survive I would have to stop and resuscitate him once more. I radioed Bronco, positioned at the Roadhead, and told him of my predicament.

'I'm going to have to stop here for a while,' I reported. 'He's not going to make it otherwise.'

It was to Bronco's eternal credit that he complied with everything I said. Never once did he question my decisions. Later, Bronco did say I sounded frantic on the radio. I was convinced I sounded calm, so will have to do a better job of hiding my emotions if the same, God forbid, should happen again.

Assisted by an uninjured climber I pitched my tent in order to resuscitate Peter further. The moment I laid him horizontal he lapsed again into unconsciousness, though I fortunately did not have to intubate him. By now he was vomiting and incontinent of urine. Dehydration was also setting in.

Inserting a drip at sea level can be difficult. Inserting one on Everest was almost impossible. I had to skewer Peter more than a dozen times before my needle found his collapsed veins. The more shocked a patient becomes, the more the veins shrink, making them harder to find when you desperately need them. After much searching, I managed to insert the needle into a vein running along his forearm. Over the needle I slid a plastic tube, the cannula, until it was also in the vein. Then I removed the needle, leaving the plastic cannula in position. To the outer end of the cannula I plugged a length of clear, plastic tubing, the giving-set. It was to the giving-set I had to connect the life-saving fluid. There are many types of fluid available, from blood to pure water. All I had was saline, a medical salt solution. Reaching for the plastic saline pack in my rucksack, I found the lifesaving fluid was frozen solid.

If I was to administer saline at temperatures lower than Nature's 37 degrees Celsius, I would potentially lower the inner, core temperature of his body, causing hypothermia. Combined with his other injuries, he would be unlikely to survive. The saline was in a plastic container, not a glass one, as the latter would have shattered in the cold. I could not heat the plastic container directly or it would melt. I chose to steam it, like a Christmas pudding. In my rucksack was a large can of orange juice. That, too, was frozen. However, it was in a metal can that I could directly heat, so within minutes I had liquid orange juice, steaming furiously on my portable mountain cooker. I suspended the plastic saline pack from the tent, letting it dangle in the steam. Within twenty minutes that, too, was unfrozen, though I had to judge 37 degrees Celsius by feel. My glass thermometer had shattered long ago.

Within moments of the saline entering the climber's body, he began to recover. His eyes opened, his breathing steadied and he became more alert. It was a pleasure to see. Despite this, I realized he was too injured to walk and would have to be carried. Now stranded above the Roadhead, it was vital he descended as low as possible as he was still perilously ill. I was terrified he would develop further breathing problems if he remained too high for too long. Every foot mattered. Often, only a few hundred feet can make the difference between life and death.

With the mountain-rescue stretcher destroyed and a fireman's lift being an impracticality, I had no idea how to carry the man down. It was Bronco's suggestion to use the caving ladder, a thirty-foot aluminium affair used to cross crevasses and other dangerous drops. It was a brilliant idea. It had taken most of the day to resuscitate Peter once again, so we would have to remain where we were for a further night. Bronco, having buried Tony near the avalanche site, joined me at my impromptu camp for the night, ready to assist with the carry the next day. All night I lay again beside my patient, listening to his screaming and shouting. Though shortly on his way to safety, he was still disorientated.

A caving ladder makes an excellent stretcher. Once padded with sleeping bags and sleeping mats, a casualty is as secure as can be. It took eight of us six and a half hours to reach the American research camp. We only dropped Peter once, though he was fortunately asleep. I had sedated him for the journey as I had felt anything could happen on the way. In reality, evacuation went smoothly. The moment we arrived, out came the tea, soft drinks and an endless supply of American candy. Meanwhile Peter was taken off my hands, being thoroughly examined and assessed by their resident specialists. Despite his broken bones, head injury and disorientation, I was now happy he would survive.

I do not envy Bronco the terrible decision he next had to make. Should we now go back up the mountain and try again? Whatever conclusion he reached was bound, in someone's eyes, to be wrong. Tony was dead. It was obvious that Peter, and Brummie, should not continue. Likewise the climber with frostbite. Brummie's neck could still paralyse him and Peter could barely speak. They would have to return to more sophisticated medical care. Four men down, from a fourteen-strong team, and significant quantities of equipment destroyed, it was unlikely the SAS would succeed. Failure is not a word that comes easily to the Regiment, but I am sure the decision to abandon Everest was correct. Exercise Pilgrims Return was over.

Four days after the avalanche, the UK still did not know of our predicament. Satellite communication was only just coming into service and our team did not have it. The Tibetan driver tasked to take us from the Roadhead to Lhasa appeared overcome by events and decided to drive like an ambulance on a blue-light emergency run. Second only to the avalanche, he was unquestionably our greatest hazard. Within minutes of leaving the Roadhead, two casualties and me on board, he ran off the track, half overturning the Land Rover. I can hear my companion's screams now. We were fortunate not to sustain further injury and wasted no time in telling the driver what we thought of him. SAS operatives are a class apart when it comes to insults. He took the hint at that point, driving sedately thereafter.

The village of Xgur was our first stop. At first sight the place had little to its name. Dusty, primitive houses, overlooked by the tatty remains of the town's walls, perched erratically on the side of a mountain. Despite this, Brummie found a telephone, so together we tried to ring Hereford. It was not easy, though we eventually made contact with the Orderly Room. This is the one location, in any military barracks, where you can be certain someone can be found at all times. The line was terrible, the only way of passing the message being to spell it out, letter by letter, using the signaller's phonetic alphabet. A is Alpha, B is Bravo, and so on. It was painfully slow, and enormously expensive, taking four hours to notify the SAS and the Defence Attaché in Peking. I also tried telephoning Louise – no answer. The first she heard of the avalanche, I subsequently learned, was when a friend telephoned her to say it had been reported on the news.

As we travelled through Tibet towards Lhasa, I was relieved to see Peter steadily improve. The lower we went, the better he became. Even so, his behaviour was far from normal. He staggered rather than walked, demonstrating that the head injury was still having a profound effect. As a matter of urgency, I felt it was important he was admitted to the nearest Western-style hospital, probably Hong Kong. The Chinese Mountaineering Association, despite the expense, pulled out all stops to help, taking us through the land at phenomenal speed. Medically this was ideal, but I felt there might be more to their cooperation than simple medical urgency. A telephone conversation I had when we reached Lhasa, with a high-ranking officer in Hong Kong, explained all.

'The Commander of British Forces wants to send in an aircraft to pick you up,' he said.

'What? Into Lhasa?' I asked.

'Yes. He's negotiating with the Chinese now.'

'There's no real need, sir,' I replied. 'Peter is doing pretty well now. I'm sure he'll recover.' I could tell I was saying the wrong thing by the hesitation at the other end of the line.

'As I said, Richard,' came the top brass's reply. 'The CBF will send in an aircraft. He thinks it's important.'

'But . . . but . . .' I was interrupted.

'The aircraft *will* come. He's talking to them now. The CBF says it's vital. I'm sure you can understand what I'm saying.'

Politically it would be desirable to have an RAF aircraft landing on Chinese soil, at a time when such things were diplomatically forbidden. To use Peter as an excuse would be perfect. I was having none of it, irrespective of the consequences. There are times in one's medical life when you must make a clear decision between what is best for the patient, and what is best for everyone else. I have always chosen the patient. Peter was recovering, I was in control and the Chinese were doing well. I bade the top brass farewell, ignored the politics and had the climber in Hong Kong within thirty-six hours. I was damned if any patient of mine was to be used as a political pawn.

Six days after the avalanche I managed to talk to Louise by telephone for the first time. I told her I was alive, uninjured and on my way home. Wasn't that good news? No one could accuse my wife of being passive – perhaps it is her Scottish roots. Her reaction was typical. 'Do you mean you're giving up?' she asked incredulously. 'Seems a waste to me.' What else, after all, would you expect of an SAS spouse?

Despite her initial doubts, by the time we reached the UK's Brize Norton airfield, she had accepted our failure. As I burst through the terminal doors to greet her, my arms spread wide for a welcoming hug, I saw the look of disbelief in her eyes. Her usual smile had disappeared, replaced by a tiny frown that puckered the middle of a normally smooth forehead. What's wrong, I thought? Hasn't she missed me? Isn't she pleased to see me in one piece? I slumped my arms in disappointment. Then I realized the problem. The beard! I had grown a respectable, hairy affair that now covered most of my face. Recognition slowly dawned as she peered through my heavy disguise to see her husband beneath. Together we spread our arms, big grins on our faces as we now hugged. 'Darling,' she whispered in my ear, 'I do love you. It's wonderful to see you again.'

It is difficult to re-enter an orthopaedic career after climbing Everest. Your mind dwells so much on other things. If I were to succeed, taking absence from mainstream surgery would not be possible for a few years. You have to become part of the system, and the system is not found perched on the world's mountainsides, even though by now the high-altitude life was firmly in my blood. My ambition to work in the Third World still remained, but for the time being I had to become familiar with a wide range of orthopaedic operations to be of any use. Fractures, replacements, funny feet, funny knees, funny hips and so on. There was much to be done. I resolved to stay based in the UK for several years learning the various tricks of my trade. However, I would still visit the Third World on occasion, both to refresh my ambition to make a life there and to teach others what I could. In my shaky stumble up the orthopaedic career ladder I spotted what I thought was an ideal surgical job in Cambridge, that unusual centre of learning in an otherwise barren landscape.

The Cantabrigians did not make it easy, giving me an interview that made interrogation seem like child's play. I struggled through it, relieved when it came to an end. Most of the questions asked were impossible. Having sent me from the room, the panel duly deliberated, summoning me from my cold cup of tea to receive their decision. I was sure I had failed. I entered the room, took my seat and waited for the axe to fall. Before me sat the eight, sombre-looking men who had grilled me. The chairman spoke first.

'Mr Villar, we are delighted to offer you the post as an ortho-paedic surgeon here in Cambridge. Do you accept?'

'Me? Are you sure?'

'Yes, Mr Villar. You. We'd like *you*. Do you want the job?'

I nodded enthusiastically at that point, detecting an irritated tone in the Chairman's voice.

'Excellent.' I saw the sombre heads nod sagely, their faces still serious, though one did wink. At least I think it was a wink, it might have been a nervous tic. 'Do you have any questions for us, Mr Villar?' the Chairman added.

This was a strange turn of events, the interviewee asking the panel questions, rather than the other way around. What was I meant to say? Ask them about orthopaedics? The time? The weather? The pay? I struggled to think of a question, if for no other reason than to look intelligent. 'Yes, I do have one,' I eventually said to the eight pairs of raised eyebrows sitting before me. 'Your mountains. Where are they?' I could not imagine life without them.

The eight faces looked simultaneously shocked and confused. I saw them look left and right, conferring in low, deep voices. Slowly each shook its weary head. One even raised its eyes to Heaven, as if to beg forgiveness for the error they had made in offering me the job. The Chairman eventually spoke.

'Mountains, Mr Villar? We don't understand. Cambridge doesn't have any mountains. Surely you are aware of that? You might mean the Gog Magogs. Keep driving south-east from Cambridge. You can't miss them. That will be all. We look forward to you starting one calendar month from today.'

I had been dismissed. Nodding my thanks, I departed rapidly from the room, returned to my car and drove hastily south-east. I drove for miles and saw nothing that remotely resembled a mountain. Not even a mole hill. After thirty minutes I reached Haverhill, a major conurbation southeast of Cambridge. That, too, was flat. Perplexed, I drew the car slowly to a halt beside an elderly lady, pushing a ropy pram stuffed with shopping bags. In her tatty tweed overcoat she turned to give me a toothless smile as I wound down the window.

'Excuse me!' I shouted across to her, raising my voice to overcome the noise of passing traffic. 'Excuse me! Can you tell me where I might find the Gog Magog Mountains?'

'What luv?' came the reply. 'Gog Magog Mountains? We ain't got no mountains 'ere. The Gogs? Yeah. Little pimples just aht of Cambridge. You'll drive past 'em if you blink. But they ain't no mountains. We got none 'ere.'

Cambridge, how could you do this? I thought, as the terrible realization hit home.

CHAPTER 9

Terra Incognita

Pain shot up my left arm like an electric shock the moment the needle stabbed my finger. 'Sod it!' I yelled, as I disturbed the peace of the normally quiet operating theatre. It had been a difficult, lengthy operation. A rabid boar had attacked the man, thrusting one tusk deep inside his chest. The lung had collapsed and bleeding had been heavy.

By good fortune the attack had occurred near the hospital, so we had been able to treat the patient before blood loss had been too severe. It was as we were closing the wound at the end of the operation, a normally simple task, that the accident happened. The hospital was so poor that I had to reuse the surgical needles. Single-use, disposable needles, commonly used in the West, were unheard-of here. The one I had selected had been used so often it was now blunt. Picking up one edge of the skin wound with my toothed surgical tweezers, surgeon's forceps, I had tried to plunge the curved needle through it. It would not go. Then, unexpectedly, the skin had given way and the needle had shot through – directly into my gloved fingertip, impaling me, and now buried almost to the hilt.

Such injuries, needlestick injuries, are part of the normal hazard of surgery. Provided neither you nor the patient have some ghastly disease, they are not a problem. But rabies. This man had been assaulted by a rabid boar and rabies was a killer. There was no known cure and no guarantee the inoculations I had received before leaving home would protect me. If any killer virus was left in the wound, however carefully I had cleaned it, there was a strong chance I would be a goner. This was the *terra incognita*, the jungles of India's Madhya Pradesh state, perhaps the most medically hazardous environment in the world.

I had been surprised by Cambridge. Surprised because I enjoyed it. I had not expected such tolerance of my peculiar ways. Having recovered from the shock of the 100-foot Gog Magogs being considered mountains (there is even a mountain-rescue team, would you believe), I settled into my new life as a fully fledged civilian. For the first time in over a decade I had no involvement with the SAS at all. Occasionally an ex-colleague would arrive in my clinic, seeking opinion on the delayed effects of some earlier war wound. Now and again I would receive strange telephone calls from unidentifiable voices, asking about peculiar tropical conditions that few in the UK had seen. Such contacts served to make me restless. My mind would repeatedly wander, as I gradually amassed experience in orthopaedic surgery.

To my horror, I found my ambitions changing. Whereas I had initially wanted to live and work as an orthopaedic surgeon in the Third World, I began to feel there might be alternatives. Cambridge, a major teaching and research centre, was giving me many opportunities. The chance to pioneer new operations, to instruct enthusiastic juniors and to set up specialist orthopaedic skills. Hips and knees I found particularly interesting, I suppose because so much of my SAS experience had involved injuries to those areas. The operatives were forever twisting knees and banging hips, so I knew a fair amount about them even before I became fully civilianized. Perhaps I would remain based in the UK, offering my services to whichever Third World country needed them, but for limited periods. That way I could maintain the UK connection, yet still be useful to the primitive peoples of the world. Louise also preferred the idea. The last thing she wanted was to be stuck in a mud hut overseas for the next twenty years. I had to sympathize.

After much deliberation, I thought I would try out my modified ambition. I wrote to dozens of charities, some of which are household names, while others are rarely heard of. 'If it is of any use,' I wrote, 'I can give you six months of my time. I am happy to do anything. You do not need to pay me.'

To my astonishment, of the 190 envelopes I posted, only two agencies replied. Voluntary service was obviously harder to enter than I had anticipated. Many of the charities had standing rules that did not allow anyone to work for less than a year, or eighteen months in some cases. Perhaps it was my SAS background, I do not know. When the first offer did arrive, it came as an unexpected telephone call, during a clinic in an orthopaedic hospital in Essex. It was the Afghanistan Support Committee, looking for someone to run ambulances into Russian-occupied Afghanistan, in support of resistance operations. I was sorely tempted at first, paying several visits to a shady-looking office in London's Shaftesbury Avenue. In the end I declined, mainly because information available about Russian troop movements was inadequate, making the venture too unsafe. By then I had also received an alternative, second offer from a Cambridge-based charity, Action Health. Perhaps I am becoming soft in my old age, I thought, but the small hospital of Padhar, in India's *terra incognita*, was enthusiastic for my help.

Study a map of India and the village of Padhar is nowhere to be seen. Situated 220 kilometres from the city of Bhopal, it is truly in the heart of the subcontinent. The village is in the state of Madhya Pradesh, a region of 450,000 hectares, an area that sprang to fame in the mid-1980s when the leakage of methyl isocyanate gas ostensibly caused tens of thousands of casualties. Defenceless locals died and choked while they slept. Their problems continue to this day. Chronic lung conditions, due to damage from the effects of poison, are a terrible way to die. Imagine being breathless to the last, when even minor exercise such as tying a shoelace makes you pant. It is awful. I have seen patients die from it and would not wish such a fate on anyone.

From Bhopal, a tiny road passes south, winding through mile upon mile of teak jungle. This is not the jungle of the Far East or Central America. It is dry, fairly open, with frequent clearings. It is not so oppressive, nor so claustrophobic, as the humid, tropical rainforests in which I had spent much of my SAS life. There is barely any habitation. This is the home of the monkey, the panther, the elephant and every other form of jungle wildlife imaginable. It is truly an unknown land – *terra incognita* – named by the British during their Indian rule. It was not a region that early mapmakers would happily enter. If they did there was a fair chance the *dacoit* would see them as prey.

Yet one man had the foresight to go against the grain. Not only did he travel freely through the area, but also lived and worked in the villages around Padhar as a missionary. His name was Clement Moss. He began work in 1939, but after twelve years felt he could do something more for the enormous health problems of India's rural peoples. He decided at the age of thirty-six to become a doctor, entering medical school in India's Punjab, despite being British to the core. As a highly articulate, intelligent man, qualification did not take him long. Medical degree in hand, off to Padhar he went. At that time there was nothing in the area beyond an orphanage, a dispensary, a church and a once warlike tribespeople – the Gond. Quite illogically, or so it appeared, Clement decided to build a hospital in Padhar, the very heart of the Indian jungle. To many, placing a hospital there, for it is truly isolated, was a futile exercise. The essence of hospital construction is to place them near populated areas. What use is a hospital without any patients to treat?

Clement guessed correctly, being driven by a faith that few have the privilege to understand. With the help of local tribespeople he physically built the hospital himself. He even supervised the manufacture of the bricks. He estimated it would make no difference where a hospital was positioned. If it was good, people would travel to it. Furthermore, Padhar was a market village, on a road of sorts and so easier than most to reach. He was right – it was a well-chosen site. Now, with 200 beds to its name, Padhar is a thriving institution that sees more than 3000 patients each month. It is a true phenomenon.

Isolation unfortunately has its perils. In particular, staff become lonely and it is difficult to fill posts as a result. That was where I was needed. Having turned my back on Afghanistan, I was looking to use and develop my surgical skills somewhere that people both needed and appreciated them. Padhar seemed ideal.

A feature of primitive areas, particularly if local people are uneducated, is the variety of disease one sees. They are often different to those back home. I was fortunate that SAS service had done me proud. I was used to living in isolated surroundings, coping with contaminated water and the strange diagnoses that go hand-in-hand with the Third World. In Britain we have our share of bunions and back pain, coughs and colds, arthritis and epilepsy. In Padhar it was more common to see diseases like tuberculosis, polio, vitamin deficiency or cancer of the throat. Your medical perspective changes once you get there.

Neglect is a problem. Patients travel for miles to visit Padhar and appear with conditions that have been present for ages. It would not be strange to see someone with a broken leg, for the first time, four weeks after the accident that caused it, or an infection that had been discharging pus for a year. Because diseases are so advanced, treatments that are effective at home do not necessarily work in the Indian jungle. Take a child's dislocated hip. In the UK I would hope to solve the problem easily with mild, albeit prolonged, treatment. The same condition in Padhar, because it will have been present for longer before detection, would require lengthy, high-risk surgery without guarantee of success.

It was into such an environment I was thrust one sunny Monday morning in September. Struggling from a Land Rover that collected me from Bhopal airport, I extended my hand to greet the hospital's superintendent, Vincent Solomon. I was feeling awful. Already, a brief stop in Delhi had managed to poison me when I had foolishly downed an ill-cooked hamburger. Vincent, an experienced orthopaedic surgeon, smiled broadly, as if he had known me for years. 'Dr Richard? Welcome,' he said. 'This is Padhar Hospital.' Though I had never met him before, Vincent's reputation went before him. He had trained worldwide, not just in India and, though an orthopaedic surgeon, was just as skilled at a variety of other operations – Caesarean sections, womb removals, opening skulls for bleeding, even repairing a birth-deformed heart. He was also brilliant at badminton. This level of surgical talent is only rarely

seen in the more developed countries as specialization has inter-
vened. In Padhar there was no choice. If the job was not done
there, the chances were the patient would die. You could not be
surgically choosy.

I was given little time to think or prepare. As Vincent walked
with me the short distance to the hospital buildings, he described
the situation in a precise, efficient tone. 'Once we heard you were
coming, Dr Richard, we advertised in the newspapers and on radio
and television. You can do that here. We have had an enormous
response. More letters than you can imagine. We have filtered out
the serious ones . . . Watch out!' He grabbed my shoulder tightly,
pulling me back from the edge of the dirt road. A massive, overladen
truck whisked by, horn blaring, exhaust fumes pouring into the
atmosphere. Even in *terra incognita* I could see pollution was a
problem. I watched the tail end of the vehicle disappear into the
jungle, scattering chickens, cows, children and dogs before it. The
driver had no intention of stopping, whatever stood in his way.

Crossing the road to the main hospital gates, I could see everywhere the thriving community that had developed around the
complex: dozens of roadside stalls offering food, refreshments,
odds and ends, even a haircut. Some poor fellow was being assaulted
by the barber as I stared. A fine head was being reduced to a
pale shiny pate before me. The barber saw my gaze, shouting
incomprehensibly to me as he brandished his comb and scissors.
Vincent shouted something equally impossible back. I saw the
barber recoil in horror at his words. 'He says you are next, Dr
Richard,' explained Vincent, obviously enjoying the occasion. 'I
told him he can cut *your* hair after you have done *his* operation.
I think he will keep quiet for a while now.'

Approaching the main hospital buildings I could hear the low
murmur of many voices, though there were few people to see.
Vincent guided me up a small wheelchair ramp, following signs
indicating 'OPD' – the Outpatient Department. Despite my distinctly unstable stomach, already sounding orchestral, I was looking forward to this. Cambridge had been turning me soft, so the
challenge of a rugged Third World clinic was something I relished.

It was as we rounded the final corner I almost changed my mind. The low murmur had now become an unbearable din, hitting us hard the moment we entered the patient waiting area. The place was jammed with people, an immense mass of them. There must have been at least 300. A clinic in the UK would be regarded as big if it saw more than thirty. Men, women, children, crutches, wheelchairs, even a few patients crawling. It seemed as if all humanity had descended on Padhar that day. Vincent's advertising would have done credit to a major conglomerate, so excellent was the response.

It was impossible for me to deal with every case, particularly working through an interpreter. Hindi and Gondi are the local languages. My abilities in either tongue are appalling. An interpreter may seem a good idea but frequently loses those little nuances of expression that are so important to a doctor. Patients often tell you they are well when, in fact, they are as sick as a dog. Particularly so when they have some ghastly sexual problem. To make the best of a clinic, you have to speak the local language, preferably like a native. Clement Moss could speak six of the things with an accent that was indistinguishable from the original. I can barely speak my own.

Women struggle to be heard in Padhar, despite the heroic efforts of Vincent's wife, Meenakshi, to raise their profile in Indian society. That first clinic showed me how far they have to go. A large, overfed woman perched herself precariously on the patient's chair to one side of my desk.

'*Namaste* – hello,' I said, hands clasped firmly together in prayer-like fashion as welcome. With this one word I had already exhausted my knowledge of the local tongue. The woman did not move. She simply looked at me – a vacant, expressionless stare, half smiling. Perhaps I had tried the wrong greeting, I thought. Never mind, there was a job to do.

'What is your problem?' I asked, now in English. I had given up with the interpreter as I had caught him asking a patient the World Cup football score instead of taking details of a painful hip. 'Is it your knee?' I added. There was a fair chance this would be so.

Vincent had known of my interest in the joint and had advertised widely.

'Oh yes, doctor. It is her knee,' came the reply. Only it had not come from the patient but from some distance away. I glanced around me. The consulting room was bursting with people, more than fifty in its tiny area, hundreds more milling outside. Orderly queues did not exist and appointment times were a forlorn hope. The rules were simple – every patient tried to be first. A clinic auxiliary would attempt valiantly to keep order, but was frequently flattened in the rush. Through all of this he would maintain a calm, controlled exterior, plying me with soft drinks and tea whenever I looked overcome. He was a lifesaver that man. Once a patient had made it into the consulting room, his next task was to find his way to the chair beside my desk. That might mean elbowing dozens of other unfortunates to one side. Crutches were ideal. When in trouble they could be used as spears. Plaster casts also made vicious clubs for fighting your way to the front.

So it was that day as I searched through the morass of bodies, trying to identify the voice. From somewhere in the middle of the crowd I could see a small, dark head bob up and down – jumping up on its toes, trying desperately to be seen. I could tell it was a man, not a big man, but unquestionably he was trying to attract my attention. 'Her knee, doctor. Her knee. Pain,' he shouted, his arm waving frantically above the heads of his fellow patients. Then, slowly, at times forcefully, I saw him push his way through the bodies to reach the side of my desk. He collected dozens of irritated glances as he moved. 'My wife,' he added as he breathlessly gained his destination, pointing to the large, silent, motionless creature in the chair. 'My lady wife.' I learned then that most consultations with women took place through their husbands. No matter that you might seek information on menstrual cycles, piles or vaginal discharge, the husband answered all.

Women also appeared to have a raw deal in marriage. I confess to a small degree of male chauvinism. However, rural Madhya Pradesh tested even my tolerance to the full. During my first weeks in Padhar, I noticed several women were admitted as emergencies with burns. Sirpandi Bai was one of them. She had awful injuries. As I walked into her small room, away from the main hospital ward, I could smell the rotting flesh. Sirpandi was a beautiful woman, what little of her I was allowed to see. Young, no more than twenty years old, with a delicate appearance. Her normally smooth face was now lined with distress and racked with pain. Her top half, above the belly button, was fine. Below that level was a mangled, infected mess. It took all my self-control not to vomit as I pulled back the single sheet to examine her. Apart from a small area at the top of her right leg, the skin was missing from the rest of her. Bright red flesh shone like a huge, bloody beacon. Small patches of black, dead tissue hung off her in thin strands, as green pus began to seep from several areas. The bed was stained with body fluids. Not urine, but serum secreted by the exposed flesh. The sight was horrific. Full thickness, infected burns affecting more than 50 per cent of her body. Sirpandi Bai would die for sure. Worse, she had no family or friends to sit with her. She was suffering her fate alone.

Sirpandi's crime had been to marry without a dowry following her. It had been promised, but had never appeared. Arranged marriages still exist in Indian society and are largely very successful, but a dowry is usually agreed beforehand. There is unquestionably a business element to many Indian partnerships. Within months of the dowry failing to materialize, Sirpandi had sustained her terrible accident. Some would say it was bad luck, something that Nature had decreed, but Sirpandi was not the only one. During my time in Padhar I saw this fate befall more than six young women. Rumour had it new wives would be disposed of by fire if the dowry did not follow over the marital threshold. Rumour is not always accurate, but six cases says more than bad luck. Often at dead of night, the unsuspecting victim would be thrown on to an open fire, or her flimsy dwelling set alight. Petrol could not be used as this, of course, would be obvious murder. Rotting to death is not a pleasant way to go. Sirpandi died two days later. Overwhelming infection of the raw flesh, combined with kidney failure, were more than her young frame could take. Fifty per cent is a large skin area to destroy. Even professional burns units in the West would have had their work cut out to save her. This was *dahej hatya*, bride burning or dowry death, in action.

Life appears cheap if you are a Gond, particularly where children are involved. Mothers become used to losing one in every four to the ravages of local disease. If you reach sixty years of age you are doing well. People have simply become accustomed to death. This was brought home to me forcibly one day, when Vincent and I went to Bhopal to meet Louise. She had decided leaving her husband to his own devices in central India was unwise. Why shouldn't she join in the fun?

That day, early in the morning, I met her at Bhopal airport. The place is like something from a Cold War spy novel. Battered rectangular buildings, largely deserted, watched over by bored security guards armed with dilapidated Lee-Enfield rifles. Each guard looked identical. Black, macassared hair painted firmly to a greasy scalp. A neatly manicured moustache decorated the upper lip while huge, symmetrical sweat stains dampened each armpit. Sleepily they would wave people by, whether or not they were boarding or disembarking the various rickety aircraft that landed from time to time. By then I had been working in the Indian jungle for two months and was totally accustomed to Indian life. Such a scene could have been repeated throughout the land at various key installations. I no longer regarded it as strange.

I wish I had taken my camera to record Louise's expression as she staggered down the aircraft steps that morning. I could tell she was overwhelmingly relieved to be alive. The airline had supplied its oldest, tattiest, rattliest airplane to fly her from Bombay. Her image of the country had been that of guidebooks, of *Passage to India*, or of *Plain Tales of the Raj*. Properly dressed in her Jaeger tropical suit, to be suddenly faced with the real, rural thing was a major shock to her normally tolerant system. 'Darling, where have you brought me?' was all she could say. 'And look at *you*!' I was now truly local, looking every bit the missionary doctor. Open sandals, battered khaki trousers and tatty shirt. I was also very thin, shabby clothes hanging from a bony frame. Gastroenteritis had attacked at least four times. Weight loss was a foregone conclusion. As I hugged my wife in welcome I could see one bored security guard perk up. For a brief moment something different was brightening his day.

'What does *she* see in *him*?' I could hear him think.

'Wouldn't *you* like to know,' I was tempted to reply. Contrast in marriage is a good thing. I have always been suspicious of dating agencies that match like with like. It sounds terribly boring to me.

With Louise and me firmly wedged into the back of the hospital's white, battered Volvo, Vincent drove steadily south towards Padhar. It was a single-lane road, more a track, full of potholes and hazards. You officially drive on the left in India, but it can take several days in the country to work that out. Blind corners, subsidence, fallen trees and reverse cambers are everywhere. Unlicensed lorry drivers, high on *ganja*, marijuana, try desperately to control their overladen charges, many of which physically capsize *en route*. This occasion was no exception. The Bhopal–Padhar road, if it can be called such a thing, is a lesson in survival. Should you meet anything coming in the opposite direction, you accelerate, hoot, flash your lights and generally play chicken. Then, in the final millisecond before disaster strikes, one of you steers from the road into the surrounding jungle. Vincent handled this alien driver's environment supremely well. You have to be brought up in the land to understand it. It was he who broke the silence, as Louise and I sat rigidly in our seats, back-seat driving incessantly. Our white-knuckled hands gripped tightly on to anything we could find.

'Oh no!' he exclaimed. 'I don't believe this. Look! There! On the road.'

I peered through the chipped, dirty windscreen of the rattly Volvo. Dust was everywhere. Several hundred metres to our front I could discern the shape of a pile of rags on the roadside.

'What about it?' I asked. 'It's only some rags. Perhaps they will be collected later.' I strained to make more of the shape as we lurched closer. Louise and I both realized what it was simultaneously.

'Oh God!' she cried, 'It's a body!' A body it was. Splayed across the road, its head split wide open and crushed. Brains stained the irregular dirt while the rest of the corpse was untouched. I had heard of it happening before, though had never seen it. Tired tribesmen, recovering from the rigours of the day, would lie by the side of the road to sleep. At times, no traffic would pass for at least an hour, so they would be lulled into a false sense that all was fine. Slowly the head would drift from roadside to road itself. The next lorry, driven by a man equally tired and possibly drugged, would run over the tribesman's head, squashing it hedgehog flat. The man was as dead as they come. Instinctively I wanted to stop, if nothing else to remove the corpse from the road. But then I remembered – this is India, and in India you drive straight past, even if you do have a car full of doctors. There was nothing to be done for the poor fellow anyway.

Water contamination is a major cause of disease in rural India. As in my jungle SAS years, human or animal faeces can easily find their way into the water supply. Gastroenteritis – gut rot – is the result. Padhar is remarkable in this respect, as water can safely be drunk from the taps, thanks to the foresight of Clement Moss and the ongoing slog by those who followed him. It is not easy to keep water drinkable in such regions. However, it can give a false impression of the situation outside the village, where drinking from a tap may be asking for trouble. Most travellers, not that many venture as far as inner Madhya Pradesh, arrive in India armed with sterilization tablets, filters and assorted items to keep waterborne disease at bay. Human nature being what it is, regular use of such things is difficult, particularly if you are in the land for more than a standard holiday fortnight. To expect a Gond tribesman to use them at all is unrealistic – he will not. Clement solved the problem by drilling deep into the dusty soil to take water from several hundred feet down. Such *tube wells*, being so deep, are difficult to contaminate, given even the most unhygienic tribesman.

Despite these efforts, gastroenteritis is everywhere. Travel by Indian train any day around dawn and you will see hundreds of locals striding purposefully across the fields to their favourite rural spot. In their left hand they will carry a small aluminium pot of water. This is their equivalent of loo paper and explains why you do not eat with your left hand in India. For that matter you do not touch anyone with your left hand either, as this can easily be taken as an insult. How many times have you eaten with your hands and noticed food stuck under your fingernails? The same is true for human excrement. Once you realize it, there is strong incentive to keep left and right hands separate on the Indian subcontinent.

Gastroenteritis can be a killer and is one of the commonest causes of childhood death in rural India. Padmi, a lovely two-year-old girl, was a typical example. Her mother, a Gond tribeswoman living twenty kilometres from Padhar, had carried her through the jungle once she realized all was not well. I can see the mother now, head covered, bowed with worry, searching frantically for assistance at the hospital gates. She was not crying, which I have never seen a Gond do, irrespective of circumstance. They are a fatalistic lot. In her arms lay Padmi, a tiny creature despite her two years. The child's skin was so wrinkled, when I pinched it between finger and thumb it did not spring back. It stayed there in a heap, like some tiny mountain. Padmi's eyes were sunken, sparse hair straggled, arms dangling limply towards the ground. With each irregular breath, her whole body seemed to jerk. Anyone could see she was dangerously ill due to gross loss of her body's water – dehydration. Cholera kills this way. The stuff pours out of the patient so persistently they cannot make it to the loo. Special cholera beds have been designed with conical holes in their centre. Patients lie flat on their backs, watery diarrhoea pouring forth until either death or cure intervenes. As treatment, all you can do is to replace what comes out.

Padmi was desperately sick and needed rehydration rapidly. It was her only chance. If gastroenteritis is treated sufficiently early then rehydration solutions can be given by mouth. In Padmi's case, she was beyond this. She was so ill she would not have the strength to swallow. Rehydration by intravenous drip would be needed. Ignoring local protocol, I grabbed the mother by the arm. The

woman still tightly hugged poor Padmi's limp frame, as I force
marched her towards the children's ward. The hospital did not
have bleeps, Louise was visiting villages in the countryside and
most of the medical staff had gone off for the afternoon. I was
sure Padmi would be better treated by the medical side; it was not
an operation she needed. I knew also how difficult it was slipping
a drip needle into a dehydrated baby's veins. So dry has the patient
become that blood vessels shrivel up and disappear. Paediatrician
– children's doctors – and that included Louise, were brilliant at
finding veins that no one else could see.

I had marched the mother only twenty yards when I realized we
would not make it to the ward. Padmi's body gave a soft grunt
and her back arched alarmingly in her mother's arms. Then, in an
instant, she died. Her eyes, dry and covered with a transparent
sticky film, were half open. It was too late. Resuscitation, I thought
I've got to resuscitate. I reached out to grab the little body from
her mother to lay it on the ground. There I could at least begin
heart massage. But the mother refused. Quietly, very sadly, head
still bowed, she turned from me. I stood transfixed as she walked
away, Padmi's body in her arms. The now lifeless head flopped
up and down as she carried the once lovely girl into the surrounding
jungle. I have no idea where she went. Human tragedy is everywhere
in Madhya Pradesh.

One French couple stand out in my mind. They had volunteered
their services to work in Padhar for several months, before going
onwards to a mission station elsewhere in India. Very bravely they
had turned their backs on everything at home, setting out to make
a new life among the poor of India. They brought with them
their small child, aged only eighteen months. Predictably, and
unfortunately, the little boy developed gastroenteritis. With medical parents able to deal with the problem before it got out of hand
there was fortunately no risk to the child's life. It did mean copious
nappy changes for several days. This was not a problem – until it
came to the Chief of Police.

It was Vincent's idea. Always keen to promote Padhar in the
eyes of both the world and Indian politics, he makes strenuous

efforts to maintain contact with various authorities both in and outside the country. It is one of the secrets of his success. During my time in Padhar, and I have returned there six times over many years, I have treated politicians, social bigwigs and influential businessmen, as well as the poor and impoverished of the land. Money from the well-off is always used to treat the poor. It is an excellent, Robin Hood style arrangement and something other health systems should notice. Late one evening, eight of us paid the Chief of Police a visit at his official residence twenty kilometres away, in the town of Betul. Louise had not joined us. However, the French couple, and their little boy, did form part of the group. At the residence, Vincent ensured I was seated next to the police chief who, within seconds, was discussing the ups and downs of medical care in the area. The remainder of the group sat patiently and quietly, listening to us talk.

So intent on the conversation did I become, that I failed to notice the general stampede, only two minutes later, when everyone except the Chief of Police and me dashed from the room. It was only as the smell struck home that I realized all was not well. It was a penetrating, pungent odour that was impossible to tolerate. My eyes watered, my nose stung, my throat contracted, trying hard to keep the vomit down. I could see the police chief change colour before my eyes, a shade of purplish green, as he, too, began to suffer. I forced myself to continue the discussion, though my constricted gullet would barely let me speak. I knew immediately what it was – the classic odour of gastroenteritis. The little boy had been caught short and the parents had decided to change his nappy. Rather than leaving the room, they had ducked down behind a high sofa to perform the task there and then. I imagine even they had not reckoned on the vicious smell of a gastroenteritis stool. Within seconds it had cleared the room of most human life. It was worse than an SAS gas assault. Choking for air, the police chief and I staggered wheezing from the room. Tears streamed down our faces. I was certain I had breathed my last. Our negotiations? Fortunately he saw the funny side, though our discussions were never completed.

Your chances of acquiring disease or injury in the Third World are higher than with any amount of service with the SAS. My experience in the operating theatre with the rabies-infected needle was a classic example. With a thirty-day incubation period, the time it takes for the disease to appear, it took seventeen days to reach some vaccine. The rabies doctors I consulted went crazy and insisted I had a full course of injections – not a happy experience. I am obviously here to tell the tale, but it does highlight the risk to health workers. The moment you put your hands inside a patient's bloody wound, whether you are gloved or not, there is danger of cross infection. Anything the patient has, you can acquire. Anything you have the patient can acquire.

Hepatitis, an inflammation of the liver, can be transmitted this way. There are three major types – Hepatitis A, B and C – and many other, more minor variations. Vaccinations exist for A and B, not for C. Even in the UK, one in every hundred people carries Hepatitis C and knows nothing about it. The carriage rate is higher in India. It can be extremely infectious and destroy the liver in no time. As a surgeon it is best to assume *everyone* has it and behave accordingly in the operating theatre. At home I wear three pairs of reinforced gloves and special protective hoods and gowns. In the Third World such items are expensive and only rarely available. You therefore take your chances if you intend to operate in such circumstances. It is quite possible you can acquire a disease for which there is no known cure. HIV is another example. What a disease. India now has one of the fastest growing HIV carriage rates in the world. When over 40 per cent of your patients have it, and still you must operate, irrespective of the risks to yourself, it concentrates your mind acutely. Even so, given a toss-up between operating on a patient with HIV and one with Hepatitis C, far more infectious, I would choose HIV any day. The risk is cumulative. The more you do, the longer you do it, the higher your chances of picking something up. Naturally, the moment you develop any one of these diseases, your career is over. You cannot be in a position to give disease to your patients. They, of course, are at perfect liberty to give one to you.

Not all treatments in Madhya Pradesh require a surgeon. As with many Third World countries, local quacks and medicine men abound. One remarkable individual is the bone setter, based 160 kilometres south of Padhar. As Vincent and I sat in the various interminably long hospital out-patient clinics, we saw several patients who had been treated by the man. It was Vincent who made the first, complimentary remark.

'He seems to be doing a good job, Richard. Look – this patient has a broken thigh bone that has now mended perfectly.' He indicated a young railway worker who had walked 120 kilometres simply to show us the excellent results of his treatment. Three months earlier he had broken the bone in a road accident. Now, he was able to walk with barely a limp. Vincent thrust the large celluloid X-ray films on to the flickering illumination box. I could see the outline of a perfectly united bone and nodded my approval. The result was good. 'Let me show you the bone setter,' Vincent added. Within an hour we were on our way in the hospital Volvo, bumping and thumping along even dirtier roads, penetrating further into the countryside.

The bone setter's clinic, if that is what one can call it, was a primitive affair. We had arrived unannounced, so it was impossible for the man to prepare. Low ramshackle buildings surrounded a dusty courtyard. Mangy dogs and sleepy, thin cows were everywhere. The fresh, clean, disinfected smell of clinics so frequently found in the West was not a feature there. Mostly we weaved our way past animal droppings and the general detritus of an impoverished society. Within the gloom of the most ramshackle dwelling of all I could see the shadow of a man hard at work. Vincent strode through the open door, shouting a greeting at the fellow. They knew each other well, though both were at different extremes of the bone-disease spectrum. Through Vincent as my interpreter, I greeted the man and then peered further into the gloom, inspecting him as closely as I dared. The bone setter was perhaps fifty years of age, unshaven, untidy, with gums stained red from incessant chewing of betel. Dressed in dirty, baggy, dishevelled garb, he smiled a half-toothless smile as we entered, indicating we should stand quietly to one side of the room. To call it a room is an exaggeration. The house was half twig, half mud, with an earthen ground floor to its one room. The front door hung precariously from its one remaining hinge, the air inside penetratingly dank.

We had arrived at an ideal moment. On the crumbly ground lay a ten-year-old boy. I could see the youngster was in pain. The lower end of his left shin bone was angled alarmingly as a result of a break – a fracture – several days earlier. The bone setter indicated I should examine the leg before he commenced treatment. I bent down slowly, taking care to make no sudden movement. I did not wish to frighten the boy. No sooner had my hand come within an inch of the broken area, it had not even touched it, than the boy began to whimper. Gently, with barely any pressure whatsoever, I laid my hand on the deformed bone. Instantly, the lad let out a violent scream – 'Eeeaargh!' In the close confines of the shadowy room, the noise was deafening.

I lurched backwards, removing my hand rapidly, as if electrocuted. 'I'm sorry,' I whispered, not that the boy could understand. 'Let me try again. I won't hurt you. I promise.'

It was no use. Whatever I did, however I tried to examine the broken limb, I could not get close. Each time I so much as brushed the broken area with my fingers, however gently, the boy would thrash his head from side to side and deliver a piercing scream. 'Eeeaargh! Eeeaargh!' It was not a good demonstration of British bedside manner.

Vincent leaned towards me in the half darkness. 'Let the bone setter show you, Richard. Watch how he does it.'

As if on theatrical cue, the bone setter held up the palm of his right hand towards the boy, who immediately fell silent. It was as if the man was saying 'Don't worry – I'm in control now. The Englishman doesn't know what to do anyway.' He was probably right. The only way I could have dealt with the situation was to put the lad to sleep with anaesthetic first. Western medical training relies heavily on certain basic items of equipment being available. The bone setter had nothing except his hands, a pile of rotting rags and some seeds in a small heap on the ground near by.

'I see 400 patients every month, Dr Richard,' explained the bone setter, via Vincent's interpretation, as he stretched out a rag on the ground to his front. 'I charge them nothing, though sometimes they will give me small gifts in exchange. Chickens, pots and pans, that sort of thing.' As he talked, he retrieved a large, smooth oval stone from the shadows, moving it nearer to him. From deep inside his baggy, stained clothing he produced a small piece of pale root, no more than an inch long.

'Who taught you your methods?' I asked.

'My father. Before him his father. And before him his father. This has been with my family for generations.' Carefully, deliberately, he placed the root on the large oval stone, reaching behind him to retrieve another, smaller stone. My eyes had by now become accustomed to the shadows.

The bone setter continued talking as he worked. 'I crush the root like this, into a fine white powder.' Deftly, within seconds, the root had disappeared as he thumped and kneaded it between the two stones.

'Then I take some oil – sunflower oil – that I have made from these seeds.' He indicated the mound of small black seeds I had seen earlier. I saw him dip one finger in a small pot of oil and make a tiny smear on the ground beside him.

'What's that?' I asked.

'In memory of my father's God. It is part of the treatment.'

I was not one to argue. The whole procedure was alien to me, though I could see the young boy was equally fascinated. He remained silent, watching the bone setter's every move. Vincent, too, was quiet. He had seen this before and I could tell was interested in my reaction.

The bone setter picked up the fine powder between finger and thumb, sprinkling it on the surface of the thick oil. Then he set to, mixing it vigorously with a small stick until the powder had disappeared. 'Once it is mixed,' he continued, 'I pour it on to the bandage like this.'

I smiled at his use of the word 'bandage' to describe the thin rag on the ground before him. Skilfully he poured the mixture on to the cloth, in a narrow line from one end to the other. 'Then I take the bandage and wrap it around the boy's leg. Watch.' As he spoke I could see the lad lean backwards in fear and anticipation. Instantly the bone setter detected the worry, again holding up the palm of his right hand in reassurance. Visibly, the boy relaxed. Then slowly, very carefully, the bone setter wrapped the now-impregnated rag around the broken shin bone. The moment the oily cloth touched the skin I saw a transformation come over the boy's face. Instantly the pain settled, his eyes relaxed and the etched lines of distress disappeared. The bone setter smiled. 'There, what did I tell you,' he whispered. 'It's better already.' I was not sure who he was addressing. Me, Vincent or the boy. The effect was astonishing. He had achieved instant pain relief using little more than his hands and a crushed root.

'How do you *do* that?' I asked.

The bone setter turned, giving a half wink. 'That, Dr Richard, is my secret.'

The result was miraculous. As soon as the oily bandage was fully applied I could pick up the boy's leg, press it, manipulate it and be rough if I wished to. Pain was not a feature. He lay stationary, without symptoms, well able to tolerate anything I wanted to do.

I was dumbfounded. The bone setter also claimed he could make a broken bone mend within three days. In the West such things take twelve weeks minimum. Months later, on my return to the UK, I took some of the root with me, handing it to the scientists at London's Kew Gardens to see if they could identify it. I was sure, if I could find the secret, I would become a millionaire overnight. Ideas for scientific trials, and subsequent marketing, flashed through my mind. I nearly formed a company – 'Fractures Unlimited' I was going to call it. No such luck. Kew Gardens could not help and the bone setter was not letting on. He is one competitor I am delighted lives thousands of miles from Cambridge. He could knock spots off me without trying.

It was not only orthopaedic conditions that were treated in such novel ways, as Louise's experience with the community midwife demonstrated. In the developed world it is often regarded as abnormal to deliver your baby at home. In Madhya Pradesh the opposite applies. Community midwives travel throughout the villages, delivering children as they go. The workload is often so great that they cannot see every delivery, local elders coping with most routine births admirably. One problem at childbirth is splitting of the vagina. At the back, near the anus, is a thin bridge of skin and some very important muscles. At the *moment critique*, the child's head squeezes past, distending the vagina enormously. This is the time when the skin bridge, and the tiny muscles, can split. If they do so, the woman can be incontinent of faeces for the rest of her days. This is not a welcome complication. The community midwife's solution was simple – the birthing stone. A smooth, flat, palm-sized stone is pressed hard against the skin bridge and anus during delivery, particularly when the mother pushes to expel the child. This counterpressure significantly reduces the chances of splitting. The device, if that is what it can be called, was the midwife's only item of equipment. No forceps, no syringes, no modern medicines – just a birthing stone. I often see Louise looking longingly at the rocks and boulders of our flowerbeds at home, wondering if she ought to demonstrate the technique to our Cambridge obstetricians. She knows, as I do, what their response will be. A Cantabrigian birthing stone would not succeed. Perhaps, one day, who knows?

In our civilised society we are spoiled rotten, however deprived we may say we are. It is fashionable to criticize healthcare in the West by saying patients will die due to lack of equipment, or drugs, or staff, or whatever. That may be true, but such shroud waving is frequently an exaggeration, particularly when much of the world has to cope with so little. Improvization in rural India is essential. You are unlikely to be given the same instruments to do the job that you would receive at home. Compressed air may not be available for your bone saw, so doing it by hand is the only way. Gauze swabs for mopping up blood may be in short supply, so are reboiled between cases, used for any number of patients until incapable of the job. Needles and knives are used repetitively until they will cut or pierce no more.

Improvisation does not only apply to surgeons, as Louise's experience with tiny, two-month-old Srina shows. The little girl had developed awful pneumonia. Lips blue, breathing raspy and shallow, her ribs strained visibly for every breath. Death was not far away. Again, the mother looked on impassively, as local paediatricians fought to keep the baby alive. The father had long since lost interest. In his mind she was, after all, a girl not a boy. At such times it is vital the child receives oxygen. The lungs, blocked with pus and phlegm, cannot absorb enough from the surrounding air. The concentration in normal air is too low. It must be delivered in high quantities for sufficient to reach the blood. For an adult there is no problem. A mask is applied to the face and high concentrations of oxygen are delivered this way. For a tiny baby, keeping a mask in place is difficult, even if one can be found to fit. Such minuscule items were not available in Padhar, being both expensive and in short supply. Louise improvised instantly by manufacturing a substitute on the spot – a headbox. Once an established method of delivering oxygen to tiny babies, it had long since faded into oblivion in Western paediatric circles. It pays to know something of medical history when working in the Third World. On one side of a biscuit tin she cut a head-sized arch, while in the other she made a small hole. Placing the biscuit tin over Srina's gasping head, and a small-calibre oxygen tube in the hole, allowed high concentrations of oxygen to reach the infant's lungs. Instantly her breathing became settled, more regular, less laboured. A tin of chocolate biscuits had saved the day. We never did learn who ate the contents.

The type of surgery required in the Third World is different to that seen at home. Illnesses in rural India are similar to illnesses in the West at the beginning of the century. Your surgical style must be similarly ancient. Modern techniques and fancy up-to-date textbooks are of little use. My favourite book for Padhar was written in 1939, a comprehensive manual of archaic operations that worked brilliantly for the Gond. Many procedures I had never seen before, let alone performed. Vincent was well used to this existence and was often able to teach me what was required. Despite an extensive experience both with the SAS and civilian practice at home, I would still find myself out of depth. Sometimes even Vincent was stumped. When that happened we would both leap into uncharted territory, doing the best we could. If we did not operate, no one else would. Padhar was the Gond's only hope. There were many successes. Little Sunita, for example, with her dislocated hips. At four years old, the balls of her hip joints had never once been in their sockets since birth. The poor thing could barely walk. Slowly, and over a period of two years, we put her hip joints into their rightful positions. Sunita, and her parents, were delighted. In a society where the marriage prospects of a young girl are a feature of success, these operations transformed her life. Taking risks sometimes pays off.

Sometimes risk-taking does not pay. All surgeons live with such events on their conscience. No more so than my experience with Suraj. It started as a simple hip replacement, an operation I have performed more times than I care to remember. Suraj was a lovely man, about thirty years old, but totally crippled with spondylitis. Spondylitis is an inflammation of the spine and hips that slowly bends a patient over until he can only stoop. It can become so bad that it is impossible for the patient to look forwards. He can only look downwards, at the ground. To get a patient vertical, one way is to replace the hips so they can stand more upright. That is what I planned for Suraj.

All went well at the start. Suraj was soundly asleep, under anaesthetic, and positioned on his side on the operating table for surgery. I knew I had to operate quickly as the operating theatre did not have a special anti-infection airflow within it. The longer a surgical wound lay open, the higher the chances of infection. Bacteria are everywhere, even in the most advanced operating theatres. For major surgery units in the West, air is forcibly blown through the operating theatre so that bacteria are directed away from the surgical wound, not into it. No such luck in Padhar. Such air systems are hugely expensive. Operating quickly was a good second best. There would be less time for air bacteria to land in the wound and infect it.

I started by making the typical long, slightly curved incision in the skin. As I did so I felt something was not right. I could not tell at first. It was more an uncomfortable gut feeling – nothing specific. Then, four minutes into surgery, I realized Suraj's blood was turning blue before my eyes. No longer did the arteries spurt forth bright red streams as I cut through and around them. The blood was a dark, purplish blue – cyanosis, like Peter on Everest. 'Damn it!' I shouted, not a good thing to say in an Indian mission hospital. 'We've got problems! There's no oxygen in Suraj's blood!'

As I spoke, my voice raised and distressed, I could see the anaesthetist move quickly. 'Come on!' he said. 'Stop operating, and turn him on to his back! We've got to resuscitate him fast!'

At such times you cannot delay. Fancy stitching is inappropriate and takes too long. Quickly, without asking, I grabbed two large gauze swabs from the theatre sister's instrument trolley and forced them hard into the wound. Their pressure would control the bleeding sufficiently to allow us to resuscitate Suraj if we could. I would worry about stitching later.

In one swift movement, we turned Suraj on to his back to start heart massage, thumping up and down on his fragile chest. I could feel the ribs break as I pushed with all my strength, each shove squirting vitally needed blood to his oxygen-starved brain. I knew immediately the hip replacement operation must be abandoned. Saving life was now the priority. The anaesthetist pumped furiously on his breathing bag, delivering the oxygen to Suraj's lungs. I would massage the heart six times for every one of his bag squeezes. It was no use. However hard we tried, Suraj continued to decline. We failed. After eight hours of continuous resuscitation, by which time the entire theatre team was physically and emotionally exhausted, Suraj died. The spondylitis had so affected his spine that he had been unable to breathe, whatever we did to save him. The extra stress of a major operation had tipped him over the edge. His weakened frame had been unable to cope.

After Suraj died I was mortified. To have a patient perish on the operating table is a most terrible experience for a surgeon. I could see Vincent, his charming wife Meenakshi and the anaesthetist, all feeling the same. We knew it was possible Suraj would have died anyway, so advanced was his disease. That is not the point. When a patient is asleep on the operating table, he is *your* responsibility. You have talked to him beforehand, you have met his family, you have encouraged him to proceed. For a brief moment, during surgery, he hands himself to you in faith you will do your best. When your best kills a patient, it is something you never forget.

Louise and I returned to Cambridge from India very impressed. We had seen doctors work for almost zero pay in conditions that can, at best, be described as primitive. The dedication to their task is astonishing. I sometimes wonder if patients fully understand the enormous sacrifices such people as Vincent and Meenakshi make when they choose to set up shop in the Third World. I doubt the patients spare it a thought. With their skills, many Third World doctors could earn what they liked, wherever they liked. They choose, driven by enormous personal force, to stay where they are.

Once it becomes known you like working in outlandish parts of the globe, offers come from everywhere. For most civilian agencies, my time with the SAS was an unknown quantity. They did not know what to make of it. The moment I returned from Padhar, the situation changed. I had earned my Third World civilian wings and suggestions poured in. For a period I worked in Bulawayo, a two-month attachment to Mpilo Hospital. Here, HIV was again a problem. The first surgeon to die of the disease in the UK probably acquired the condition in that hospital. The day he pricked his finger while working inside the belly of an HIV-positive patient has now become hospital legend. My first stop on returning to Cambridge from Bulawayo was the virology laboratory for an HIV test. I was negative, I am relieved to say.

From Bulawayo it was off to Romania, in the wake of the Ceauşescu regime. This time, instead of orthopaedic surgery, it was my knowledge of medical appreciations that was required. A full report of a Transylvanian hospital, in the town of Zalau, was needed. It could have been the Third World. Facilities were appalling, training neglected, and one X-ray specialist had already died of leukaemia, a bone-marrow disease. I could never prove it, but I suspect this was due to the leakage of X-rays over many years. X-rays destroy bone marrow and doctors take great care to avoid unnecessary exposure as a result. An astonishing, highly motivated Cambridge character, Patrick Colquhoun, turned my recommendations into reality. The hospital was transformed. A remarkable man.

I did miss one thing, however. It is a terrible thing to say. It is, of course, entirely the fault of the SAS. I missed war. I hate it and yet I love it. I hate the misery it creates and yet I love sorting it out. I hate the worry it gives me and yet I love the challenge to control my fears. It is completely illogical and I cannot explain it. What I needed was another war zone to keep my system honed.

CHAPTER 10

Tortured Lebanon

I could see alarm on Fatimah's face as the Arab voices became louder. Rapidly, nervously, she shifted from one foot to the other, side to side, tilting her head to gather each word spoken.

'I hope there is not going to be trouble,' she said, craning her neck to see through the small, high window. No sooner had she spoken than the air was broken by two massive explosions, shaking the very fabric of the building in which we stood. My ears rang, a high-pitched whine, as the explosions died. AK47 shots at close quarters, fired in a confined space, make a terrible noise. Military training took over. Instinctively, I dived for cover under the examination couch beside me, flicking off the light switch as I fell. This was southern Lebanon, near the Israeli Occupied Zone, in the heart of Rashidiyeh Refugee Camp.

As I lay on the cold concrete floor, waiting for whatever might happen next, I looked up at the patient I had been examining before fighting broke out. He was an elderly man, perhaps seventy-five years old, with a previous gunshot wound to his elbow. His arm now stiff and immobile, he wanted me to return his elbow's movement. I had explained, through the good offices of Fatimah, my interpreter, that undoing the damage of war is often impossible. I had been about to suggest surgery, with all its limitations, when the shooting had started. The old man had seen it all before. Unlike Fatimah and me, he was unperturbed by the fighting and sat nonchalantly on the edge of the couch, one leg swinging impatiently to and fro. He looked disdainfully down at me grovelling on the floor and pointed at the stiff elbow with his good hand. I could see his eyes rolling Heavenwards. Briefly he said a few words in his deep, gruff voice. Despite my S A S Arabic training years earlier, I did not understand one syllable. Fatimah translated from behind her chosen cover, a rickety medicine cabinet in one corner of the consulting room.

'Dr Richard,' she mumbled, her voice trembling and unclear, 'he says, "Forget the shooting – what about my elbow? That's the only important thing here." What do you want to reply?'

Lebanon had seemed a good idea at the time, but as I lay on the damp floor I confess to having second thoughts. I had responded to a plea for help from Medical Aid for Palestinians, MAP, an enthusiastic and efficient charity based in London. When at home, I had been completely unaware of the enormous political and medical implications of such a task. The Palestine–Israel problem was not something I understood. Television broadcasts showed violence in both Lebanon and the Gaza Strip. Quite why it should occur had never crossed my mind. It was someone else's war, in someone else's country. To most of us, it meant little more than that.

It was only by going to Lebanon that I recognized the passionate views held by either side. Furthermore, it is my opinion that *we*, the British, have much to answer for. Somehow I do not think Winston Churchill liked Arabs. The scene was set before his time, with the Balfour Declaration of 1917, publicly proclaiming British support for a Jewish homeland. In the few years after the Second World War, and with British Government acceptance, almost one million Arab Palestinians left that part of Palestine the United Nations had decreed should become Israel. The majority left due to terror of what would happen if they stayed. They took with them their front-door keys, title deeds, insurance documents and a promise they could soon return. They never did and have been a people without homeland ever since. I can understand why emotions run so high. 'Why do you come to help us when your people caused the problem?' was said to me on numerous occasions in Lebanon. It was a difficult question to answer and a subject I tried to avoid.

It is difficult to travel that middle line, taking neither one side nor the other. I have both Israeli and Palestinian friends, some of whom are very longstanding. I hold them all extremely dear and wish desperately they could somehow reconcile their differences. I fear it will be a long and painful road before it happens.

My visit to Lebanon fortunately coincided with a phase of relative quiet on the battle fronts. This was important as it allowed opportunity for the after-effects of war to be treated. One naturally imagines that to be shot means death. In practice this is infrequent. More often, to be shot means permanent injury or handicap, not death. To correct damage caused by warfare represents some of the most demanding surgery known. There is no standard recipe for success. Each case is different, each patient a challenge. The combination of earlier SAS experience, and orthopaedic surgery, put me in the fortunate position of knowing how to handle both the immediate, and the after-effects, of war. These were the skills MAP sought.

Bullets quite naturally cause a significant degree of damage to the body. In order to appreciate why they can cause serious after-effects, a surgeon needs to understand how they cause their damage in the first place. There are two types of bullet – high and low velocity. High-velocity bullets are fired from modern rifles and machine-guns, travelling at speeds over 1100 feet per second. Low-velocity bullets come from handguns and older rifles, at speeds less than this. When a high-velocity bullet hits you it makes a small entrance hole in the skin, but explodes the flesh beneath to form a huge cavity – cavitation. From the outside, you can be unaware cavitation is present. All you can see is the bullet wound in the skin, the real damage being deeper inside. Cavitation only lasts a fraction of a second, but in that period sucks in dirt and debris from outside, contaminating the flesh. The bullet then travels onwards, often leaving a large, gaping exit wound. Occasionally it can ricochet off a bone, making it possible for a bullet to enter a thigh, for example, but exit the chest. Along this tortuous path everything cavitates. The damage such an injury causes is enormous and the shock to the body extreme. You do not have to be shot through a vital organ, such as the heart, to die. Shoot someone in the upper arm with a high-velocity bullet and it is quite possible shock and impact will be sufficient to kill outright, even if the bullet passes directly through. Should you be unlucky enough to be shot in the first place, that is.

Low-velocity bullets cause much damage, as one might expect, but no cavitation. Their effect on flesh is less and contamination is not a major problem. That is why it is vital to the success of early treatment to obtain an accurate idea of what weapon caused the injury. Looking at the entrance wound is of no value. Low- and high-velocity bullets can have entrance wounds that look identical. The two bullet types are handled in different ways. High-velocity injuries require radical surgery. The surgeon must cut open the whole bullet track, from one end to the other. If the bullet has entered the foot and exits the shoulder, for example, the patient is surgically opened from top to bottom. It is the only way to remove flesh contamination. If you then close the wound immediately, it is possible a small quantity of contaminated tissue can be left behind as it is very difficult to see each tiny piece of damaged flesh with the naked eye. Sometimes tissue continues to die *after* a bullet injury has occurred. For this reason, surgeons leave the track open for several days and then stitch it up later. If you do not do this, bacteria in the contaminated flesh can multiply and create a horrifying condition called gas gangrene. A particularly poisonous bacterium causes it, rotting the flesh and destroying the kidneys. Death is almost assured.

Low-velocity injuries, provided nothing major has been perforated, still require the surgeon's knife, but in a less radical way than their high-velocity cousins. It is often sufficient to clean and close entrance and exit points, and leave the track alone.

Once you realize that a bullet wound is not always a simple matter of two holes being created, one on the way in and one on the way out, with a perfectly clean track between the two, it becomes easier to understand why serious after-effects occur. Cavitated muscle may not recover, nerves that cause fingers and toes to move can be destroyed, or tissue can be so damaged that amputation is the only solution. Whole bones and joints can be shattered beyond any hope of reconstruction. On two occasions I have seen patients where the bullet has ended up inside the ball and socket of the hip. Both later developed arthritis as a result. Another, a ten-year-old girl, was shot in the head, survived, but developed a gradually expanding lump above her right eyebrow. For two years this became bigger until someone thought to X-ray her. The lump was a piece of bullet slowly working its way out of her skull.

My visit to Lebanon began well before leaving the UK, when a very overladen postman arrived at my Cambridge home. He was struggling with a thick pile of large brown envelopes. X-rays, the items he was carrying, are heavy in bulk. Arabic writing stood out on the various envelopes, though I was unable to decipher a word. On each one I could see the bright red stamp of the Red Crescent, the Palestinian equivalent of our Red Cross. As I studied them, I soon realized what an enormous task lay ahead. In the various Palestinian Refugee Camps of south Lebanon, a physiotherapist had been hard at work. She had gathered together a massive collection of war-wounded injured over several years. Some young, some old. Civilians, soldiers, men and women. The X-rays, and their accompanying case histories, said all. 'Bombed', 'Caught in blast', 'Shot', 'Sniped' and assorted vivid descriptions appeared in every case report. Each X-ray showed the typical bright, white, metallic shrapnel fragments, often surrounding smashed and macerated bone. Shrapnel, named after Major-General Shrapnel, describes the pieces of metal that fly in all directions when something explodes. Some are small, some are huge. Whatever the size, the damage shrapnel creates can be immense.

The physiotherapist, Miranda, had done an impressive job. It is rare to receive such detail of likely cases before visiting locations overseas. Normally you must do the best you can when you arrive and without prior warning. To realize what lay ahead allowed me to prepare and to advise Miranda of likely treatments so she could warn the patients what might happen. Some of the surgery needed was huge, often needing more than one operation. Certain deformities created by bullet wounds, particularly high-velocity ones, can be so serious that a single operation is insufficient to correct them. You may need to operate five or six times, each time correcting the deformity a few degrees. By the final operation you leave the patient with a limb that is perfectly aligned.

Miranda wrote seven times over the succeeding weeks, on each occasion enclosing a further mound of X-rays. 'Excellent physical training this, Doctor,' the postman would comment as he lugged another massive weight of envelopes along the gravel drive to my front door.

I began to worry Louise would think I had struck a secret affair with a woman she had never met, so frequent were the missives from Lebanon. It is a feature of most charities that everyone is immensely cheery, amicable and supportive. By the time Miranda and I had written to each other for the seventh time we were communicating like long-lost friends, though in reality we had never met. I did my best, involving my family in all arrangements, though knowing they could not accompany me on the eventual trip. Out came the maps at the kitchen table, the Lebanese guide-books, the histories of Palestine. I also listened carefully to Louise's sound medical advice as to what she thought I should do with some of the children's cases. Thus it was, by mid-September, I waved farewell to my family once more, now comprising Louise and three children, and set out for Lebanon. I cannot pretend I was relaxed. I was not.

Four of us went, two surgeons and two nurses, as I felt the work required was more than I could handle alone. Some of the operations were particularly complex and would need two operators at least. None had been to Lebanon before and each was full of anticipation, mixed with some worry, as to what lay ahead. The media does not help. Close-up shots of Palestinian youths throwing petrol bombs, or Israeli soldiers sporting Galil machine-guns appear every day. By the time your airplane has landed at a humid Beirut airport you are convinced your chances of returning home are lessening by the second. Modern warfare has never been a great respecter of the medical profession, many members of which have been kidnapped, tortured, murdered, shot and raped in various parts of the world. As a civilian, you are more exposed to these dangers than in the armed services. No longer do you have the protection of soldiers or Government behind you. Native wit and instinct are your only weapons.

We staggered from the exit doors of Beirut airport, though I noticed my surgical colleague, Fred, staggering more than most. A mammoth rucksack creaked and groaned on his back, his normally strong frame struggling to stay vertical. Had we been walking on sand rather than chipped concrete he would have disappeared to his knees. 'What on earth have you got in that rucksack?' I inquired.

'Just books, Richard,' came the reply. 'I thought we might need to look a few things up. Didn't know what they might have over here, so thought I would bring my own.'

Fred had, I think, brought every book to Lebanon he possessed, in case of being caught out by an unfamiliar disease or operation. It was his first time in a war zone. I laughed, having overconfidently assured him before we left England that I had seen it all before and there would be no need to worry. I would show him what was necessary. By the end of our short stay in Lebanon, I was eating humble pie. So horrendous were the cases, so insoluble the conditions, I, too, pored over Fred's books for answers.

It is difficult to know what to bring as a surgeon to such places. Do you take every hi-tech item known to man, or do you do the best you can with what is available? I have always chosen the latter course. Hi-tech equipment usually has to return home again, and cannot be left behind. It seems unfair to raise local hopes for the short period you are there, only to dash them once you leave. On one occasion I was visiting a Third World country in company with several surgeons, in order to demonstrate certain modern surgical procedures. One of my companions, a charming fellow and with the interests of our hosts at heart, took with him in his suitcases every item of equipment needed for major surgery. They rattled and clunked furiously through each security check, and were a guaranteed manual search whenever stopped. His luggage weighed tons. He could barely carry it and had left himself room for only a single pair of underpants as a personal item. By the end of our two-week stay, not only did he smell overripe, but he had not had an opportunity to use any of the instruments. Due to various reasons, the locals had cancelled our operation schedule. The mass of equipment returned to England unused and, by then, much hated.

The medical lot of a Palestinian in Lebanon is not a happy one. Money is unavailable for private care, while Government-run hospitals do not always offer the full spectrum of possible treatments. As a result, diseases, wounds and children's deformities can remain untreated for years. This was the country into which we stepped. Like Northern Ireland, every eye that stared was a potential kidnapper, every backfiring car a terrorist assault. Though it was early evening, I felt the cold trail of sweat run an isolated course down my back as I searched the mass of unfamiliar faces crowding the passenger reception area. Were we expected? God knows. Please come and meet us, somebody, I silently cried.

'You must be Richard Villar,' I heard a gentle voice say to my left, interrupting my incipient panic. I turned to see who it was and was glad to see a woman of European appearance, tanned, well-dressed and smiling in welcome. A gentle hand was extended as greeting. 'Hi,' she added. 'I'm Miranda.'

It is always a shock to meet someone for the first time to whom you have previously written on numerous occasions. So it was outside Beirut airport that evening. The occasion was slightly awkward, but we both had work to do, so there was little time for discussion. With the briefest of handshakes I was ushered into her dilapidated, certifiable, though much-loved car and driven south along the coastal road towards the town of Sidon. My colleagues were squeezed into a more modern version of the same, following close behind.

Miranda was a remarkable person. As a physiotherapist she spent much of her time dealing with bone and muscle problems, many of which had been caused by the ravages of war. A bullet through a child's spine, for example, can cause paralysis of everything below the point of injury and spasticity of the muscles. Spasticity makes the arms and legs rigid and tight, so the patient can barely move them. A physiotherapist can work wonders, loosening them up, eliminating the inevitable deformities prolonged spasticity creates. This is one tiny example of the many conditions they can treat, but however much physiotherapy you offer, some deformities will not correct without surgery to allow treatment to start. Once tight tissues have been released, the physiotherapist steps in once more. Miranda largely masterminded our visit as a result. Scheduled to leave the country shortly, after a long tour of duty with MAP, she wanted to be sure she had done as much for her patients as possible.

As we thumped our way along the cratered and potholed road in her rattly car, Miranda explained in her mild New Zealand accent what was involved. I was feeling uneasy. I always feel uneasy in war zones. Though Lebanon was reported to be quiet, such terms are relative. I now realize I was being unnecessarily alarmist, but my mental image of Lebanon then was one of bombs and kidnappers round every corner. Miranda, meanwhile, was completely relaxed, continuing her briefing as if she was driving down the centre of England's safest motorway.

'You'll be working from Hamsharry Hospital. It's in Sidon, next to one of the refugee camps,' she explained. 'It is the main Palestinian hospital in Lebanon. You are badly needed.'

As she spoke I felt the car slow. We were approaching a haphazard arrangement of oil drums on the road. I had heard of Lebanese roadblocks, the second most common point of kidnapping after Airport Road. The isolated trickle of sweat on my back was fast becoming a torrent. Miranda was unfazed, oblivious of the unnecessary worries continually flashing through my mind. She must have been through hundreds of the things. Road blocks were two-a-penny. I never did learn who controlled them though I believe the majority were run by the Syrian Army. On this occasion a good-looking young man, no more than twenty years old, put his head through the driver's window and smiled. On his shoulder was a gleaming Kalashnikov, oiled perfectly. I could tell from the way it lay against his shoulder the magazine was full. Most so-called armed guards in the UK carry a rifle loaded with thirty rounds of fresh air. The bullets either have to be kept in a tunic pocket or in the guardroom near by. Whoever thought that rule up had never been in a real-life contact with an enemy. The opposition is hardly going to wait while you run to retrieve your bullets so you can return fire. This young man had a fully loaded, and cocked, weapon. Arguing with him was not an alternative.

'We are travelling to Sidon, *al-Hamdu lillah*,' Miranda announced in excellent Arabic. 'This man is a surgeon who has agreed to work there.' She pointed towards me disdainfully, as if I was a piece of baggage. I felt exactly like one at that moment – a very sweaty mess.

The young man smiled further, revealing a sparkling gold filling in a lower tooth. Looking at me carefully, he inspected me in detail. Then, with a brief closing of his eyes, a mild facial sneer and a casual wave of his right hand, we were ushered past.

Hamsharry Hospital is a dominant building, standing immediately beside a Palestinian Refugee Camp in the city of Sidon. Of 1960s design, square and ugly, it is for most Palestinians their only real medical hope. Pockmarked by shrapnel, it houses several wards and two operating theatres. All around is evidence of rebuilding and reconstruction, an attempt to eliminate any trace of war. In some areas of Lebanon, particularly the Israeli Occupied Zones, this is a forlorn struggle. As fast as rebuilding progresses, another assault knocks it down.

In the cellar, now a storehouse, sit the remains of an old courtroom. Now untidy and neglected, one can imagine the earlier scenes of judgements made and punishments issued. Many would have been terrified to enter that room. Outside the hospital perimeter, day and night, gunfire can be heard. Normally intermittent, it can occasionally be continuous and severe. Stand on the hills that surround Sidon and you would be forgiven for thinking full-scale conflict was still in progress. Admittedly there are no major explosions, but rifle fire is persistent, the sound of either skirmishes or sniping. Southern Lebanon is unquestionably a paradox. It really is a land where you can sit outside in the evening with your ice-cold drink, looking at a sunset in one direction, but murder being committed in the other. Peace and war can take place at the same time in the same street. After a long day in the operating theatre, we would occasionally play games, trying to identify a weapon by the noise it made. As there was no way of confirming our various opinions, I imagine we were always hopelessly wrong.

Hospital staff were a hard, motivated crowd. They welcomed us with open arms, particularly as our way had been paved by Miranda. Most were very fit and very tough. Many had been fighters at some stage. Firm handshakes, and incredible courtesy, were the order of the day. You would always look a man in the eyes when you spoke to him. The slightest hint of an Israeli assault on a refugee camp or village, and the hospital would empty immediately. Staff of all grades would disappear to the area under threat to help. For most, an attack on any Palestinian was the same as an attack on themselves.

I never understood the various groups – Sunnis, Amal, Hezbollah, Palestine Liberation Organization, Popular Front for the Liberation of Palestine and many others – it was best not to ask as it would mean entering a political conversation that I wished to avoid. The uniting factor for all groupings was their universal dislike of the other side. Being a fighter, for whatever Palestinian cause, was respected. Those I met were astonishing people and had led a precarious existence for years. In certain of the camp wars, when the refugee camps had come under direct attack, irrespective of the vast number of defenceless civilians within them, the Palestinian fighters could spend weeks defending a tiny area no more than 200 metres square. Pinned down from all sides, and shot at if they showed themselves for more than a second, it was little wonder these people were tough. If it had not been for my Army experience I would have been daunted.

As well as the Palestinians, there are certain doctors who have upheld the best name of the profession under the most arduous of conditions. None more so, I believe, than Pauline Cutting in Lebanon. I had, of course, heard of her. Working as a surgeon during Beirut's Bourj al-Barajneh Camp siege, she continued supporting sick and injured Palestinians under the most deprived and stressful conditions imaginable. To read her book *Children of the Siege* is to see war surgery in its true perspective. Quiet-spoken, charming, I have never before met a doctor so admired by her former patients. Mutual danger and discomfort bonds mankind tightly – I had experienced that with the SAS. The same applied to Pauline and the Palestinians. They love, cherish and admire her. I know she would be too modest to admit it. It was certainly my privilege to meet her. One cannot underestimate the enormous stresses placed on someone under the terrible conditions she was forced to endure. Scars can remain for life.

Sometimes, when a patient walked into my consulting room I could sense the power inside him. Take Kayed, for example. He was both leader and fighter, standing high in local society; he came surrounded by several tall, heavily armed bodyguards. Running a clinic with Kalashnikovs in the room takes some getting used to. Fatimah, my young interpreter, did her best to translate.

'My knee,' said Kayed, his voice little more than a growl as he rolled up one trouser leg to mid-thigh. 'I cannot bend it. Please cure me.' His request made it appear as if success was a foregone conclusion. His guards nodded their heads silently in sympathy and agreement as they toyed ostentatiously with their weapons.

'How did the knee get like this?' I asked, trying hard to bend the stiff leg at the joint. It would not move. The skin was scarred and pockmarked like a Beirut wall.

'Israelis,' he replied. I could see the hatred in his eyes. 'I managed to kill several before they did this to me.' I knew I was on dangerous ground. It was important to take neither one side nor the other. I could see he was searching for compliments. I stuck to my trade, kept my head down and looked intently at the knee. However hard I looked, the thing would not budge. If he was to walk normally again, I would somehow have to free the knee up.

From a large, tatty, brown envelope one of the bodyguards produced two equally tatty X-ray films. Holding them to the dim window light I could see the white, metallic specks of shrapnel still buried deep inside the leg. Much of the thigh bone was missing, though time had done its best to fill the gap with irregular, thickened scar tissue. I nodded as sagely as I could.

'It's bad,' I said. 'Very bad. But I think I can help.'

'Can you make it normal?'

'No. That is impossible. But I can help you bend it slightly.'

'Can you be certain you will succeed?'

'No.'

'Why not? The people say your team is the best in Europe.'

'The damage is too great,' I replied, not wishing to be drawn into discussion as to whether we were good, hopeless or indifferent. 'There are some things even we cannot achieve,' I added, capitalizing on whatever reputation was being given us behind the scenes.

It never pays to bluff in surgery. In many countries patients will travel from surgeon to surgeon, physician to physician, faith healer to faith healer. Each will give a different opinion. Some will offer guarantees that are scientifically impossible. Being truthful and open is always best.

For a brief moment Kayed fell silent, then glanced either side to his bodyguards. All three nodded quietly. 'Then you must do it,' he eventually replied. 'You must do what you can.'

Kayed's problem was a straightforward one, despite the horrible appearance of his knee. He had been caught in a mortar burst two years earlier, a large number of shrapnel slivers, over twenty, penetrating his leg. The bigger fragments had been removed at the time, the wounds healing over the remainder, now lying deep inside him. The residual shrapnel was best left where it was, it was doing no harm. It is a common misconception that it needs to be removed. Trying to find tiny metal shards deep inside a bleeding wound is difficult. A surgeon's efforts may do more harm than good as the messy tissue makes it so easy to cut the wrong thing. Kayed's stiffness was due to much of the muscle having been destroyed at the time of the injury. His previously muscular thigh was now wasted and thin. When tissue is damaged, by whatever means, the body tries to heal the area. It does this by the formation of scarring. Though we normally talk about scars on the skin, they also occur anywhere in the body that damage has previously occurred. That includes muscle. In Kayed's case, scar tissue had replaced the muscle and scar tissue does not bend. If he was to bend the knee again, all scarring had to be removed – surgically excised.

Fred performed the operation while I looked on. It took ages. With a scalpel he made a long, vertical cut down the front of Kayed's thigh and knee, dividing the skin to expose the underlying bone and scar tissue. Scar is white in colour, like a tight, inelastic band covering a joint. You have to cut transversely across it first, so it is completely divided, then you force it further apart, bending the joint by hand. It requires both surgical dexterity and muscle power. You must be strong enough to grasp a large knee in both hands, bending it until it gives way. Orthopaedic surgery is not for the faint-hearted. Painstakingly slowly the knee began to flex, degree by degree. By the end of the operation the once stiff joint was able to move to a right angle or more. It was a masterpiece of surgery.

It is one thing making a knee bend under anaesthetic, as in Kayed's case. It is another to ensure the patient maintains the improvement once he wakes up. Bending a knee that has been stiff for two years, and has required radical division of scar tissue, is very painful. The natural temptation is for the patient to lie motionless after surgery, not daring to move his leg for pain. Within a few days the scar tissue reforms if the knee is not kept moving. Fred's work would have been in vain.

Our plan had been for Miranda, or a Hamsharry physiotherapy colleague, to provide intensive treatment once surgery was complete. We had not reckoned on Kayed's demands. He felt his bodyguards would do the job better. Perhaps he had something to prove. No sooner had he regained consciousness, back in bed on the hospital ward, than his men set to work. Ignoring their leader's cries for mercy, they worked the long stiffened knee to and fro. Straight and bent, straight and bent, straight and bent. You could almost hear Fred's carefully placed stitches breaking, one by one. It is difficult to argue with an armed physiotherapist, even if he is unqualified, but within a day the careful surgery had been ruined. Try as I might to explain to the bodyguards that operations of this nature needed careful handling after surgery, they would not listen. The result, within forty-eight hours, was that Kayed needed his operation repeated. This second time the bodyguards stayed their distance and Kayed's knee was a success.

Not all injuries in war are caused by bullets. Mines, particularly antipersonnel mines, are major problems. To a doctor they represent an unforgivable act of war. So often the injured are defenceless civilians. Should you see a civilian in a war zone minus an arm or leg, you can be fairly certain a mine has caused it.

The Hamsharry clinics were full of women and children with horrific injuries. It is immensely distressing to see a beautiful six-year-old girl, radiating health and charm in every way, yet absent a leg. Staggering into my consulting room on crutches, young Lamia was a pitiful sight. Her wide brown eyes begged me to do something that might help. 'Can I have another leg?' she asked. I could only say no, tears stinging my eyes. The best I could offer was a lifetime with an artificial limb. Hamsharry highlighted the immense civilian toll of the Palestinian–Israeli conflict. More than 90 per cent of the patients we treated were civilians. People without any clue as to how a weapon should be handled.

You only have to see an amputee child in a war zone once to hate mines for life. There are millions scattered worldwide. They are of two sorts: anti-tank (AT) and anti-personnel (AP). As an ex-soldier, the former I can understand, the latter I cannot. The object of anti-personnel mines, from a military viewpoint, is to deny certain areas to an enemy. For example, should you have to withdraw from a building or trench system, scattering anti-personnel mines is a quick, simple method of being certain the enemy cannot use the same building or trench for his own ends. Being small, the mines may also be used for booby-traps. For example, under toilet seats, behind doors, under doormats. Once the enemy moves on, the AP mine stays behind. Children frequently play on wasteland and derelict areas, favoured locations for mines, and are prime victims for AP injuries.

The object of an AP mine is to maim, though some are designed to kill. The intent is to place as much strain on the enemy's logistics as possible, by having to evacuate the wounded. There are two sorts of AP mine: blast mines and shrapnel mines. Blast mines are normally buried in the ground, requiring the victim to step on the device in order to trigger it. The dreaded Black Widow mine from Russia is barely two inches high and five inches wide, and needs only three kilograms of pressure to set it off. It can kill, but will certainly cause major leg injuries to above the knee. Amputation is likely.

Shrapnel mines are designed to maim or kill over a wider area, perhaps up to twenty metres from the device, often injuring more than one unfortunate at a time. They can be activated by pressure or a trip wire and will frequently spring to chest height before exploding. They are manufactured in many countries, including China, Portugal, the Czech Republic and, I am afraid, the United Kingdom.

Once a blast AP mine explodes, the human damage it causes is immense. Bones do not break cleanly, they shatter. Skin does not split smoothly, it rips. You are faced with a mangled mess that is impossible to reconstruct. If a bone breaks cleanly in two, it is simple enough to screw a metal plate across the break, or pass a metal rod down the centre of the bone, across the damaged area, supporting it until healing occurs. Orthopaedic surgeons do such things all the time. With AP mine damage, all you can do is tidy up what is left, maybe skin-grafting defects where the blast has blown the victim's skin away; and this usually requires amputation as well.

If you have to do this terrible operation, it is best to make the decision quickly, as soon as the injured patient presents. The shock of the moment is so great, you can capitalize on it and remove the limb rapidly, before the patient starts to worry how he or she is going to manage the rest of life without a leg. In reality, life with a good artificial leg is a thousand times better than life exposed to a sequence of major operations, trying to preserve a totally shattered limb. If the leg is not removed, two years later the victim can be jobless, spouseless and depressed – the result of repeated admissions to hospital with a still unsatisfactory result by the end.

The higher up a leg you perform an amputation, the worse the result. If you must lose a leg, best choose a below-knee amputation, rather than above-knee. Modern artificial limbs are so good that it is sometimes impossible to tell someone has had a below-knee amputation without very close inspection. They walk almost normally, sit naturally and do all manner of things like skiing, climbing and scuba diving. Amputate through the thigh, or worse still through the hip, the dreaded hindquarter amputation, and the situation is very different. Walking properly is impossible, often requiring a stick for support, and the artificial leg is a much bulkier arrangement. In short, do not step on an AP mine. It will upset you and certainly upsets me.

Throughout my time in Hamsharry I was impressed by the intense and close friendships between hospital staff. These were people who had witnessed more than anyone should see in a lifetime. War is a horrific institution, particularly when large numbers of civilian casualties are involved. No doubt the official line would be that civilian casualties are unavoidable in war. At times it was difficult not to think civilian targets were the prime object, so many innocent folk did we see. For some the psychological effects of war were extreme. After my experiences during the Falklands conflict I had to sympathize. Some would twitch, or scream, or simply breathe deeply the moment gunfire was heard. At times I felt like taking such people to one side, putting an arm around them, in an attempt to reassure. They were a pitiful sight – psychologically and physically shattered.

Bomb and blast injuries are a major cause of death or injury in war. These come from high explosive, delivered by guns, grenades or mortar. As well as creating shrapnel, high explosive causes blast. This is a huge pressure of air flying ahead of the shrapnel. If the metal does not get you the blast surely will. Because blast is an air effect rather than due to solid matter, hiding behind a wall will not help you. The only way of protecting yourself from blast is distance. The further you are away from the explosion, the less likely it is you will be harmed. The concept of blast causing damage is difficult for many people to understand. Imagine a massive shock to one side of the body, from top to bottom, only lasting a millisecond. The skin may stay intact, but the shock is transmitted deep into the body itself. The solid organs, bones particularly, can remain unaffected. Those containing gas or fluid, such as lungs, heart, ears or guts, can rupture as they are compressible. Eardrum rupture is particularly common, with permanent hearing damage not unknown.

'Blast lung' was a well-recognized condition in the Second World War. This develops after the explosion, often several days later and quite unexpectedly. Damage occurs to the lung tissue, reducing the body's ability to absorb oxygen from the air. Fluid also pours into the lung cavity, making it still harder to breathe. Victims require urgent Intensive Care treatment to survive, but in a war scenario such facilities are rare. You can therefore withstand metal shards flying past you, and think the blast was not a problem, only to perish later. Blast lung, should it happen, can be a killer.

Hamsharry Hospital showed us all of this, and more. Fighters, and defenceless civilians, would attend the clinics we held. Day and night theatre staff would pack, repack and sterilize the instruments we needed for our operations. It was an exhausting task. Not everyone we treated was Palestinian. The conflict has attracted its fair share of soldiers of fortune – mercenaries. One morning a tall, powerful African stumbled into my clinic, barely supported by a long wooden pole. Like his associates he had a hard, impassive gaze that looked directly through you. His problem was a hip replacement that was going wrong. Many years earlier he had injured his hip, the only solution then being to replace rather than repair it. Quietly he looked at me, his eyes unable to show pain, whatever he might be feeling.

'I can't move sometimes, doctor,' he said. 'My leg becomes stuck and I have to stay where I am until it loosens. It's a problem with the fighting.'

'You're fighting with that? With a hip replacement?'

'Of course. You look surprised. Is it a problem?'

I had to admire him. The mercenary's life can be a perilous one

– I have many friends who do it – but a hip replacement is not normally associated with successful soldiering. In the British Army, a hip replacement in a soldier would often mean medical discharge from the Services. Yet for more than ten years this huge man had done just that. Fighting for other people's causes with an artificial hip, albeit well paid. When I X-rayed the leg, it did not surprise me to find the replacement had come loose. Instead of being tightly fixed to the man's own bones, it was flopping about inside them. Any normal person would have been unable to walk.

The mercenary was desperate for help. In his precarious existence, when life could be snuffed out at any time, he had to be able to fight well. I suspected he was not qualified for anything else. I contacted our operating theatre staff and told them we needed to reattach a loose hip replacement. Though this is major, complex surgery, it has now become almost routine in the UK. In my mind, the job was as good as done.

'We cannot do it,' the theatre administrator replied.

'What do you mean? This man is in terrible trouble.'

'That may be so. But it is not possible for us. We do not have the equipment.'

'If he gets into battle again, he could easily die. There is no way he can run for cover or dash from building to building as he is.' As I spoke I could see the mercenary stagger around my consulting room, supported by the pole that bent alarmingly each time he applied his weight.

'Doctor,' the administrator answered finally. 'We cannot afford it. Funds do not exist. You will have to leave him.'

I wanted to argue, to insist the soldier's only hope of life was through my services. I knew it was hopeless. I was expecting too much – the door had been shut. The surgery was too involved and too expensive. I hate turning people down for treatment. I have always felt it was my job to keep going to the bitter end. Naturally a patient can turn me down, but not the other way round. It is an awkward realization as a surgeon that some treatments are not possible, due to the costs involved. It happens at home too, but it is difficult when you are the one who must tell the patient. When

I told the man there was nothing I could do, I was worried how best to explain the situation to him. I started to mumble, to um and to ah. The mercenary was not daft. He could see me hesitate, stumbling my words, and understood immediately.

'No money, Doctor?' he said bitterly, walking awkwardly to the consulting-room door. 'I thought that might happen. I guess my time is over.' With a brief look of hatred and resentment over his shoulder, he disappeared through the door. I shall remember that look to the end of time. If he had been armed that day I would surely have been shot.

For many years the Palestinians have existed in refugee camps at various locations throughout Lebanon. The original intention had been for these camps to be temporary. Before I visited, I imagined a camp would be line upon line of tents, communal water stands, poor sanitation and the like. I had in my mind an image of displaced people living under canvas for years. However, Palestinian camps can be thriving institutions, with schools, health centres, shops – a wide variety of modern conveniences. Some are very well cared for. Well-constructed buildings, running water, decent sanitation, are often found. This surprised me. Life has not been made easy for the Palestinians, irrespective of which side you support. At all levels they are a people who have had obstructions put in their way, whether it be negotiating a peace accord or buying a spare part for a dilapidated car. Full credit to these people for creating such an organized life in the face of such resistance, when all around refuse to help. I was very impressed.

Leadership is a vital part of this success against such difficult odds. A strong people needs equally strong control. One morning, searching for more surgical cases in a frenetic camp clinic and under Miranda's discerning eye, I came across firm leadership first hand. Fred and I had travelled south, near the beautiful harbour town of Tyre, to a Palestinian camp beside the Israeli Occupied Zone. Such camps are now in the firing line, being close to the Israeli border. You never refer to 'Israel' when discussing borders with a Palestinian. To them, Israel is Palestine.

The clinic was in full swing with Fred and me working in

separate parts of the small camp hospital. Miranda had done, as usual, superb homework before we arrived, filtering out only the most severe cases for us to see. I had examined more than twenty patients in the first hour and my mind was spinning with ideas. Fatimah, meanwhile, was interpreting well. Hospitality was immaculate. I was being plied with soft drinks regularly, as many as I could consume. The inevitable occurred. My bladder distended – I had to relieve myself.

I dashed next door to the tiny toilet. As I stood there, I heard the gentle scuffing of feet outside the door as a number of people filed past into the adjacent consulting room. It was a relief to hide from the chaos outside in this tiny, cramped haven of temporary tranquillity. I am a leg specialist at home, so the majority of patients I saw had leg problems. To assess them I naturally need the patient's trousers down, or skirt lifted. As I walked back into the consulting room my head was for some reason bowed, my eyes on the floor. 'OK. Take your trousers down,' I instructed, aware that another patient had entered the room while I had been absent. 'Let's have a look at you. Hop up on the couch,' I added.

As I spoke, I looked up to see Fatimah standing quietly, and very humbly, in the corner shaking her head from side to side. It was her way of saying, 'Not now, Dr Villar! Just shut up and keep quiet!' Beside her sat a smartly dressed man, small worry beads in his hand, wearing a perfectly pressed grey suit. Impenetrable sunglasses covered much of his clean-shaven face. As he looked at me he did not smile. To either side stood two tall bodyguards, each armed with an AK47 assault rifle. The man in the sunglasses, whoever he may be, was important. If you merited bodyguards, you were very important indeed. He indicated an empty plastic seat to his left. 'Sit,' he instructed in English. That was all. His voice was clear.

Obediently, like a domestic pet, I did what I was told. I could sense the power in the room. It was obvious that Mr Big, for that is what I will call him, was in control. I glanced across at Fatimah, raising my eyebrows quizzically, and as surreptitiously as I dared. She understood immediately, mouthing the silent letters 'PLO' back at me. PLO, the Palestinian Liberation Organization, was not something I knew much about.

Mr Big turned to look at me, his face breaking into the tiniest of smiles. Suddenly I felt very alone. Fred was still busy with his clinic elsewhere in the hospital, unaware of what was taking place. Nobody knew we were in the camp. We could disappear and no one would be any the wiser. Civilian aid workers, of which I was now one, take grave risks at times. Mr Big spoke.

'I have just one question for you, doctor,' he said. 'It is simple, but it is important.'

I could feel a tight hand gripping my chest as he spoke. That same hand seems to have travelled with me to many parts of the world, appearing suddenly and without warning. I could tell Mr Big was not a man accustomed to lengthy negotiations.

'What is it?' I asked, my mouth dry and barely able to speak. There was silence around us. Out of the corner of my eye I could see one of the burly guards quietly shift the position of his AK47. The muscles of my thighs began to shake minutely as my whole frame began to be overcome by an uncontrollable fear. Thank God I was sitting down. I felt I would physically have been unable to stand.

Mr Big spoke quietly. 'Doctor, tell me one thing. Are you here because your Government sent you or are you here of your own accord?'

What was I to say? There was obviously something very important about the question. Mr Big had travelled a long way, with his guards, to ask me this. I had now learned Palestinian politics are not easily understood by those outside. It is difficult enough for the people involved. What one man finds acceptable is, to another, a declaration of war. Would it be better to claim British Government involvement to lend authority, and hence safety, to my presence? The temptation was strong. However, the British Government had no idea one of their surgeons was currently absent without trace in southern Lebanon. The truth it would have to be.

'No, sir,' I replied, trying hard to penetrate the dark, forbidding, sunglass wall. 'I am here of my own accord. My Government hasn't a clue.'

The moment I answered, I felt the tension disappear in the air. The guard's hand shifted from his AK47 to a more relaxed position near his pocket and Mr Big smiled – a huge, broad smile. 'Good,' he said, 'that is the correct answer.' Then, instantly, he sprang to his feet and left the room, taking his entourage with him. 'Give him all the help he needs,' he ordered as he departed. I had been given Mr Big's blessing. A near miss? I have no idea.

For an impoverished people, and for many charities, cost is a limiting factor. My experience with the African mercenary had already shown me this. Furthermore, there is always someone who attempts to make a quick dollar from the situation. Take Mohammed, a fourteen-year-old Palestinian who had been shot in the hip joint two years earlier. He survived the bullet, but the damage it created was so severe that arthritis set in. By the time he was fourteen pain was crippling him. He could barely walk. I looked at the poor lad in the clinic, racking my brains as to what I could do to help. There were many alternatives, but the safest would be fusing the hip joint straight. We call such an operation arthrodesis. It is a big procedure, involving a large incision over the front of the hip and the damaged bone being cut away with a high-speed, compressed air saw. Once the damaged area has been removed, the remaining healthy bone is fixed together until it heals. Though surgery only takes two hours, the subsequent healing takes three months. The hip area must be held rigid during this period, so a large metal plate, with multiple screw holes, is needed. The plate is fixed to the pelvis above and the thigh bone below, bridging the hip area. It is an unusual operation to do, so the metal plate must be specially designed. It is shaped like a cobra snake and is called, not surprisingly, a cobra plate.

The moment I saw Mohammed, and made the decision arthrodesis was correct, I requested a cobra plate be obtained. It is not something you would expect to find in every hospital's storeroom. Even in the UK, a cobra plate would most likely be specially ordered. Several days passed, Lebanon being searched from north to south, without one being found. It appeared the only way of obtaining one would be an appeal directly to the manufacturers in Switzerland. This would be too expensive, so it was beginning to look as though Mohammed would join the mercenary and be deprived of his operation. Then, unexpectedly, a mysterious benefactor came to our rescue, or so I thought at the time. A cobra plate had been found and would be available whenever I wanted it, but would cost US$1000 for the plate alone. A thousand dollars! I could not believe it, but Mohammed's needs were great. Without it he was destined to spend the rest of his days in either a wheelchair or walking with crutches. To the credit of MAP, they never blinked. Without hesitation they agreed to pay.

It was on the day of surgery the plate arrived. I carefully unwrapped it from its green cloth towel to inspect it. I could not believe what I saw. The plate was appalling – scratched, chipped, bent and burnished. It was not a new one at all. Our so-called benefactor, already charging a thousand dollars, had most likely given us a second-hand plate. The device had already been used in someone else. For all I knew it could have come from a dead body. 'How could anyone charge a thousand dollars for this rubbish!' I shouted, tempted to throw the thing wildly away in disgust. Even worse, how could anyone imperil a fourteen-year-old boy, just to make a buck? I would have to do the best I could. Mohammed was in too much trouble to be left untreated.

Later that day we had surgery under way. With the patient asleep under anaesthetic I made the incision, clotting all the haemorrhaging blood vessels with an electrical coagulation device as I worked. Blood transfusions were in short supply, so it was vital to be sure a patient did not bleed unnecessarily during surgery. Once I had removed a number of muscles from their attachments, the hip joint appeared. I could see the terrible damage the bullet had created. The gristle had become eroded and soft, huge lumps and knobs had appeared around the edges of the joint. This was a hip on its very last legs. It was a quick job to cut it away with the compressed-air saw, blood splattering everywhere as I did so. I turned to the theatre sister and asked for the cobra plate.

I looked at the plate again, still horrified by its condition. I placed it in Mohammed's wound, holding it this way and that, trying hard to find a suitable position to screw it home. It was no use. However much I prayed otherwise, the plate was too damaged to do its job well. How could I give it to young Mohammed? So battered and bashed had it become, it would not have held the hip joint rigid for long and might well have broken before healing was complete. Eventually, I improvized by taking a metal plate designed for the shin bone and refashioning it during surgery to fit the hip. Unquestionably a second best. My only consolation was our so-called benefactor did not receive his thousand dollars. I heard months later that Mohammed did well.

A common request when working overseas is to perform a demonstration operation for local surgeons. I am always happy to oblige, provided I am not expected to do something too unusual. Hamsharry requested I demonstrate a hip replacement operation. As I do hundreds, if not thousands, of the things back home it seemed simple enough. Fresh in my mind, however, was the memory of a similar operation in Teheran, the previous year. There, with cameras in the operating theatre around me, a simple operation nearly turned to disaster when the thigh bone fractured in mid-surgery. Fortunately we spotted the problem at an early stage. We managed to salvage the situation, and complete the operation, without anyone else realizing what had taken place. It was not an easy task and certainly not a performance I wished to repeat in Hamsharry.

News of the demonstration spread like wildfire. One of the major orthopaedic manufacturers flew in a massive quantity of equipment from overseas for the occasion, accompanied by several support and marketing staff. It was to be the first replacement of its kind in Lebanon and they wanted to be sure they were there. The day arrived and the operating theatre was bursting with onlookers. When that happens, a major difficulty is to ensure surgery goes well, while still affording a good view to those who have travelled many miles to see you. The greatest risk is infection. Though it is an unpleasant thought, all people teem with bacteria.

The skin is covered in the little beasts, though they cannot be seen. The sites of maximum contamination are the nose and groin. Anyone who wears a skirt pours the things on to the floor. For this reason trousers are much preferred in operating theatres as they contain the bacteria inside the clothing until released into the changing room later. Those performing the operation wear special clothing throughout surgery to seal off their bacteria from the patient. Those watching do not. If the observers come too close to the patient during surgery it is easy for bacteria to infect the open wound.

As surgery began, all appeared to go well. The incision was made, bleeding controlled and the hip dislocated. There is always a wonderful graunching sound when that happens, enough to test the strongest stomach. The observers were fascinated. Someone was also using a videocamera, its dangling lens cap swinging perilously close to the patient. At times it hovered only inches away. The observer would not have achieved a better view had he climbed into the wound itself. Behind me voices were arguing.

'Out of my way.'

'Give me room.'

'Let *me* have a look.'

'Come on, it's my turn.'

People elbowed their way forward to see more. The only way those of us operating could prevent transfer of bacteria into the wound was by sticking out our bottoms to ward off the observers. We struck a strange sight doing so, but fortunately completed the procedure successfully within an hour. Never could one see a happier surgical team. When we inserted the final skin stitch to close the huge surgical wound I breathed an immense sigh of relief, only then removing my buttock crowd barrier. It was as I removed the restraint that the entire mass of observers almost collapsed on to the still sleeping patient. I had to smile, so close to the wind had we sailed. You can never tell when overseas. It will be a few years yet before I feel brave enough to try a demonstration operation again.

Maintaining sterility of the patient during operations is a skilled, difficult task for which surgeons and their teams train for years. Essentially, the moment you have scrubbed up and donned your gloves, mask and gown, you can touch nothing except the patient until surgery is complete. Should you develop an itchy nose, become desperate to have a pee or become uncontrollably overwhelmed to smoke a cigarette, it is tough luck. Touching anything other than the patient risks infection being transferred to the wound from elsewhere. You must stay at your post, whatever the consequences, until the task is complete. Imagine my discomfort on one occasion when I had to perform a single operation that was nine *hours* long. My bladder had by then distended upwards to my diaphragm and I could barely breathe without wetting myself. Imagine also Fred's predicament when his trousers fell down in mid-operation. Surgeons' clothing was at a premium in Hamsharry and he had been obliged to wear the only remaining pair that day. They were far too big for him and, predictably, ended up around his ankles during a particularly difficult operation. Baring your backside to unsuspecting theatre staff, male or female, is not a recommended act in Arab society, however unwitting the occasion. Fortunately, and judging by the laughter echoing round southern Lebanon that day, Fred's involuntary display was taken in good spirit as theatre staff queued to pull up the offending items.

I was sad to leave Lebanon, most particularly its Palestinian people, who must be some of the bravest, most resilient, individuals alive. During our stay we had seen and treated several hundred patients who had borne their conditions valiantly, often for years, before corrective surgery was possible. It had been exhausting work, for both surgeons and patients. Perhaps I'll go back one day, if they'll have me. Who knows? They might even have a homeland by then. They certainly deserve it. By saying so, of course, I enter politics at my peril.

CHAPTER 11

The Forgotten People of Sarajevo

The Hercules was descending rapidly, its frame rattling and shaking with strain. 'Hold on tight!' I heard the loadmaster scream over the deafening noise of the throbbing engines. I glanced over the mound of freight lashed to the aircraft's floor to see him grip the edge of his flimsy seat. Determination was written on his face. Surface-to-air missile attack was a genuine risk. Already one Hercules had failed to make it.

Sarajevo, this is where I meet my Maker I thought, as the angle of descent grew still steeper. One engine whined loudly as we picked up yet more speed. Through my mind flashed images of Serb snipers aiming their telescopic sights upwards, indiscriminately firing at whatever they could see. It was not unusual for United Nations aircraft to land peppered with bullet holes. The Germans were favoured targets. Sweating, I tucked the protective groin flap of my body armour still further between my legs, and perched myself on top of my Kevlar helmet. It would be my backside or privates the bullets would hit, if I was to be the chosen one.

'Oi!' yelled the loadmaster at the top of his lungs, addressing our motley group of eight terrified individuals. 'Listen in you lot! When we hit the ground I want you out fast, and running! Grab any two bags, it doesn't matter if they're your own. We can sort that out later!' Each of us nodded slowly, faces worried. The war beneath us was in full throttle. Every brokered ceasefire had failed, the land was alive with ruthless, gunhappy militias. God help me, I thought. I had made it through a lot of things in the past. This? I had no way of knowing.

It had started with Irma, a young Sarajevan girl caught as an innocent victim of the Bosnian war. Stranded in Sarajevo's State Hospital, doctors had felt she was dying due to lack of basic medical care. The world had thrown up its arms in horror as her plight touched millions of hearts. John Major, on the UK's behalf, had stepped in to fill the breach. At the time, the conflict was a distant affair to me. Genocide was not something I really understood. Naturally, I had heard the news reports but putting figures and faces on the situation was impossible. It was another person's problem, not mine.

The situation changed one damp Thursday afternoon when the letter arrived from a charity, World Orthopaedic Concern. It looked lonely, lying on my doormat, the envelope creased, stained and accompanied by a misspelt note from doctors in Sarajevo. A non-governmental organization, an NGO, was seeking surgical support for the beleaguered city and had approached WOC for advice. For some reason, they had recommended me. The NGO wanted surgeons on the ground, deep within the city, in a matter of days. Could I help? I should have known better. I was becoming accustomed to my relegated role of armchair warrior. Deep within me, however, still existed that voice of adventure. However old and crumbly I become, the voice speaks now. As I read the letter, struggling to understand it in places, I could feel the tiny spark become a blaze. Someone had to do it. Someone had to show it was possible. It might as well be me.

Louise thought the idea crazy. 'It's not your war,' she observed, her voice tense. She could see my distant expression the moment the envelope appeared.

'I know that,' I replied. 'But can't you imagine how awful it must be to live in Sarajevo? Think if it was Manchester, or Exeter, or Bristol. Those people are just like us.'

You cannot expect a mother with three children to support such things, whether or not she has undergone military training. Her whole being cries out for the security of her family. For two days I pounded the narrow corridors of our house, struggling to balance family duty with what I had been asked to do. It was an impossible decision to make. I knew if I did not move fast, the opportunity would be missed. As an SAS doctor I had resolved always to say 'Yes'. So 'Yes' I said to Sarajevo.

It was an immense task, not something I could handle alone. Sarajevo's orthopaedic surgeons were lacking large quantities of vital equipment. They were also short of people. Death, injury or evacuation had reduced their ranks to the few still able to work and survive. Within four days I had made contact with almost every orthopaedic consultant in the United Kingdom – there are more than a thousand – and had twelve volunteers able to drop everything at short notice. They were helping with an enterprise they, or I, knew little about. Suddenly, television news broadcasts assumed a most intense meaning. Every death or massacre filled me with dread. No longer were broken ceasefires other people's problems. Now they were mine as well.

The NGO was small, though highly motivated. Its chief field worker was Simon, intelligent, well-used to conflict and an obvious adventurer at heart. Earlier work in Afghanistan had made him fairly war-wise. However, twelve surgeons, eager to help, were more than even he could handle. Within a few days I had whittled this number down to four, one nurse and a tough, capable operating theatre assistant. The pruning largely took place by natural selection. As the time to departure grew nearer, so I would receive more telephone calls and letters withdrawing initial enthusiasm. Wise folk, I secretly felt, sympathizing with the anxieties felt in orthopaedic households up and down the land. This was not to be a low-key charity task in some warehouse far removed from the fighting. We were being asked to work in central Sarajevo, only yards from a bloody front line. For myself, I was now thoroughly committed and could not opt out if I had tried.

Going to war as a civilian is totally different from conflict with the Services. The Government guards its intelligence jealously – such information is not for general consumption, certainly not for civilians. No satellite photographs, no detailed maps, no emergency evacuation routes, no briefings on the warring factions. The SAS would have told me all this. No such luck in the UK's civvy street.

You must start from basics. Obtaining volunteers is just the start. Thinking as pessimistically as you can is the only way to survive. What happens if I die, I thought? I had to see what I would be worth if a Serbian sniper decided I was flavour of the day. Already I had upset Louise by volunteering for Sarajevo and had disrupted our planned family holiday by offering the same dates to the NGO. The last thing I wanted was to leave her penniless if I was killed. I contacted the handful of companies who have the misfortune to insure my life. 'No problems,' they proclaimed to a man, or a woman in one case. 'We'll pay the lot if you die. Good luck to you.'

I felt mightily relieved, until a colleague asked me one morning, as I sat in another terrified daydream, 'What about injury, Richard? Say you get your hands shot off? What then?'

Confidently I replied I was sure there would be no problem. As I spoke, doubts were ringing noisy alarmbells in my mind. In peacetime I insure myself for such things. If I lose a hand, or my fingers drop off, I should be worth a fortune. In war, as I soon discovered, the situation is different. No one would insure me for injury, only for death. The risks were too great. Everything I had ever subscribed to protect against injury would be null and void if I returned, unable to work. War zones were major exclusions.

This was a problem. For a moment I considered aborting the project. I already knew that the chances of injury were far higher than the chances of death. Simon saved the day through contacts at Lloyd's of London. They agreed, at enormous cost, to insure our team. My premium alone was ten thousand US dollars each week, the other team members being extra. The NGO was still in full support, so determined was it we would go ahead. Anything we required seemed fine.

By now Sarajevo was becoming even hotter. NATO jets were making bombing runs over Serb gun positions and the city wanted us there as fast as possible. Apart from Simon, only two of the group had previous war experience, an ex-Marine and me. The remainder had never seen such things before. It was colossal bravery on their part. Every news bulletin carried further evidence of death and destruction, with aid workers now appearing to be legitimate targets. I could see obvious worry in their eyes whenever we met to discuss our plans. Wills were written, relatives and parents telephoned and retelephoned, personal equipment packed and unpacked a hundred times. I knew the feeling so well, having sat for days awaiting my certain death during the Falklands War. You daydream and ponder. You lie awake at night. Permanently you carry a pale, stressed expression.

Protection was vital, both physical and political. The physical side was well catered for with body armour. Theoretically you can cover yourself from head to toe with armour, like a personal tank, but the weight makes walking impossible. Protection is a compromise between safety and mobility. Both suffer to a degree.

Once you start choosing designs it is impossible to know where you should stop. There are blue ones and red ones, even white ones and purple ones. Some go under your clothes and some go over them. Some have high-velocity protection plates front and back, others do not. The choice is mind-boggling. Kate Adie, the UK's renowned BBC television journalist, came to our rescue, though she never knew it. I had always been impressed by her. When all hell broke loose around, she had that uncanny ability to appear relaxed and controlled. She is like that, too, when you meet her. On this occasion it was her body armour we loved. It appeared perfectly tailored, ready for anything war could throw at it. At every broadcast we scrutinized her form, not for the content of its journalism, I must confess, but for her design of body armour. '*That* is what we want,' we universally agreed. 'If it's good enough for Kate, surely it will be good enough for us?'

If you are male, the most important part of body armour is the groin flap – psychologically at least. Being shot is one thing, but being shot in the balls is another. When I go to my grave, however God chooses, my manhood goes with me. The groin flap is your salvation. Normally concealed within the body armour it can be pulled out any time you wish. If you genuinely think a Serb is about to take a pot shot, pull it down. It won't alter his aim, but it will certainly make you feel safer. I look at male war correspondents with renewed interest now. If their groin flaps are down I know they are *really* worried.

Political protection was also essential. What, I asked, would happen if the Serbs overran Sarajevo while we were there? When the project was first suggested, no contingency existed for our rescue whatsoever. We would be on our own. Operation Irma saved the day. The young girl, perilously injured, had been evacuated to London's Great Ormond Street Hospital. The politicians wanted Britain to appear fully involved as soon as possible. Our group was poised to move, which suited the UK's Overseas Development Administration well. Suddenly, after a mere handful of telephone calls, we changed from an independent charity to a team under ODA control. Having ODA backing would not force a sniper from his target, but was a major layer of protection for the team. If the SAS had taught me nothing else, it showed successful survival is based on precise organization and anticipation of impending disasters.

First stop, via a tiny Fokker aircraft chartered specially for the team, was Ancona in Italy. Its airport was a hive of activity, Hercules transports from a variety of countries coming and going regularly. It was the home of Maybe Airlines – maybe you'll make it, maybe you won't – the unofficial name of the massive United Nations airlift needed to keep Sarajevo alive. Ancona also high-lighted one of the tragedies of war-relief work. In the pouring rain stood tons of flour being ruined by damp. Damaged medical equipment lay scattered in puddles of water to one side of the runway, in company with several discarded containers of military rations. Service life trains you to be a magpie, so within minutes I had encouraged the others to take what they could carry from the pile. If it was no use for us, we could certainly leave it behind in Sarajevo. Looking at the mound of damaged goods and equipment made me doubt how coordinated such massive relief projects can ever be. Public funds, and individual donations, had probably been used to bring the items together. I would be horrified if my hard-earned charitable donation lay in a puddle of water somewhere in the world. The fantasy of aid to an area of conflict is a sharp contrast to reality on the ground.

War zones are not pleasant places and Sarajevo was no exception. The first thing to strike you, surprisingly, is the silence. Much of the time there is eerie quiet interspersed with the occasional thump of a mortar round, or crack as a bullet flies by. That day, Sarajevo airport was deathly silent. All around lay evidence of the intense shelling that had gone before. Shattered glass fragments, earthen craters, surrounded by the hulks of burned-out personnel carriers and aircraft. The soldiers were similarly silent. No smiles, no warm welcomes. Just a lifeless stare as you walk by. Many had seen friends killed or maimed by the conflict.

Sarajevo airport stands outside the city itself. No APC, 'armoured personnel carrier', was available to take us to the United Nations Headquarters at the post and telecommunications building, the PTT, so a routine minibus it had to be. Largely unprotected, I could see the bullet holes crazing the driver's window. Despite their white colour, and blue UN flag, minibuses were fair targets in this crazy Balkan war.

As we drove towards the PTT, the true horror of a city under siege became apparent. Everything was destroyed. Not one window intact, not one wall spared the irregular pitting of shrapnel damage. Every building was gutted, roofs in tatters, their bare and charred beams in full view. It was a depressing sight, as if a huge tornado had passed by, destroying everything in its path. Occasionally there was an oddity. A bright orange Volkswagen Beetle, completely untouched, parked close beside the ruins of a house. Perhaps the pride and joy of its owner, I have no idea how it had escaped. There was no petrol to run it, but why a bored Serb gunner had decided to spare it was a mystery. Our minibus driver remained silent throughout the journey. I learned later he had been wounded three times since the conflict began, and had lost every member of his family. His sister had been raped before she was murdered. When he eventually told me this, I was struck by the impassive way he described events. War does suppress emotions – for both hunter and hunted.

The PTT was a busy place, people and vehicles coming and going continuously. When we arrived, our driver exited the minibus without saying a word, leaving us where we sat. No one had said where the Serb front line was positioned, so I had no idea whether or not we were in a firing line with a sniper at the other end. Consequently, I felt the only safe place was tucked away in the parking area between two large APCs. We crept from the minibus and cowered there until I noticed the strange looks from passing UN staff. One eventually beckoned me forcibly. 'Come on!' he said. 'There's no problem at the moment. You don't need to hide there.'

Walking into the PTT itself I could see a complete mixture of people. Long-haired, ragged aid workers worked alongside immaculate UN soldiers. Meanwhile many well-known television journalists flitted to and fro the various offices, gleaning what little information they could. No office had curtains, or very few, and every exterior window was criss-crossed with sticky tape. The PTT fared well during the siege, though came under attack occasionally. Communication with the outside world was difficult, as fighting had destroyed most telephone landlines. However, there was one satellite fax, running night and day, and a telephone in the office of the United Nations High Commission for Refugees, the UNHCR. They guarded it for their own needs closely, as it was one of the few ways of communicating elsewhere. To use it without being caught or challenged was one of the only ways of having fun in Sarajevo.

Our contact at the PTT was a charming Scandinavian, working on behalf of the World Health Organization. He had seen most of the war through its various stages and knew everything about the conflict and its warring sides. He greeted me as if we had known each other for ages when, in fact, we had never met. After an initial, warm handshake and the only smile I had so far seen in Sarajevo, he looked at me seriously.

'We were going to cancel you,' he said, his voice quiet and low.

'Cancel us? Why?' I asked.

'There didn't seem any point in you coming. All electricity is off, there's no water and gas is non-existent. We didn't think you could do very much without basic power.'

'I'm sure we can do something to help. Prepare an appreciation if nothing else. Perhaps it would be best for us to find out what Sarajevo is lacking and set the scene for later visits.' After so much anxiety and emotion to come this far, we were not giving up at such an early stage.

The Scandinavian appeared to agree. 'Yes, I thought that too. We decided to let you come and do the best you can. I understand you've done this sort of thing before.'

I nodded and avoided saying I had never before entered a city under siege. 'Where will we be going?' I asked.

'The State Hospital. It's where little Irma came from. No teams have been there before. At least no team has *stayed* there before. But I'm afraid it's a little close to the front line.'

'How close?'

'A hundred, maybe a hundred and fifty metres.'

'Shit.'

The drive to the State Hospital was an adventure in itself, directly through the heart of Sarajevo. To get there, our sad little minibus had to negotiate the lethal Sniper's Alley, so-called because of its proximity to Serb snipers. The Alley *was* the front line. Snipers would sit, or lie, in buildings only fifty metres from the Alley. You survived a journey down that road from the goodness of their hearts, what little remained. It was impossible for even a one-eyed beginner to miss. Naturally it was important not to draw attention to yourself. You did not drive the route with headlights blazing or sirens wailing. You drove fast, steadily and looked neither left nor right. Unless, of course, your name was Beverley.

Beverley, Bev, is one of the best operating theatre sisters in the trade. In a moment of weakness, her weakness, I had persuaded her to join the Sarajevo project. Keen for adventure, she had agreed. It is astonishing what some will do to escape the National Health Service. Despite what were undoubted worries for her, she never once expressed those concerns to me. Bev had not been to a war zone before and had come armed with her tiny camera, poised to take photographs for what I assume will one day be her memoirs. The camera was one of those automatic affairs that decides for you whether or not to use its flash. As we drove down the middle of Sniper's Alley, each minibus occupant looking steadfastly forwards, I suddenly realized not everyone was trying to remain inconspicuous. There was a whirr, a click and a rustle from my left. Then, as bright as sunlight on this overcast evening, Bev's flash went off. Every one of us jumped out of our skins. I was convinced I had just been shot. 'Oh bugger it! I'm sorry!' she said. Worse still, the picture never came out.

How we survived the Alley, I do not know, but the Serbs were feeling kind that day. At one end, though a little beyond, stood the State Hospital. As we rounded a final corner I could see it to our front. It was a mess, its high-rise structure completely shell-blasted and destroyed. The hospital was also a military hospital and, as such, fair game for Serb gunners in the early days of the war. The Geneva Convention was not widely honoured in the Balkans. Such things are excellent ideas, but practice is so different from theory. No wonder its local name was the Swiss Cheese Hospital. Full of holes, it was a dangerous place to be.

By the time we arrived, the war had been running for eighteen months. The once-attractive Sarajevo had been reduced to a barren hulk. From a pre-war population of over 500,000, only 350,000 remained. Sixty-four thousand Sarajevans had been killed or wounded, of whom 16,000 were children. Of those who died, most had perished from explosive blast; but bayoneting, strangulation, rape, cold and starvation had killed many more. Of the 38,000 women, and girls, raped in Bosnia, 3000 had been assaulted within Sarajevo itself. More than 9000 pregnancies, 200 of which were Sarajevan, had been the result. This was ethnic cleansing, *etnicko ciscenje*, in all its horror.

No establishment is more exposed to the realities of war than a hospital. The Swiss Cheese Hospital was a classic example. For most of the war it dealt with up to thirty operations every day, week in, week out, month in, month out. It had to do this without an external electricity supply, limited fuel and a maximum of two hours' running water each day. So extensive was the damage that all hospital activity above the fourth floor had been abandoned. Most clinical work took place on the lower four floors, and as much as possible on the first two. Red still stained the hospital forecourt where, at times of enormous casualties, buckets of scarce water were used to wash the blood away. Large concrete paving slabs rested against ground-floor windows as protection against blast, while a damaged, non-functional ambulance stood uselessly to one side.

The hospital's orthopaedic surgeon was waiting at the front door, greeting us with open arms. 'Welcome to Sarajevo,' he said, an impressive smile across his otherwise pale, drawn face. 'We have tried to make your visit as safe as possible, but I am afraid it is going to be difficult.'

Staying outside, in the exposed, open air of Sarajevo made us feel naturally insecure. We were delighted to be taken indoors, breathing a sigh of relief as we entered the moderate protection of the hospital building. Our host led us through the gloomy maze of hospital corridors. Every window was either shattered, or contained several bullet holes. Even internal walls had been fragmented and destroyed. As we passed the kitchen, he indicated a sequence of large, irregular, gaping cavities extending through several walls, from street outside to kitchen itself. 'Tank round,' he said. 'It went through five walls and killed our cook. He was a good man.' He spoke without emotion, devoid of feeling, as if it was an everyday occurrence that an innocent cook should die. I looked at the surgeon's face. It was an expression I got to know well. I saw it on every face in Sarajevo. Passive eyes, expecting nothing from life or the world, pale sallow skin and slumped shoulders.

Only rarely did anyone venture outside. Lack of daylight, for months on end, living like rabbits in a burrow, made the Sarajevans look terrible. Yet staff would walk the hospital corridors, heads silhouetted against shattered, uncovered windows for any sniper to see. At night it was common to sit in uncurtained rooms, by the light of a candle or single electric bulb, for all outside to view you. It was as if the Sarajevans had now seen so much, endured such hell, that they had become acceptant of their fate. Each one had a tale to tell, of near misses, or woundings, or families lost and killed. 'Every day is a black day,' one surgeon said to me.

Unlike Sarajevo airport, the air around the Swiss Cheese Hospital was full of continuous noise. Crack! Crack! Boom! *Sniper putsa* – 'Sniper shooting' – could be said over two hundred times each day. High-velocity bullets cracked everywhere. Due to the urban environment it was impossible to say from where the round was fired. In open areas it is easier. First you hear the 'crack' as the bullet flies past – you naturally do not hear it if it hits you – then the 'thump' as the metal breech of the rifle moves to and fro. It is the 'thump' you listen for, not the 'crack'. It gives you the location of the sniper. The time and interval between 'crack' and 'thump' tells you the distance. 'Crack-thump' demonstrations are commonplace in the Army, where rounds are intentionally fired over your head in training to teach you this direction-finding skill. In Sarajevo, using crack-thump was difficult due to noise deflection and echo off the buildings. Any thump you might hear was normally the bullet hitting a body or brickwork, not the metal breech of a rifle. It was safer to assume that snipers were everywhere and take precautions accordingly.

When you first visit such a place, where to go in safety, if there is such a thing, and how to do it, is confusing. No one briefed us where the Serbs were to be found, nor on how to stay alive should we venture on to the streets of Sarajevo. I had given the team a short talk in Ancona, before our ordeal with Maybe Airlines, explaining the basic principles of avoiding death during war. Cross intersections at a sprint, peer round corners at ground level rather than standing up, vary your speed of travel to make it difficult for a sniper to hold his aim. Do not wear bright clothes, and use dead ground – areas the enemy cannot see – as liberally as you can. Though such advice is better than nothing, there is no substitute for experience. Unfortunately, for most team members, war experience was something they lacked. A skeet shoot was an unfamiliar event, let alone life under genuine fire.

The locals did their best to make life difficult for snipers. Ropes were attached to the first floor of buildings each side of the narrow streets and blankets suspended from them to disrupt the sniper's view. Certain no-go areas were commonly known. It was sometimes safe to walk down one side of a street, but lethal to walk on the other. Bev nearly died one day, returning from another city hospital after completing her assessment of operating-theatre facilities. She had been fortunate to beg a lift in an APC, a rare occurrence for aid workers, even with ODA blessing. The APC driver had refused to go near the Swiss Cheese Hospital, claiming it was too dangerous. Bev was left, 300 metres from the hospital, dressed in a bright yellow T-shirt. She could not have offered a better target if she had tried. I should have warned her to wear dark, inconspicuous clothing. Off she set on foot, only days into her first visit to her first war zone, in full view of every Serb sniper for miles around. I have no idea why she was not shot. Perhaps it was the opposition being kind to the fair sex – many snipers were themselves female – perhaps it was simple good luck. It took her several minutes to realize everyone else was walking on the opposite pavement to herself and that the old lady on the other side of the road was wildly gesticulating at her for a reason. Bev sprinted hastily to safety. I imagine several dozen telescopic sights were trained on her by then. She now gives an excellent description of what it sounds and feels like when a high-velocity bullet passes by, millimetres from your left ear. APCs were a dirty word that day.

Added to snipers, Sarajevans were regularly bombed. Not by aircraft, but from mortars. As many as 600 mortar bombs could land in a day, though this had reduced to about thirty during our time there. Firing a mortar is now an accurate art, so I could not understand how bread queues, schoolchildren or marketplaces could be hit without absolute intent to do so. As a surgeon in Sarajevo you rarely dealt with wounded soldiers. The majority of patients were unarmed civilians. My first ward round with our host was an education in this respect. Virtually all the hospital's 250 beds were full. Patients lay in curtainless wards, each window again shattered by blast or gunshot. Even a patient in bed was fair game for a sniper. Women, children and the elderly, lay motionless, many paralysed and dozens without an arm or leg. People like Mika, a beautiful twelve-year-old Bosnian girl, the victim of rape on two occasions, who lay stranded without legs in her ward. Her parents had been murdered months earlier. For many of the patients I saw, perhaps even her, death would have been a blessing.

War has a habit of creating multiple injuries, rather than damaging one part of the body at a time. This can sometimes cause immense problems for medical staff. Take Viktor as an example. It was nine o'clock in the morning and had been a busy night. More than twenty major explosions near the hospital had kept the operating theatres permanently active.

A few minutes after breakfast a massive blast shook the hospital to its core, jolting free the few remaining shards of glass that hung loosely in the multitudinous, damaged window frames. Seconds later came the sound of frantic shouts from outside the casualty entrance. It was Viktor, caught within several metres of a mortar blast, again an innocent civilian. His two children, lovely twin girls aged no more than eight years, were hanging desperately to the bleeding body of their father as two burly friends dragged him to the entrance. Long, bloody smears on the chipped pavement tracked their course as they manhandled their colleague to the hospital. Viktor's crime had been to accompany his children to a makeshift school. 'For their protection,' he muttered through a blood-soaked mouth. 'Their mother was shot last week.'

The blast had created terrible damage. His right leg was a bloody stump below the knee – a traumatic amputation – though reasonably clean. Strangely, he was not bleeding badly from the injured area as the blood vessels had constricted tightly to control the blood loss. It is one of Nature's miracles that arteries contain muscle in their walls. Cut one and the muscle will immediately clamp down to prevent excessive bleeding. Viktor's other leg was also a bloody mess – mangled bone, dead muscle, tendons flapping uselessly through destroyed skin. Small particles of grit, or perhaps shrapnel, peppered the area, a large piece of jagged metal protruding visibly from the depths of the wound. It was tempting to remove it. You could easily grasp it between finger and thumb and pull, but if you did so there was real danger bleeding could increase. Remove a foreign body and the arteries have nothing to clamp down upon. I have seen patients nearly die as a result. Never remove such things, however tempting it may be, until the patient is safely inside the operating theatre and an intravenous drip is running fast to allow instant blood transfusion.

Added to his leg injuries, small pieces of shrapnel had peppered Viktor from neck to groin, though his face had largely been spared. Some of the wounds were deep, some superficial, but there must have been thirty separate wounds in all. You could see it was going to take some time to save Viktor, if he could be saved at all.

Apart from his visible injuries, it was difficult to be certain whether or not the blast had damaged internal organs, such as liver, kidney or spleen. Viktor was therefore treated by 'peritoneal lavage', sterile fluid being injected through his abdominal wall and allowed to circulate before being removed again. The normally clear fluid was tinged red. 'Damn!' That meant he was bleeding into his belly. Not only would surgery have to deal with his legs, and the multiple shrapnel wounds, his abdomen would have to be opened as well. Two macerated legs, thirty shrapnel wounds, and an abdominal operation were injuries only the strongest could survive.

Viktor was taken immediately to the operating theatre, his two children crying inconsolably as they saw their father being wheeled down the hospital corridor away from them. It was a heart-rending sight. There was no one to help, no one to cuddle or console them. Medical staff were too busy struggling to keep Viktor alive. Large iodine-soaked dressings were slapped firmly in place by the casualty staff, heavy pressure being applied to control any bleeding. Arterial spasm does not last for ever. Two drips were set up, one in each forearm, to allow rapid transfusion, though whether enough blood existed in Sarajevo for Viktor's needs was in doubt. His problems did not end there. No one was available to operate on him. Everyone was busy dealing with other casualties, and all surgical staff were operating in theatre. Viktor had to be left on his trolley in the theatre reception area, unaccompanied, without painkilling medication as supplies had been exhausted long ago. His pain was immense, soon overwhelming his initial self-control. He screamed, and he screamed – a horrible penetrating cry. You could not avoid it, it struck to the core. 'Please God,' you prayed, trying hard to concentrate on the patient before you, 'Somehow, anyhow, please release Viktor from his agony.' But release did not come, nor death. Viktor was a strong man, an agricultural worker in more normal times. He lay on the trolley, eyes tightly closed, uninjured hands gripping the side of the battered mattress and continued his incessant cry.

It took an hour to finish the previous case, a simple bullet wound through the upper arm in a Bosnian soldier, one of the few military casualties that day. Then it was Viktor's turn. The moment he was wheeled into the operating theatre, his screaming stopped, his eyes opened and he looked up imploringly at the masked surgical team now poised to help him. You could tell he was certain he would die. 'Look after my children,' he slurred as the general anaesthetic took hold. Then there was silence, blissful peace, as work commenced.

For Viktor's right leg there was little to be done except tidy damage the blast had created. This meant sawing away a few more centimetres of tibia bone to a smooth end and closing muscle and skin over it. It seemed safe to close the skin on this occasion as the blast had not heavily contaminated the tissue. The left leg was different. Engrained with dirt, it took two hours to remove each piece of shrapnel – more than fifty – and a further hour to cut away damaged muscle and skin. While one team dealt with Viktor's legs, another opened his belly, an operation known as 'laparotomy'. A long, vertical incision was made to one side of his belly button, from ribs to groin. Rapidly this cut was deepened to enter the abdominal cavity itself. Then the search for a bleeding point began. It is not as easy as it sounds. Viktor's bowels, bruised from the blast, were still wriggling. Each time you push guts to one side, they always slither back to their original position, making it hard to obtain a good view of every nook and cranny inside a belly. It was a slow process, but it was eventually apparent that Viktor had not damaged an abdominal blood vessel at all. The red tinge obtained at peritoneal lavage had probably come from general, mild bruising. This was good news, if there was such a thing in Sarajevo. At least Viktor's belly would recover. His abdomen was thus closed and attention turned to the many shrapnel wounds dotted over his body. Each needed to be carefully cleaned, each one sutured. It was a laborious task.

By eight o'clock that evening, surgery was complete. Everyone was exhausted, having operated continuously for more than fourteen hours. Importantly, Viktor was alive, and would now survive, despite appalling multiple injuries. After a long period in theatre, feeling so physically drained, it is sometimes difficult to realize why you do these things. For Viktor there was no mistake. It was as he was being wheeled out of theatre that a tear came to each man's eye. His two little girls had found their way to the reception area, unbeknown to anyone, and had sat patiently throughout Viktor's operation, hugging each other tightly. They had nowhere else to go. Instinct told them they should stay as close as possible to their father. Hour upon hour they had sat on the cold, plastic bench, tears streaming down their faces. All they had was each other. The moment they saw Viktor on his trolley, squeaking slowly by, they leapt to their feet, squealing with delight. Huge, happy smiles stretched across their faces as they whispered, 'Daddy, Daddy, Daddy,' clenching his semi-conscious hand tightly for extra security. Such occasions make surgery very worthwhile.

For many, the severity of their wounds meant that infection was unavoidable. Contamination by high-velocity missiles, combined with lying in the dirt for hours before rescue, and an inadequate supply of appropriate antibiotics, made it commonplace. At such times, a surgeon should not sew up the wound. After cleaning, damaged areas should be left open for several days, however big they are, until the wound looks healthy. Surgical closure is then safe. Otherwise, bacteria are trapped in the wound when it is sewn up and gas gangrene is the result.

Nerve damage was common. This was not always full paralysis, as happens when a bullet passes through the spinal cord, but more localized trouble. One pleasant, middle-aged woman, a teacher in peacetime, showed me her paralysed arm. A bullet had passed clean through her shoulder, dividing the nerves to her arm and hand by destroying an area called the brachial plexus. The damage had been so great that repair was not possible. Her right arm flopped uselessly by her side, the feeling absent from her fingers. She looked at me appealingly, grasping my white coat with an intact left hand. 'Please help me,' she pleaded, in faltering English. 'I must have my right arm.'

I could do nothing, but how can you say so to a patient who believes that miracles are possible? I knew that nerves sometimes recover, but very rarely fully. For her, any improvement would be astonishing. She would have to wait at least two years to see, as nerve regrowth is agonizingly slow. All I could do was to look her sympathetically in the eyes, squeeze her uninjured hand and smile. She knew from my expression there was nothing I could do.

Nerves to the leg were also vulnerable, particularly a large one that passes behind the knee – the lateral popliteal nerve. Several patients had injured it due to gunshot wounds or shrapnel. The nerve's job is to lift the toes and foot upwards. When it is damaged the foot flops downwards as the patient walks, making it easy to trip over – the 'footdrop' deformity. One way of immobilizing a prisoner, if you are so inclined, is to smash the outside of the knee with a rifle butt. That damages the lateral popliteal nerve so the prisoner cannot run away. Again, it is a matter of time and good fortune to see if the nerve is going to recover. Healing is only rarely complete.

There were also tales of great heroism. Benyic was an example. A mortar bomb had landed on a Sarajevan street in the midst of a gathering of children, but failed to explode. Benyic, a young man aged only twenty-four years, saw the danger immediately. Without any hesitation he barged his way through the terrified children, picked up the bomb and ran with it, preparing to throw it as far away as he could. As he started to run, the device exploded in his hand. His action saved the life of everyone present, as his body shielded them from the blast. Benyic had not fared so well. His right hand, and both legs, were missing. Unable to pass urine due to the enormous damage created by the bomb, he now relied on a thin catheter passing up his penis into the bladder. That one astonishing act of bravery, over within seconds, would remain with Benyic for life. It is so vital people like him are never forgotten. Throughout Sarajevo similar stories could be told. For most, the world will never hear of them.

Some of the bravest were the ambulance drivers. Proper ambulances did not function in Sarajevo. They had either broken down or been destroyed months earlier. Battered, high-mileage civilian estate cars were used instead. These were painted in camouflage colours, plying between front line and hospital whenever they could. It appeared the Serbs regarded such vehicles as legitimate targets, so driving an ambulance car was one of the more dangerous tasks in Sarajevo. Daylight evacuations were rare events, they were simply too hazardous. Most casualties would therefore be held over until nightfall when the drivers would make their way at full speed, and under fire, from the front line. You could hear them. Suddenly, as if from nowhere, the sound of a high revving engine would break the night air. This would be followed by the screeching of tyres as the ambulance car hurtled furiously through the narrow alleyways to the hospital. As it drove you could hear the intense sound of Serb automatic gunfire trying to stop it in its tracks. In the pitch dark, the ambulance cars would arrive, no lights, no sirens, no horns and discharge their grizzly cargoes at the casualty front doors. Often these were the dead bodies of young soldiers killed in action. It was a pitiful sight – another life finished in this futile war.

Food in Sarajevo was in short supply. The population was kept alive largely by outside aid. The Serbs had long ago prevented other supplies entering the city. What did filter in was often in poor condition, limited quantity and cost a fortune in Black Market Deutschmarks. Bosnian money was worthless. Each morning I would see the long lines of Sarajevans standing in their bread queues, those at the tail end invariably being disappointed. In the hospital we fed on aid rations. These were appalling and insufficient to keep an adult alive for long. Most meals would comprise two small slices of bread, yellow tasteless paste masquerading as butter and pale brown liquid pretending to be tea. Rumour had it the tea was boiled cardboard, though I never dared ask. In contrast, the French troops billeted in the PTT wined and dined like royalty. As much food as you could eat and a bottle of wine with your meal. No wonder Sarajevans regarded the UN with suspicion.

Water was scarce. The hospital received only two hours' supply each day. This made washing difficult and it became a challenge to see how little you needed to clean yourself from head to toe. I managed it on one occasion with an eggcupful, including teeth, but the acrobatics I had to go through were unrepeatable. Generally, a litre was sufficient for most hygiene purposes throughout the day, though in the operating theatres more was required. Because of water scarcity, the incidence of waterborne disease steadily increased within Sarajevo. People simply did not have enough to wash their hands as often as they should, and disease was the end result. Hepatitis and gastroenteritis were particularly common. In one month alone 2000 cases of gastroenteritis were reported.

A major reason for our visit to Sarajevo was not only to help surgically, and to prepare an appreciation, but to show its people we genuinely cared. Simon did staunch work with the media, ensuring frequent bulletins on Bosnian Radio and keeping our profile as high as he could. By taking up residence in the Swiss Cheese Hospital we ran the risk of being seen by the Serbs as taking sides. I had repeatedly stressed to anyone I met that, as medical professionals, we could not be seen to support one side more than the other. I tried hard to arrange a crossing of the front line to show our faces to the Serbian opposition, but on each occasion failed. In practice I am sure we were supporting those most in need, but it was important we were regarded as neutral, if there is such a thing in genocidal war. Sarajevo, of course, wished us to be viewed as an entirely Bosnian arrangement.

Local Sarajevans helped us as much as they could, as we gradually amassed evidence from throughout the city of appalling medical conditions and shortages. For most local people there was only one ambition – to escape by whatever means possible. There were few avenues left open to them. One route was as a medical evacuee. Each month, sometimes more often, a medical evacuation committee would meet to consider the plight of often 300 applicants at a time. Rarely more than four would be chosen. It was a desperately distressing task for those having to decide. Sarajevans who, before the war, were in well-paid professional jobs would do anything that might lead to an opportunity for escape. Those working for the United Nations were the most fortunate, being in frequent contact with those in influential positions.

I talked to many Sarajevans when there. For most, they would have done anything to escape. One, an attractive woman, had been an eminent academic in her own right before the conflict. Her job, and position in Sarajevan society, had gone long ago.

'Everything changes in war,' she explained. 'Your standards change, you forget those you love, your morals and behaviour reach rock bottom. Even so, I intend to survive and I intend to get out. Whatever it takes.'

I did not ask for more detail as it seemed inappropriate, though I was clear in my mind what she meant. She had a young daughter to care for and wanted her evacuated by any means. Her tactics, whatever they were, worked eventually. Two months after I left the city, I received a message from a central European location that she had escaped and all was well. Not everyone was so lucky or, for that matter, so determined.

One of our most important tasks was a simple one. To talk and make friends with local medical staff. For so long they had felt abandoned, their hopes repetitively raised and dashed by consecutive ceasefires. They had no idea what people felt in the outside world and were unaware of the enormous wave of sympathy and understanding that dominated the thinking of so many other countries. Long into the night we would talk. Complex, convoluted, political discussions that ended nowhere but made everyone feel better. One night in particular I remember well. We had found an ancient guitar in a bombed-out building. Despite a long split down its back, its tatty strings were still able to play a semblance of a tune. At great expense, I persuaded the PTT to use its satellite fax for selected sheet music to be sent from England. My secretary, with wonderful enthusiasm, could not decide which songs were best, transmitting everything I possessed. She dominated the fax machine for the best part of an hour.

It was worth it. That night, by the light of a candle, our team sat round a hospital table with local Sarajevan medical staff. We took it in turns to sing or play a tune. One of their surgeons, a habitual chain smoker whenever he could obtain cigarettes, had once sung at the Llangollen Eistedfodd. He gently strummed the guitar, sniper rounds and blast noise in the background, singing a Bosnian love song in a most wonderful, penetrating tenor voice. It overwhelmed us at the time. It was the first opportunity any of them had been given to develop new friendships and behave normally since the war began. Of anything we did in Sarajevo, such social activities were perhaps the most vital.

Before we had arrived in the city I was uncertain what to expect as far as local surgical skills were concerned. The tatty letter I had received highlighted lack of equipment, but made no mention of medical or surgical abilities. The moment I went on that first ward round I knew I was in the company of professionals. These people were excellent at their job. When it came to war surgery they could teach me far more than I could ever teach them. They had been unable to publish their experience in the medical journals, but there can be few professionals in the world with the expertise of Sarajevan surgeons and I can only pray that in time international surgery can learn from them. One technique in particular was widely used – the operation of external fixation. This is best for gunshot wounds that have totally shattered the bones. Implanting metal plates and screws directly on to the fragmented bone to reconstruct it is technically straightforward, but leaves metal inside the patient. Bacteria love metal, so the chances of infection after surgery are high.

External fixation involves placing long pins through the skin, directly into the underlying bone and connecting the outer ends of the pins with a thick metal bar. Nothing is permanently implanted inside the patient, as the bar and pins are removed once the shattered bone has healed. It is an excellent way of reducing the chance of infection while still allowing bone to mend. External fixation is used worldwide, but not many have the experience of Sarajevo. By the time we arrived, the city's surgeons had used the technique on over 1100 patients. With equipment in short supply they had been forced to design and manufacture their own fixation devices – improvization at its best. The 'Sarafix' had been born.

Equipment shortages meant surgery had to be kept simple. Fancy techniques, with the implantation of expensive pieces of metal, were not appropriate. Even scrubbing up at the start of surgery had to be undertaken with care. Without functioning taps, an assistant had to pour water from a plastic container over your hands as you washed furiously with an iodine solution. Operations had to be as quick as possible to reduce the amount of anaesthetic used, the patient being put to sleep on the operating table rather than in a room next door. You would also prepare the patient's skin, and apply the surgical towels, before anaesthesia was performed. Patients would cooperate with this fully. It is not surgical behaviour that would be regarded as acceptable by many in our peaceful United Kingdom. War forces you to challenge established practice. It is only right that it should do so.

Josip, a twenty-two-year-old former student, was a particularly difficult case. He had been wounded in the thigh by a high-velocity missile, probably a sniper's bullet. An area of the city had come under mortar attack while he had been walking through it. It was bad luck, nothing more, as Josip had survived the siege for many months by becoming war-wise. As the first bombs landed, he had hidden behind a small wall, but in his panic had not noticed one leg protruding from cover. Though Josip was dressed obviously in civilian clothes, a sniper had taken aim and shot. The bullet had entered his upper thigh and exited his lower shin bone, macerating and destroying everything in its path. Damage was immense. Several centimetres of bone were lost, much of the muscle and the major blood vessel to the leg was divided.

Despite the pain, Josip had used his own belt as a tourniquet around the upper thigh, keeping blood loss low until he could be taken to hospital. Carried and dragged by friends once the attack had finished, he was dumped unceremoniously on the hospital doorsteps. Then the surgical work began. The on-call team had its work cut out to save the leg. More than four hours without an intact blood supply and it is simpler to amputate. Tissues will not survive for much longer without blood. By the time Josip reached the operating theatre, his leg had been bloodless for two and three-quarter hours. By using an undamaged vein, stripped from his healthy leg, it was turned upside down and joined to each end of the damaged artery. The direction of blood flow in the vein has to be reversed as veins contain valves that only allow flow in one direction. Arteries do not. Almost four hours to the minute after injury, blood was returned to Josip's leg. Then the damaged muscle had to be cut away. Typically, the high-velocity bullet had caused cavitation, destroying tissue for a wide radius along its path. Once muscle is killed, it cannot recover and must be surgically excised, or it becomes a perfect focus for infection. By the time all damage had been cut from Josip's leg, an operation called 'debridement', more than half of his leg muscle had been removed.

The damage to the limb stretched for almost a metre, and a specially extended Sarafix had to be used to hold the leg straight. The upper pins were inserted into the thigh bone, immediately beside the hip joint, the lower ones near the ankle. Long metal fixator bars then bridged the huge gap between the pins. Even then the problem was not solved. As so much bone had been lost, however long we waited, it would not heal. The only way out was to use bone grafting. Bone was taken from Josip's pelvis, broken and minced into tiny morcels, and placed into the bone cavities the bullet had created. The smaller bone in his lower leg, the fibula, was also removed and used to help bridge the gap. Bone grafting like this is a very useful procedure, as not all bones heal reliably. Many need a kick start, the tibia in particular.

From time of wounding to complete bone healing took Josip ten months, and eleven operations. On occasion surgery had to be performed without anaesthetic as medicines were in short supply. Josip could not fail to impress you. Wheeled into the operating theatre on a patient's trolley, he calmly slid himself on to the operating table, his externally fixed leg rigidly stuck out before him. Then, cooperatively, he held up the leg with one hand by the fixator bars, helping the surgeons paint antiseptic iodine on his skin to sterilize the area before surgery began. He showed no fear and never whimpered once.

Once the bone had healed, Josip had an intact leg, but was barely able to bend his knee. It had taken so long for the bone to recover, what few leg muscles remained had scarred and contracted. Even a radical operation similar to Kayed's in Lebanon was unable to improve the situation. Josip was destined to limp for the rest of his days. That one bullet, unfairly placed by a Serbian sniper, had forced him to pay a terrible price. Seen from a Serbian viewpoint, I imagine the sniper had done a good job. Their task was, after all, to maim, not kill, thereby jamming the Bosnian logistics. The last thing you want as a sniper is a clean head shot. By the time Josip had healed, he had required more than fifty hours of surgical time and the services of more than eighteen medical staff. Had he been shot dead the hospital would never have seen him.

Leaving Sarajevo was an immensely emotional experience for me. I daydreamed and pondered most of the way home. War does force unreasonable reflection on the meaning of life. To hold my own progeny, to see Louise, uninjured, limbs intact, was an indescribable delight. I felt guilty too, that I had escaped while others lay maimed and dying. It is a strange combination of feelings that only those who have been shot at would understand. Yes, I resolved, it is time to hang up my boots. Peaceful surgery beckoned.

Whatever the emotions, or personal promises, reality always returns – in my case with a flash. It was as I opened the front door of my home that I heard the telephone ringing.

'Yep? What is it?' I panted, out of breath in my haste to answer, indicating uselessly to my family they should keep silent.

'Mr Villar? Is that you? Mr Villar?' came the earnest female reply.

'That's me.'

'Mr Villar. Thank Heavens we've got hold of you. I've been telephoning for days. It's the World Rescue Foundation. We've a spot of trouble with war-wounded in Sri Lanka.' Her voice prattled on, a mixture of monotone and enthusiasm, as she described the horrors of the Jaffna Peninsula. The children, the mines, amputations, torture, the inhumanity of mankind.

A strange feeling came over me while I listened. I knew that sensation so well. I had lost count how many times I had felt it before. It was that tiny voice again.

'Keep quiet!' I said forcibly to myself, looking towards Louise. I had made my resolution. England, family, it had to be. I had done my bit for warring society. I had risked myself enough. Then the little beast took over. It always does. Say 'Yes!' it cried. What the hell, I submitted, I have never been good at resolutions anyway. Sri Lanka? Maybe just this once.